Doing Good and Doing Well

Inspiring Helping Professionals to Become Leaders in Their Organizations

Michael L. Kaufman

ROWMAN & LITTLEFIELD
Lanham • Boulder • New York • London

Published by Rowman & Littlefield
An imprint of The Rowman & Littlefield Publishing Group, Inc.
4501 Forbes Boulevard, Suite 200, Lanham, Maryland 20706
www.rowman.com

86-90 Paul Street, London EC2A 4NE, United Kingdom

Copyright © 2023 by Michael L. Kaufman

All rights reserved. No part of this book may be reproduced in any form or by any electronic or mechanical means, including information storage and retrieval systems, without written permission from the publisher, except by a reviewer who may quote passages in a review.

British Library Cataloguing in Publication Information Available

Library of Congress Cataloging-in-Publication Data

Names: Kaufman, Michael L., 1967– author.
Title: Doing good and doing well : inspiring helping professionals to become leaders in their organizations / Michael L. Kaufman.
Description: Lanham : Rowman & Littlefield, [2023] | Includes bibliographical references. | Summary: "Helping professionals are committed to doing good in the world but often don't realize that they also possess distinct characteristics and aptitudes that uncommonly equip them to rise to top positions within service organizations. This book aims to encourage them to follow their passion and ignite their power as they seek organizational leadership"— Provided by publisher.
Identifiers: LCCN 2023028164 (print) | LCCN 2023028165 (ebook) | ISBN 9781475868296 (cloth) | ISBN 9781475868302 (paperback) | ISBN 9781475868319 (epub)
Subjects: LCSH: Social work administration. | Leadership.
Classification: LCC HV40 .K37 2023 (print) | LCC HV40 (ebook) | DDC 361.3068—dc23/eng/20230706
LC record available at https://lccn.loc.gov/2023028164
LC ebook record available at https://lccn.loc.gov/2023028165

Contents

Introduction: From One Helping Professional to Another	vii
Chapter 1: So You Don't Think You're a Leader, Huh?: The Top 10 Reasons You Already Are	1
Chapter 2: The Rise of Female Power	11
Chapter 3: Now Is the Time for Individuals to Make Their Mark	27
Chapter 4: Putting Your Personality Traits to Work for You	35
Chapter 5: Learn as You Go	53
Chapter 6: A Spotlight on Leadership in Education	85
Chapter 7: What Did COVID-19 Teach Us about Getting through Crises?	103
Chapter 8: Managing Personnel Issues	117
Chapter 9: "Money" Isn't a Bad Word	135
Chapter 10: Succession Planning and Growth	143
Conclusion: What Kind of Leader Do You Want to Be?	165
Notes	169
Acknowledgments	185
About the Author	187

Introduction

From One Helping Professional to Another

It's 1994, wintertime on the Busch campus of Rutgers University in Piscataway, New Jersey. Even though I'd graduated from Rutgers two years earlier with my master's in social work, I was still living in the Richardson Apartments housing as part of my compensation as the psychological evaluator for the college's Office of Residence Life—my part-time gig in addition to my full-time day position at the time as the crisis intervention director for a nearby school district.

This particular night, I was reclining on my bed, propped up against a bunch of pillows, watching a boxing match on TV. I guess I could have been anywhere else doing anything else with anyone else—at a party, out on a date, grabbing a late-night movie—but I was on call in the evenings (the university's counseling center only operated from 8:30 a.m. to 4:30 p.m.), and I never knew when a call was going to come in from anywhere across the university's vast system.

I didn't mind being home alone at night, and I didn't mind still living on campus. As a single guy in my mid-twenties residing in a state with one of the highest costs of living in the nation, a free room with free cable and utilities seemed like a pretty sweet deal. Besides, I was used to the job by then, not only accustomed to its on-and-off nature—some nights with no calls, others with four in as many hours—but genuinely enjoying my role in helping students of all types, from all walks of life, from all over the world, deal with things that, well, they needed help dealing with. So I was right where I wanted and needed to be, comfortable enough to start dozing off.

At 2:11 a.m., my pager went off. A second later, my adrenaline followed suit. Yeah, I relished my work, and I was good at it, but the beep-beep-beeping always rattled me, every time.

Last week, I'd been called over to an off-campus apartment to be present when a young woman learned that her boyfriend had just died in a car crash. A few weeks prior to that, I'd had to break up a group of rowdy drunken guys whose behavior had gotten so out of hand that their floormates had reached out to the crisis line for help. Another recent call had involved a junior who was doing *really* poorly in school and who was *really* terrified to tell his parents that he wanted to drop out. What would this call be about?

This one was about Amanda, a 19-year-old freshman on the Livingston campus, who eventually told me through sobbing breaths in her dorm room that she just didn't want to go on anymore. She just didn't have it in her. Other people were strong, she said, but she was weak. She wasn't going to class, she wasn't sleeping, she had no appetite, she'd isolated herself from her friends. The antidepressants she'd been prescribed back home—my eyes immediately shot to the half-full, open bottle on her nightstand—weren't working, and her psychiatrist wouldn't be available until Monday.

It didn't matter anyway, she told me when I continued to gently probe for information, her family would be better off without her and so she'd come up with "a plan." In the meantime, she didn't have anyone up here yet, at her new school hundreds of miles from home, to call for support. So I'd been called in.

"What's wrong with me?" she asked in a whisper, staring at me with eyes so full of desperation, it was palpable. "Why does everyone else know how to be happy but me?"

In that moment, nothing else in my life mattered. Not who won the boxing match, not my favorite cousin's planned visit next week, not the new dent in my blue Ford Mustang. My job in that moment—no, my calling—was to somehow lead this young woman out of the darkest dark and toward the dawning of the faintest light.

Counselors are trained to assess the degree of suicidal ideation at the scene, to determine if immediate hospitalization is warranted or if next-day follow-up would suffice, to make the call between dire crisis and manageable situation. But in that moment, I wasn't thinking as much as acting on instinct. Training and education are one thing—they'd gotten me here and equipped me with the tools I needed to be here—but real people in extreme pain hyperventilating inches from your reluctantly withheld embrace are quite another. They need more than statistics and procedures right then. They need full-on humanity and heart.

In that moment, I felt like this young woman's lifeline, and I wasn't about to let that line slip from my grip. Despite the fact that we weren't that far apart in age, that we'd never seen each other before that night, and that I'd never had a suicidal thought in my life, I had to trust that I'd find the words that would reach her, do the things that would make her feel safe, plant the seeds of belief in her that she would be able to come out of this on the other side, that she would be okay.

I did and she was. It took a little while. It took intensive interventional counseling well into Mandy's sophomore year with a local therapist we referred her to, but she was eventually okay.

Why did I tell you this story? Open a book on career advancement with this story? Because for helping professionals, it's not just a story—it's an everyday occurrence: the teacher of a nonverbal child with autism who guides that child to functional communication; the shelter worker who doles out equal parts necessities for daily living and dignity; the paramedic who keeps the heart beating all the way to the hospital; the juvenile justice caseworker who gets a youth back on track; the halfway-house counselor who painstakingly and repeatedly keeps the resident from self-sabotage; the nurse exposed to all sorts of health threats on behalf of the health of the patient; the reading specialist who leads individuals out of illiteracy; the geriatric-care worker who turns bodies to prevent bedsores, brings ice chips to stave off dehydration, and holds hands to deliver crucial human contact; the food bank clerk who stocks shelves while nourishing souls.

On a regular basis, day in and day out, helping professionals meet and treat people in crisis and in need. They form almost-instantaneous bonds with people who were strangers only minutes ago. They innovate, improvise, and impact. They're keen observers, adept listeners, and skilled analyzers. They're short on judgment and long on patience. They're innately empathetic and naturally insightful. They're master-level problem solvers and top-tier crisis managers. I don't think it's too great a stretch to say that they make the world go round (or maybe it's more accurate to say that they form the center pole around which the rest of the world revolves)—that they categorically change lives each and every day.

And yet . . . and yet, they don't always believe they can change policy. Enact reform. Effect large-scale improvements. Make headway eradicating systemic injustices. They don't usually believe they were "meant" for positions of power, "cut out" to lead programs or initiatives, "well-suited" to be the boss," or "built" for roles of great authority and responsibility.

And, for the most part, society at large plays along with these prewritten scripts. "Bleeding hearts" are too soft to make tough decisions. "Right-brained people" were born to create, nurture, and dream, not spearhead, direct, and take charge. People who "care" don't care about fame, fortune, clout, or personal gain—they're just in it for the emotional rewards.

In other words, helpers aren't supposed to be interested in doing well. They're supposed to paint the world all rosy and keep hope alive and sit around the campfire singing "Kumbaya." I don't know when this lovely folk song became a disparaging punch line, but evidently, wanting to end suffering, seeking unity and harmony, and working for global peace are no longer in vogue, or at least are "unsophisticated" and "unrealistic." If you do want these things, if you devote your career to these things, you're deemed naïve, softhearted, tender, sentimental, or, God forbid, idealistic! In a word, you're a "do-gooder," and do-gooders were meant to follow, not lead.

Do you buy into any of these myths and preconceptions? Do you accept that you're ruled by your heart and not your head? Do you believe that your principles would be compromised and your values trampled if you tried to ascend the "corporate ladder"? That you just don't have what it takes to drive the whole damn vehicle in which you're currently a passenger?

Maybe you think you can't handle the stress of being in charge, the acrimony of board meetings, the demands of stakeholders, the seemingly endless parade of personnel issues that would walk through your office door if you became the boss. I didn't either. As a 27-year-old, newly minted MSW in charge of thousands of college students spread out across three campuses in a metropolitan area in the wee hours of the morning, I didn't yet have a true understanding of what that kind of pressure meant. I had no idea how much I could handle. But really, what's more important than saving a 19-year-old's life? What will happen to you in your life that's more momentous than that?

We helping professionals can handle so much more than other people might think we can, than *you* might think you can. In the work that you're doing right now, not in some imaginary future, you already endure a high level of stress. You're already skillfully navigating situations that take you to the brink. You're already facing serious implications, dealing with heavy experiences, and making weighty decisions. Every day at work, you're touching lives, contributing to those lives, advocating for those lives. Fighting for those lives.

And if you can do *that*? If you can take a life in your hands—shape it, protect it, defend it, even *save* it—then surely you can do anything. Lead a team? Head a division? Run a whole company? Yep, you got this.

WHY THIS BOOK?

So we've already talked a little about the historical assumption that helping professionals doing good out there in the world is somehow antithetical to doing well from a business perspective. But being a helping professional doesn't preclude you from being a business leader—quite the opposite, actually. That's the whole premise of this book: that the skills, traits, and mindset you possess are the very things that equip you well for (and do not at all exclude you from) positions of organizational leadership.

Now, not every helping professional wants to enter the leadership space, and that's how it should be. Some educators want to remain in the classroom. Some caseworkers want to remain on cases. Some physical therapists want to stay hands-on PTs instead of supervising the clinic or string of clinics they work for. And thank goodness for that—for the boots-on-the-ground, arms-in-the-mud, out-in-the-field professionals who are committed to staying in the field, doing the work they feel they were meant to do.

This book is not for them.

This book is for the person who went to school and got their degree in the field of their choosing—say, social work, education, psychology, nursing, or public health. Then this person—say, you—was quickly hired straight out of school and has been gainfully and (mostly) contently employed in said field ever since. There's been a cost of living raise here, a merit raise there, even a promotion or two along the way that brought a fancier title and a few more job duties. You've accomplished what you set out to do in college, you're established in your field, you've got the lay of the land.

So now you're thinking, *That's it, this is probably it.* You earned your degree in a particular area of study and that area will likely be your whole career: one direct route as an elementary school science teacher or a nursing home aide or a guidance counselor or a mental health advocate. That's what you've been trained to do, that's what you worked your butt off to do, and that's what you're doing. You'll stay in this role—maybe at a few other organizations, maybe under a few different bosses—until it's time for retirement.

You should be happy with that, your best friend says. You should be so proud of staying the course, your parents say. And you are happy, you are proud of the path you're on. Sort of. But what if you want to widen that path? Not take a complete detour from it, not take the exit ramp or make a U-turn, just add another lane to your professional highway, maybe even a whole new parallel highway? You don't want to abandon your field—you're still dedicated to your work and your heart's still in it. You know you're doing good. You know you make a difference. But what if there's more of your original blueprint to unroll? What if you can have a big heart *and* have a big job, a big title, a big staff, and—dare I say it—a big wallet to boot?

This book is for the person who knows they're on the right path (like I did), they're in the right field for them (as I was), but they don't want to stay in place there (as I didn't). They're no longer as fulfilled as they once were, they're ready for new challenges, and they have a different vision for themselves in their mind's eye. They might stop at midlevel management, they might try to get to the mountaintop, but they're interested in stretching their wings and seeing how high and how far they can fly.

I wrote this book for the fellow helping professional who thinks they might possibly stay in their current role indefinitely, but who secretly believes they might have an untapped well of greatness inside them to explore. I want to inspire others to get excited about their potential to advance to top-tier positions in the agencies and organizations they're now a part of, to feel empowered to ascend to whatever level of leadership they aspire to, in whatever business sphere they choose. I want you to open your mind to more than the possibility, but the *reality* that you are able and qualified to be the director of the show, not just an actor taking cues on someone else's stage.

You *can* go from point B to point M or even V, quite quickly. You *can* stay true to your North Star and still expand your life map. You *can* repurpose your current skill set, work beyond the credentials listed on your résumé, succeed at things you've never tried before, learn more, do more, and be more. You can do anything you set your sights on doing with the tools you've collected in your toolbox and with the know-how you've stored up thus far. Best of all, you can get where you dream of going with your integrity intact, the same integrity and noble ideals that led you to the helping professions in the first place.

Put succinctly, you can continue to make people's lives better and also make change, make policy, and make money. You can do good *and* do well.

How do I know it can be done? Because I did it.

MY STORY: THE ABRIDGED EDITION

I didn't always know I'd end up a helper. Not even close. In fact, having had a somewhat unstable and inconsistent childhood, I quickly settled on an accounting major when I entered college to afford me a safe, steady, predictable career as a CPA. But something interesting happened as I was earning my undergraduate degree: though I did well in my classes and progressed quickly, it was actually my extracurriculars at Rutgers that filled me with a sense of authenticity and value: For example, my role as an RA—a resident assistant—which was initially taken to pay my way through school but which turned into an awesome avenue to serve as my building's unofficial guidance counselor (and, come to think of it, my first leadership experience); the community activities I engaged in through my fraternity that exposed me to many populations in need in surrounding neighborhoods; my involvement with the Rutgers Community Outreach Program, through which I was able to work with local kids and start our own university-sponsored "big buddy" program modeled after the Big Brothers Big Sisters of America organization; the volunteer work I was just naturally drawn to—at a homeless shelter and a cognitive rehab clinic, where I learned far more from the people I met than they ever did from me.

Through it all, I felt like I had a purpose, an inner peace I'd been lacking, a place of belonging. It was my experiences working with people, I realized—not my business coursework—that made me feel vital and useful. So it was a surprise to everyone but me when I turned down an opportunity at Ernst & Young upon graduating and instead decided to enroll in the Rutgers School of Social Work to earn my master's.

During graduate school, I was fully absorbed in the interesting classes, the work that didn't feel like work, and the string of intriguing but equally intense internships I completed that formed the basis of the man I am today: the husband and father, the son and brother, the friend and partner, the special education leader, the business owner. In both one-on-one and group counseling settings, I worked with psychiatric patients, war veterans, individuals with PTSD, abandoned children, and bereft parents. I'm not sure how effective I always was—I was very green and very emotionally attached to all my charges—but I did my best to alleviate suffering and improve quality of life.

At every turn, I felt more and more fulfilled, more and more at home. My gut told me I was on the right path, so after grad school, I dove headfirst further down that path, happily and eagerly paying my dues in the field that so many others pay on their way to being truly skilled and compassionate helping professionals. I've always gravitated toward children with challenging home lives, so my early jobs centered on them: counseling coordinator for the Boys & Girls Club of Newark, crisis intervention director for the Keansburg School District, clinical supervisor at Calais School in Whippany.

In 1995, when I was working in a school for students with disabilities, I bonded with the boy I'd mentor for the next 30 years. He's more like a son to me now, and he's a father of three himself, but I still see him about once a week and our relationship has been life-altering.

All the while, I was moonlighting in what I now understand were some of the most dangerous neighborhoods around, making house calls to visit some of the most disenfranchised kids you'd ever meet. I was teaching graduate-level courses at Rutgers—one of the most educational and enriching experiences of my life. And I was working toward my doctorate, which I eventually earned from the International University for Graduate Studies in 1999.

Long story short, although I'd started my PhD in social work at Rutgers, I ultimately shifted my focus to clinical psychology so that I could broaden my formal education in psychological theories and concepts and, thus, extend my reach in terms of what and whom I can counsel. Later, this training greatly informed my managerial perspective.

I witnessed a lot of strife and hardship in those early years: the child whose bedroom was a closet, the little girl whose cupboards were always bare because her mentally ill mother forgot to get groceries, arrests and incarcerations, drug overdoses, far too many funerals of far too many people who died far too young. But they were also immensely rewarding—like, beyond-the-ability-to-capture-in-words rewarding. Still, by the time I was working as director of student services at an elite prep school in Somerset in 1998, I was ready for a change—the biggest issues the kids there faced were what to wear to prom and which car to drive to school.

I saw an ad in the paper for "directors in training" at a Maryland-based special education company (no LinkedIn or Indeed back then), and I answered it. Cue the climax of my career.

Getting hired at the privately owned company eventually named Special Education Services, Inc. (SESI) was the most fortuitous professional opportunity that could ever come my way. It's not that I didn't work for it. It's not that I didn't have champions to whom I'll be forever grateful, who seemed to pluck me from the sea of candidates to dub me their protégé and heir. It's just that part of one's life journey is being in the right place at the right time, and this is that part of my journey.

I was at SESI from 1998 to 2015, first as the director of the High Road School of Baltimore (after the requisite training period) for two and a half years, then as regional director of all the Maryland schools for three years, next as COO from 2004 to 2006, and finally as CEO. During my tenure there, the organization grew from fewer than a dozen East Coast schools serving K–12+ students facing moderate to severe social, learning, and behavioral challenges to a nationwide network of 60+ whole-school and in-school programs in 14 states and Washington, DC, with a total staff numbering over a thousand, in charge of the holistic education of 3,000 special and alternative education students. To this day, SESI serves a vast population of students aged 5 to 21 with intensive special needs.

I can't begin to adequately convey here all the duties that fell to me in these various roles, all the know-how I accumulated along the way—everything from building leases, budget forecasting, and staff leadership development to model replication, program innovation, and trust-building with our district partners—but it was never lost on me, even when I was knee-deep in Excel spreadsheets working on salary structures or loan covenants, that all of our joint efforts were solely for the purpose of effectively and expertly meeting the individualized needs of students most in need. And never was that moral imperative weightier than when I was CEO, no longer having anyone above me to pass the buck to when tempted by the stress, now fully in charge of the ultimate health of the company.

McKinsey & Co. calls the CEO "the most powerful and sought-after title in business, more exciting, rewarding, and influential than any other. What the CEO controls—the company's biggest moves—accounts for 45 percent of a company's performance."[1] True, all true, but nothing quite prepares you for total responsibility for everything, and I won't pretend it wasn't intimidating at times. I savored my role and arrived at work each morning raring to go, but the challenges were as many as the triumphs, and the demands were as great as the rewards.

In each and every job, I learned on the job. I learned a lot by trial and error. I learned a ton from the company's owner. I learned so much from my staff—how to lead them and what to lead them in by closely analyzing our daily operations and identifying what they needed most to thrive. Critically, I learned to delegate. (Ask anyone who knows me, and they'll tell you I'm a first-rate delegator!) Many of this book's chapters follow my career progression and share what I learned at each turn.

I had a wonderful, wild ride at SESI that I'd recommend to anyone who feels up to the task. Some of the highs included the privilege of attending the Key Executives Program of Harvard Business School in 2004, which markedly broadened my outlook on the business aspects of running a service-oriented organization and further ignited my zeal for leadership; the quarterly SBUs we held, where I was most directly able to channel that zeal by gathering together in person all of the company's regional directors, school directors, assistant directors, and essential management and support staff for group interaction, collaboration, and team building; and being part of advancing and promoting the careers of others, watching my staff members grow and flourish—hands-down the most rewarding part of any job I've ever held.

Oh, and I even got to host my own call-in radio talk show for a short while when I was living in Maryland. I had a *blast* combining many of my interests and talents in such a fun and creative way—humor and entertainment, public speaking, public service, and, of course, doling out advice—regardless of the ratings the show got!

There were lows, of course, too. Relocating from New Jersey to Maryland when I first joined the SESI team wasn't something I looked forward to. Now, looking back, I'm glad I pushed myself out of my comfort zone and learned to adapt in new settings, as this isn't something that comes naturally to me. Juggling everything early in my career was also hard: I was working by day, teaching by night, volunteering on the weekends, and finishing my PhD during stolen off-hours—all of that at once is a young person's game, and I don't think I'd have the stamina now. (Hell, I know I wouldn't have the stamina now.)

And the traveling I was required to do as COO and CEO (to get face time with my directors before there was FaceTime) eventually took its toll on me. I used to love hopping on a plane and checking into a pristine hotel room with HBO and the air conditioner set as low as I wanted it, but once I had a baby girl at home waiting for me, I'd do whatever had to be done to depart and arrive back home within 24 hours.

And then there were all the "in-between" points, neither good nor bad, just part of the business of doing business, like the purchase of a controlling stake in SESI by a private equity firm in 2009; having to report to a board as a consequence of that sale; and, eventually, our 2015 merger with another education outfit similar to ours, but larger.

Being supervised by a board turned out to be a worthy growth experience for me, as it exposed me to the value of having a global strategy consulting firm create a future road map for our organization, it forced me to more strategically and fiscally scrutinize each measure we took, and it taught me how to connect the dots between our student-based organizational mission and equity's focus on positioning our organization at the forefront of the special education landscape for an eventual acquisition. Initially, I was concerned about how much my hands might be tied, but the equity firm respected our culture and gave me leeway to keep shaping it, and I remain grateful for that.

But the merger turned out to be a buyout, and although I hung in there for a while—staying as enthusiastic as I could about the new joint venture's prospects and lending my expertise specifically in special education to the schools division—by the end of the year, I'd grown weary of resetting my lens to someone else's vision, of the pressures of profitability always over my head, of no longer looking forward to work when I got out of bed in the morning. Though I wouldn't trade my days at SESI for anything, I left in December 2015 and never looked back.

It wasn't that I didn't enjoy the climb—not at all; I actually found the most joy there and would encourage you to do the same, making the rhythm and reason of each step entirely your own. The whole point of this book, in fact, is to inspire you to make your career entirely your own. It's just that for everything there is a season. It was incredibly satisfying to have played such a large role in building and growing an organization, and it was bittersweet to have to walk away when the time came. But come it did, and I knew in my heart it was time to move on.

After a brief period of reflection and regaining my footing, I realized I wanted to return closer to my roots, get back face-to-face with people I could help. I led the launch of a start-up that provides online therapy services, and I came *very* close to accepting the CEO role for two amazing companies that do amazing work for young populations in need; but in the end, I decided I wanted to remain my own boss. So, I started an education consulting company with two partners (both from SESI, who'd soon followed me out the door), and we provide highly customized, tailor-made management and oversight to highly specialized schools for students with the full array of exceptionalities.

We're small, and I like it that way. I like having cofounders and co-owners to huddle with, I like having full discretionary power over the handful of programs we currently run, I like investing our profits back into the kids who attend them. I don't know what else the future holds for me—who or what may come knocking next on the door of our three-man band, when I'll be able to return to teaching and, hopefully, chairing a charitable organization—I just know I look back on my road traveled thus far with equal parts pride and passion. And I'm looking forward with great excitement, great humility, and a sense of great honor for the chances that have befallen me—those I've been given and those I've taken.

ENOUGH ABOUT ME: WHAT ABOUT YOU?

I wanted to share some of my story with you before diving into the real meat of this book so you'd know a little about where I've been and how I got there, about what qualifies me to fill these pages with advice and guidance for your own advancement, in case you're interested in following a similar path. And I hope you are. Because the helping professions need feeling, kindhearted, and empathetic people in corner offices and in conference rooms as much as they're needed in clinics, classrooms, and group homes. Our related fields need intuitive, not just intelligent leadership; perceptiveness *and* professionalism; benevolence *and* business sense.

It's funny, the "corporate watchwords" that have become trendy in recent years—"passion," "mission," and "values"—they come from our world, not the business world. It's service organizations like ours that have always put those ideologies at the forefront, and now it's finally been recognized that they matter everywhere, that they at least *should* matter everywhere. But they mean nothing if you don't mean them.

You? My guess is you mean them. My guess is that you wake up most days mentally reciting what might as well be our group mantra: "I want to make a difference in this world by helping others." And my guess is that you already are . . . I just want you to believe you can do so on a larger scale. And that's why I've set out here not to *convince* you that you can be any kind of leader you aspire to be, but to *explain* to you why you've already stocked your toolbelt with what you need to get there.

There are a lot of books out there on business leadership, but I haven't come across a lot of them written by proven leaders in the helping professions. Most are by multimillionaire tycoons, corporate VIPs, manufacturing magnates, and captains of industry—everyone loves a rags-to-riches (or silver spoon to gold spoon) story, right? But you know what I find fascinating? That books on business leadership so often focus on cultivating the qualities helpers already have. Yep, leadership guidebooks teach others how to be like you already are!

And yet so many people in our fields don't seek to lead, so many just don't recognize the prized abilities they possess and, in turn, the opportunities that await them because of their natural skill sets. Helpers bring deep-rooted value to organizations, and because of that, they're prime candidates to lead those organizations.

Maybe you're at the very start of your career, maybe you're a few years in, or maybe you're about halfway through. No matter where you are in your progression, there's no end in sight unless or until you declare your own end. If you want even greater success, you can have it. If you know you have a business-oriented side to your brain, you can develop it further. If you want to make the decisions instead of just implementing them, allocate the budget instead of just following it, you have that capacity.

Whatever type of helper you are—community health educator, substance abuse counselor, midwife, youth leader, behavioral tech, home health aide, or any one of the other myriad helping professionals who each do utterly essential and invaluable work every day en route to creating a more moral, just, fair, and caring society—you can continue to do good in the world and still make a good living running a company, leading a for-profit or nonprofit organization, or being an entrepreneur.

There's a path there—it's one you're likely already on, and you've already got what it takes to travel it.

Still don't believe me? Read on.

Chapter 1

So You Don't Think You're a Leader, Huh?

The Top 10 Reasons You Already Are

Helping professionals possess the personal constitution, education and professional training, and hands-on field experience that not only prepare them, but already equip them, to hold positions of organizational leadership. They may not think so, but they do. They may not believe they're qualified or calculating enough to be the head honcho (or the head honcho's sidekick!), but leadership, like almost everything else, is about people far more than about balance sheets and quarterly reports, and the realm of people is where you excel.

Business is often about dollars and cents. The helping professions are often about life and death. And people who are entrusted with young, impressionable, and vulnerable lives can certainly be trusted to handle the kinds of challenges and obstacles that populate a typical business executive's day.

Let's take a look, David Letterman–style, at the many ways and reasons you're already poised to advance to positions of leadership in the organizations in which you want to make the greatest impact . . . and why you're particularly well-situated and well-suited to do so.

REASON #10: YOU'RE A NATURAL

Some things just come naturally to people. Certain kids seem to come out of the womb knowing how to draw, others put a mitt on their hand and it's like an appendage that belongs on their arm, and still others take to foreign languages or early reading remarkably easily. Proclivities, natural aptitudes, inborn talents, inclinations, call them what you will, we all have a collection of assets inside us that will unfold over the course of our lives and set us on the courses that are right for us.

Your assets include things like feeling compassion for those who are struggling, a compulsion to reach out your hand when you see someone in need, the desire to want to *do* something to correct an injustice instead of just standing by as a spectator. You know how to properly treat people, your communication style invites camaraderie and connection, and you reliably choose right over wrong—not because you consider yourself morally superior but because you recognize that it's just easier, and better, to do the right thing. People would say that you have an admirable character, that you're innately altruistic, and that you emit an aura of trustworthiness and genuineness. You are as concerned about others' well-being as you are your own.

We're not talking about skills here as much as what's called a "helping mentality." Helpers have it in spades. And although it's a muscle that *can* be overworked or taken advantage of, if you learn to harness its energy so that it leads you to accomplishment rather than burnout, your helper mindset is one of the strongest mechanisms in your arsenal of personal power. It's what led you to become a helping professional in the first place, and it will stay with you wherever you go, whatever you do, because it's a *part* of you.

Raise your hand if you want a boss who has a "helping" mentality as opposed to a "help me" mentality.

REASON #9: YOU'RE ALREADY VIEWED THIS WAY

If you're a professional helper of any sort, people already see you as a fixer, a problem solver, a confidant, a doer. That's why they come to you seeking advice (don't they?), why they depend on you to point them in the right direction.

You know how to keep a level head when things get unbalanced; you're accustomed to upset people venting to you, maybe even blaming you for this or that dilemma; and you know how to be rational when the situation calls for it, how to lead with emotion when compassion is more in order. You can see solutions where others see complications, and you're ready and willing to step in to assist.

Perhaps you're the teacher who's asked to teach the most difficult-to-reach students. Perhaps you're the physician's assistant called into the room to assuage the most irritating patients or the caseworker the rest of the agency turns to when an especially complex case is assigned by the county. If so, these are all signs that people think of you as a professional guidepost, and they look to you to guide them.

Someone who fixes problems, listens to others' needs, is counted on to dole out fair and just counsel, and always at the ready to help? Hmm, sounds like leadership material, wouldn't you say?

REASON #8: YOU DON'T NEED AN MBA

This is a biggie that trips people up, that makes them think they can't pursue their dreams because they don't have the right degree. Simply not the case. That's not to say an advanced business degree can't help you in business—of course it can—only that someone who wants to advance to management or lead an organization isn't required to have one.

In North America, 46 percent of CEOs lack an MBA.[1] Like who? Like Mark Zuckerberg, Bill Gates, Barry Diller, and Ralph Lauren (among many others), that's who.

Some form of higher education or graduate degree certainly can and will advance your career, but it doesn't have to be an MBA; in fact, an MBA might not do you much good. A 2019 analysis by *Institutional Investor* found that CEOs with an MBA and those without performed equally well, leading to the conclusion, "MBA programs simply do not produce CEOs who are better at running companies."[2]

And an MBA holder can actually *weaken* a business. One 2015 study found that MBAs focused more on their own welfare than on their companies' and, thus, let market value decline.[3] MBAs may also refuse to ask for help, like drivers who get lost and won't pull over to get directions. But helping professionals will ask for help—they're in the business of help—another reason they make great leaders.

Point being, the lack of an MBA is no bar to leadership. You will need some specific business skills—you'll need at least a basic understanding of finance, accounting, marketing; you'll need to be able to read spreadsheets and profit-and-loss statements, comprehend the implications of debt and operating expenses. But you can acquire such knowledge from alternative sources, like books, evening or online classes, your organization's accounting department or CFO, a mentor.

What you can't acquire from books or classes or colleagues, however, is passion for your job, vision for your organization, and an appetite for expanding the good for the one into the good for the many. That's your terrain, that's your university.

REASON #7: YOU HAVE ESSENTIAL TRAINING

Both your formal education and your fieldwork have trained you quite a lot—trained you more than you probably realize—to manage both people and situations. As a helper, any decision you make at your desk—or in your car or on the street, or in a school office, or anywhere else you deliver your hands-on expertise—affects more than just you (sometimes not even you at all). By default, just by being a helping professional, your role is to serve others, and so you're already conditioned to put their best interests first. That's what leadership is about.

Maybe you're saying, "Doesn't everyone do that?" No, actually, they don't. Graphic designers design. Electricians wire. Woodworkers craft, housepainters paint, and authors write. Now, their work certainly reaches others, touches others, and is usually commissioned by others, but their output is a reflection of their own proficiency and talent—it's a direct manifestation of what they choose to create or produce or repair in return for compensation by a second party. You get paid for what you do, too, but your work is a direct response to a societal need, and you deliver it through the vehicle of service: human service.

To succeed in your job, you've learned to listen to both the words and the silences, you've become attuned to what motivates people, you've figured out what rewards they are seeking, and you know how to read the "vital signs" of a room. The ER worker is trained in triage. The teacher is trained in behavioral interventions. The youth counselor is trained in self-esteem building.

Additionally, you've been trained in the tools of your trade. The eco-maps used by social workers are a good example. An eco-map is a graphical representation that depicts all of the systems at play in a person's life—a structural diagram of that person's primary relationships with people, groups, and organizations that, in turn, identifies the resources available to them within their community. In employing and executing such tools, you've learned to measure, measure, measure. You know how to gauge outcomes, to evaluate improvements, and to separate results that don't matter from results that do matter.

All of this adds up to a pretty cool (and useful) kind of leadership training!

REASON #6: YOU KNOW HOW TO DEFUSE CRISES AND FORMULATE PLANS

Suppose you're a family therapist. One night you're called to make a home visit after neighbors called the cops about the angry ruckus next door. When you enter the house, the adults are red-faced and shouting. One seems to be wielding a weapon in their hand. The kids are cowering in a corner, and a baby is crying from another room. You viscerally absorb the stress in the room as you walk in, but you're there to do a job, as quickly as possible.

That job is to immediately conduct an on-the-scene assessment and make on-the-spot decisions. Risk analysis, basically. *What is the probability of actual violence here? Are there any illicit substances in sight, any alcohol involved? Should the kids be taken away or just sequestered elsewhere? Is there a need for an ambulance, for child protective services . . . or just for a sit-down calming session? Have the adults' reactions since I entered the room given me reason to believe we can talk this out peacefully?*

Well, you do what you're trained to do, everything and everybody calms down, and the police feel it's safe to leave. But skillfully managing the crisis isn't the last stop on this train. Now what? What do you do next to help deter such incidents from happening again among this particular group of people, in this particular setting? Well, you create a plan to enact the next time the same tensions flare, and you get buy-in on this plan from the involved parties by pointing out the likely incentives for cooperation and the likely consequences of noncooperation.

You're able to create this plan so promptly because your skill set includes astute examination, analysis, and interpretation of the facts and circumstances of troubling situations so that you can guide people away from them and toward effective solutions.

Sounds a lot like what business leaders do in their roles.

REASON #5: YOU SEE THE WHOLE PICTURE

Just as the family therapist in the last example had to gather the pertinent details of a particular situation to generalize them to a larger pattern of behavior or performance, so any helping professional makes it their business to investigate whatever background information is needed to make an informed decision that best addresses the issue at hand in the foreground. So you use a combination of specific and wider observations, both concrete facts and abstract principles, to reach conclusions and then plan actions based on those conclusions.

We've all heard the expression "can't see the forest for the trees." It's about focusing too much on the little stuff at the expense of seeing the big stuff. Scuba diving is another relevant analogy. The joy of the sport lies in going down deep enough to see the minutiae of the biome there, the very particles in the water beyond your mask. But the farther down you go, the darker the water gets, until you're in utter blackness, unable to make out any dangers in your path. Only once you start rising toward the light can you regain the vision of what's below.

Most organizations are similar—the nitty-gritty happens at the lower levels, but things can get awfully murky and confusing down there. The day-to-day operations happen on the ground, but if you're just looking at leaf after leaf hanging from tree after tree, you can't make out the whole of the forest from the bird's-eye view, which helps you see exactly where you're situated and in what direction you need to head.

You know how to do this. You know how to notice the details but also the larger perspective to which they point. You know how to deduce that the senior citizen's refusal to eat his rice pudding isn't because he doesn't like rice pudding; it's because he has a swallowing issue that he doesn't want to admit because he's desperate to be released home. You grasp that the kids weren't fighting on the playground because Theo dropped the ball; they were fighting to release the hostilities bottled up inside from events at home.

Helpers have excellent micro- and macrovision because they're regularly tasked with scrutinizing the plight of one human being while simultaneously endeavoring to comprehend the human condition at large. And this is a precious skill to have: "When you step back and look at your entire enterprise—the 'whole picture'—you see how all the small individual elements of it need to fit together with other pieces to create something masterful."[4]

REASON #4: YOU HAVE INSIDER INFORMATION

Lynette is a BCBA (a Board Certified Behavior Analyst) who works with individuals with autism in various home and educational settings. At lunch with a friend recently, she was overheard saying, "We're getting a new director—another corporate suit who has no experience with autism. This has happened to me before, people coming in from the outside who actually hold us back. If I were an alcoholic, would I want to be in a recovery program run by someone who was never an addict? Why should I have to be directed by someone who doesn't even understand what I do?"

Alcides Marte, a teacher in the Bronx, feels much the same way: "I went into teaching because I love the work. I love working with children." But, she adds, "You really don't have as much power as you're told that you do. There are people above me that are making the rules for a population that they're vastly out of touch with."[5]

There's a huge advantage to coming up through the ranks within your own organization over coming into a leadership position from the outside, both for you and for your staff. In an organization where you have performed the client-facing jobs yourself, you know what the people in those jobs need to succeed. You know their frustrations and complaints, their pressure points and victories, what they're happy with and what they're not happy with about their bosses.

You already understand the organizational milieu and the environments in which the organization operates. You understand the services being rendered and the functions being performed because you've delivered and done them yourself. Most importantly, you're intimately familiar with the populations being served.

When that "end user" is placed at the start of all processes and procedures, satisfaction levels soar for both the provider and the providee.

There's a reason that all the head coaches in the NBA's 2019–2020 season were former players at some level.[6] You don't just need to know the rules of the game—if you played the game yourself, you'll have instantaneous creditability with everyone with whom you'll work.

REASON #3: YOU RESPECT OTHERS

We're in the midst right now of a new phenomenon: the Great Resignation. People have been leaving their jobs *in droves* since early 2021, in spite of precarious global conditions, in spite of massive pandemic-related layoffs, in spite of the current economic downturn. Certainly, there are generational and societal influences affecting quit rates, including evolving goals like an improved work-life balance, but generally and historically speaking, it's safe to say that people quit their jobs when they don't feel heard, seen, valued, and recognized. People leave when they don't feel respected.

But respecting others is built into your very constitution. You couldn't be an effective helping professional if you didn't view all human beings as equal; equally worthy of the dignity, decency, and opportunities you want for yourself and your loved ones. When you truly believe in egalitarianism, as helpers habitually do, you don't condescend or patronize because you truly don't see yourself as superior. You may know more than someone else or be more qualified in some areas, but you see that as an opening to share knowledge, not to embarrass or belittle someone else.

And the "toxic environments" everyone's talking about these days? That's something you'd never allow to stand on your watch, for you are dedicated to health and well-being. As you know, you don't need to be in the medical field to be dedicated to well-being.

Professional helpers are usually adept communicators who wouldn't allow disrespect or inequality or toxicity to take root in their workplace because they prefer to talk out issues rather than letting them fester. In fact, they're very uncomfortable when things fester, and so they build conversations around and take measures to establish and maintain collegial harmony and goodwill.

As adept communicators, helpers are also prone to alleviate turmoil, to put people at ease; and because we work with people from all different types of backgrounds and education levels, we've become pros at breaking down complex information into accessible, easy-to-digest bits. We explain things to people in ways they can understand, meeting them where they are in the present moment, and they can *feel* that. They can feel when you're talking *to* them and not down to them.

You can try to lure people with money, with promotions, with a bigger office window. But, ultimately, if they don't feel you respect them for who they are, what they have to say, and what they bring to the table, they won't stay. They won't follow your leadership.

A good leader knows how to acknowledge and appreciate the contributions of others. That's what you do every day, with virtually everyone you meet.

REASON #2: YOU CHAMPION OTHERS

The concept of "standing up for your people" originated in the helping professions in reference to clients. It translates directly to the business sphere as standing up for your team. It's the same idea no matter how you look at it or how you phrase it. It's more than having someone's back. It's more than encouraging them, providing emotional support to them, or believing in them. There's *action* involved here too.

In your current job, championing others (both your coworkers and those you serve) looks like face-to-face coaching and mentoring when guidance would be helpful. It's tracking down referrals and resources that people need to make positive shifts in their life. It's sharing your knowledge and tools so that they can more closely approach their goals. It's defending them, verbally and in writing, when they need protection, fighting for their rights when they're being infringed upon, even acting as their guardian when they need family. Sound familiar?

In the tiers of organizational leadership, embracing the role of champion for all members of your team means promoting people based on merit, rewarding them based on performance, backing their creative ideas, investing in them by sending them to professional development workshops or covering the cost of their continuing education, and preparing them for advancement. Champions aren't afraid to broadcast loud and clear to anyone in the organization who will listen that this person is a rising star; they're not threatened by others' progress; they're actually bolstered by it and take pleasure in their contribution to it.

Helpers who fill essential roles in society champion people naturally—they apply empathy and a generosity of spirit that cultivates fellowship and mutual respect, and the people on the receiving end of the champion's efforts grow, evolve, and push themselves to do more because of that.

It's the same in an office building as it is out in the field: "When you stand up for people, you show that you're 'on their side' when they need help. This builds long-term loyalty, trust, credibility, commitment, and morale in your team, and it gives your people a confidence boost. It also shows that you are focused on your team's well-being and interests, rather than on yourself. This helps to create a positive working environment and shows everyone that you're a leader worth following."[7]

Ten to one—no, a hundred to one—that the people you work with now would say that virtually everything about you, your attitude, your dedication, your work ethic, your "cheerleading," creates a "positive working environment" for them. That makes you a "leader worth following."

REASON #1: THE WORLD NEEDS YOU

And the number one reason you're ready to be a leader? Drumroll, please. Because the world needs good-hearted, good-intentioned, ethical people in charge, now more than ever. There is not one entity, network, association, institute, organization, consortium, or company the world over that cannot benefit from *more* understanding, *more* compassion, *more* righteousness, *more* benevolence. More *humanity*.

No matter what field you work in and for what employer, you can make it better. Your sheer humanity will make it better. (Not to mention your skills, smarts, know-how, discernment, competencies, and expertise!) Right now, you're making things better for at least handfuls of people. As an organizational leader, you can extend that reach to all the people in that organization, who in turn better the lives of everyone *they* touch through the organization's work.

You believe in community involvement and community immersion.
You practice the art of reciprocity.
You do good things for people and good things come out of that.
You know how to build relationships and rapport.
You work for the greater good over your own self-interest.
Your work is exhausting but it exhilarates you.
You regularly empower and encourage people.
You make a difference *just by being you*.

Someone like that—someone with those qualities and so many more—is *exactly* what the American business landscape needs right now, from sea to shining sea and from the mountains to the prairies: new and fresh seeds of promise and positivity to counter all the adversity and divisiveness flourishing around and among us.

Do not doubt your worth. Do not doubt the tremendous impact you can make. Do not doubt your power.

But you know who does? Women. Study after study shows that women are less confident than men,[8] that they're far less likely to self-promote,[9] and that they undervalue their performance and leadership efficacy.[10] They shouldn't. There has never been a better time in U.S. history for women to lead, and there's no better sphere in which they're qualified to lead than the helping professions—a sector they have dominated since its inception.

Chapter 2

The Rise of Female Power

Once there was a girl whose father worked in the same company factory for 39 years. As a teenager, she became an inspector on the factory's assembly line. After earning her MBA, she rose in the company's management to head of several engineering divisions and then human resources. The field was male dominated, but she performed well, and by 2011, she was head of global product development, one level below the top spot. In January 2014, she became the CEO.

The company is General Motors (GM), and her name is Mary Barra. She's the first woman to lead a major American carmaker. And she got there in no small part using a certain set of qualities—the same qualities you possess as a helping professional.

Barra has a helper's sensibility, though she never worked in a helping profession. As she rose, she said, "I realized that I had a role to play with people—to help others be their best selves."[1] Described as a world-class listener, she would stop people in the hall for their advice and input. "Listening leads to understanding," she shared, "and understanding leads to respecting other points of view." She brings people together to solve problems and thus gains different perspectives and group buy-in. Yet if consensus is impossible, she doesn't hesitate to make a call.

GM has thrived with her hand on the tiller, earning a record $9.7 billion profit in 2015 and another record, $10 billion, in 2021.[2] She puts customers first and stresses the safety of the cars, because she doesn't want anyone to die in a car accident. How many CEOs do you hear saying that? Seriously, how many? Barra has also committed GM to replacing all gas-powered cars with electric vehicles by 2035. One analyst said of her, "If there were a designated slot in the Automotive Hall of Fame for the most important GM chief in the last three quarters of a century, Barra already may have won the votes."[3]

However, rising in a corporation is not the only route to female leadership.

Nancy Santiago grew up in a frightening home. Her drug-addicted father told her repeatedly that she was worthless, that she'd never amount to anything, and he abused her physically as well. She acted as a buffer to safeguard her younger brother and sister, taking slurs and beatings in their stead. Her helper mentality was evident even in her youth.

But would she ever succeed at anything without being raised in a supportive environment that nurtured self-belief?

After earning her undergraduate degree in communications/political science from Temple University, she continued on there to earn a master's in education, then worked with kids in the criminal justice system. It was a major challenge, but also, she said, "the most fun I've ever had." And she saw how bad policy leads to deprivation and pain and how decent policy brightens lives. "I realized I had a bigger problem to help solve than just all the trauma they had experienced," she said.[4]

Santiago went on to serve two terms in the Obama administration, and in September 2021, she became the deputy director of engagement at the Office of the U.S. Surgeon General.

Barra and Santiago are hardly alone. No one would argue that the global stage in general and the U.S. workforce in particular haven't posed obstacles to female leadership throughout the majority of history. But in the past half century or so, many of those obstacles have fallen . . . and they keep falling.

It is the time of the high-powered woman in the world.

FEMALE LEADERS EVERYWHERE

Who hasn't has heard of Oprah, Ruth Bader Ginsburg, Beyoncé, and Gloria Steinem? Virtually everywhere you look, powerful women like these have been blazing trails and breaking down barriers, some from recent history (like diplomat Madeleine Albright) and some blossoming this very day (like poet Amanda Gorman).

Think of a domain, any domain, and you'll find copious examples of females leading the way for decades: in government (Sonia Sotomayor and Condoleezza Rice), in entertainment (Shonda Rhimes and Kathryn Bigelow), in sports (Danica Patrick and Dawn Staley), in music (Madonna and Nicki Minaj), in journalism (Christiane Amanpour and the team of Megan Twohey and Jodi Kantor), in fashion (Vera Wang and Anna Wintour), in aerospace (Sally Ride and Mae Jemison), in business (Meg Whitman and Indra Nooyi), in anthropology (Jane Goodall and Louise Leakey), in civil rights (Shirley Chisolm and Billie Jean King), in mental health advocacy (Selena Gomez and Naomi Osaka), in self-empowerment (Brené Brown and Iyanla Vanzant), in body positivity (Lizzo and Winnie Harlow)—just to name a very small sample from a very small selection of fields.

Women are kicking ass and taking names in the hard sciences and soft sciences, in technology and engineering, in finance and in the arts. And some have reached their full power only after separating themselves from their male partners, like the astounding philanthropy of Melinda French Gates and MacKenzie Scott.

As for women in politics, their numbers are breaking records. In the United States at the time of writing, 32.2 percent of all state legislators were women,[5] 27 percent of Congress was composed of women (a 50 percent increase over 10 years prior),[6] more women were running for office than ever before,[7] and for the very first time in American history, during the Biden administration, both the first and second seats of the presidential line of succession were simultaneously held by women (Kamala Harris and Nancy Pelosi). Given that females comprise 51 percent of the world's population, "one-quarter" and "one-third" statistics might not sound so notable to some, but there's no denying that the half-full glass is getting fuller by the day.

Women aren't just chairing House and Senate committees, running cities as mayors, and heading states as governors; they're leading nations. Female heads of state are too many to list, but they include Najla Bouden in Tunisia, Tsai Ing-wen in Taiwan, Maria de Lourdes Pintasilgo in Portugal, Sahle-Work Zewde in Ethiopia, Sanna Marin in Finland, Sandra Mason in Barbados, Paula Mae Weekes in Trinidad and Tobago, and Mette Frederiksen in Denmark. In countries like Sweden, France, Canada, and Bulgaria, women hold over half the top ministerial positions.

And they're doing a bang-up job! During the pandemic, New Zealand's prime minister at the time, Jacinda Ardern, was praised for enacting policies that minimized the spread of the COVID-19 virus in her country, which led New Zealand to become the first country to reopen safely. Iceland's prime minister, Katrín Jakobsdóttir, reenvisioned her nation's economy in the aftermath of the 2008 financial crisis and is working to make her country carbon-neutral by 2040. Saara Kuugongelwa, head of Namibia, is known for her stance against corruption and for sound fiscal policy and has spearheaded her country's first budget surplus. Bidhya Devi Bhandari advocates for gender equality in Nepal, and former political prisoner and now prime minister of Bangladesh, Sheikh Hasina Wajed, has welcomed refugees from Myanmar fleeing genocide.[8]

This level of leadership seemed unimaginable throughout most of the twentieth century. Back then, Golda Meir and Margaret Thatcher were the exception; today, the Angela Merkels of the world seem to be the rule of the land. As of early 2023, the IMF is headed by a woman (Kristalina Georgieva), the U.S. Secretary of the Treasury is a woman (Janet Yellen), the FTC is chaired by a woman (Lina Khan), and four of the top positions at NASA are held by women.[9]

Yes, females today—in all realms, across all parts of the globe, and with all types of populations on both large and small scales—are making tremendous inroads, improving policies, and changing perspectives everywhere they wield their growing power. This shouldn't come as a surprise, however. Women have shown their leadership mettle throughout the course of history and have proven it time and time again.

THE FOOTPRINT OF FEMALE HELPERS IN HISTORY

No matter where you look on the timeline of human development, you will find women who made their mark by breaking the mold.

The ancient and classical ages had such luminaries as Cleopatra, Nefertiti, Hatshepsut, and Empress Wu Zetian. The Middle Ages were illuminated by the likes of Hildegard of Bingham, Eleanor of Aquitaine, and Joan of Arc. Queen Elizabeth I has her own age named after her, and the modern world has produced a pipeline of female superstars: Catherine the Great, Sojourner Truth, Elizabeth Cady Stanton, Harriet Tubman, Babe Didrikson, Virginia Woolf, Maria Montessori, Amelia Earhart, Anne Frank, Frida Kahlo, Billie Holiday, Chien-Shiung Wu, Eva Perón, Eleanor Roosevelt, Rosa Parks, Katherine Johnson, Rachel Carson, Indira Gandhi, Wilma Mankiller, Serena Williams, Sandra Day O'Connor, Toni Morrison.

Obviously, this is just the tip of a massive, solid, and ever-growing iceberg that has often been less visible than the male pillars, but no less mighty.

Certain women stand out in terms of advancing the development of the helping professions by making the world a much better and much healthier place to live. Two-time Nobel Prize winner Marie Curie (1867–1934) is the ultimate female icon in the fields of scientific research that allow medicine to progress. By changing our understanding of radioactivity, she changed the course of history.

No doubt the leading female scientists of today—including Donna Strickland and Andrea Ghez in physics and Jennifer Doudna and Emmanuelle Charpentier in chemistry, Nobel winners all—would credit the zeal and brilliance of female pioneers like Curie with inspiring their work in (not to mention granting them access to) the hard sciences upon which human knowledge is based.

Nursing can assuredly be attributed to female origins. Caring for the sick has been a societal need since the birth of society, and women have generally been the caretakers. Though the first U.S. hospital opened in 1751,[10] doctors knew less about medicine then than astronomers knew before the telescope. Health care still relied mostly on the "four humors" (air, phlegm, black bile, yellow bile), bloodletting was common, and hospitals were therefore pretty filthy places.

But Florence Nightingale (1820–1910) began to change all that because she understood a crucial fact: cleanliness saves lives. In the Crimean War (1853–1856), she led a team of nurses who kept wards sanitary, cutting the mortality rate from 40 percent to 2 percent.[11] This was the first step taken toward professionalized nursing.

Then the bloody American Civil War (1861–1865) spurred an intense demand for nurses, and although the volunteers knew very little about medicine except what they had gleaned from family and friends, they learned what they could on the battlefields. Clara Barton (1821–1912) was one of those nurses, and after risking her life to care for soldiers in the field, she founded the American Red Cross in 1881 and led it for the next 23 years. Today, the ARC provides assistance for 70,000+ disasters per year and is the largest supplier of blood in the United States.[12]

Prior to the Industrial Revolution in America, women rarely held jobs outside the home—there was simply too much sweat labor required there, like pumping and heating water, washing clothes by hand, chopping wood, tending fires, and sweeping ashes. Not to mention the endless cooking. But once modernization (steam-powered factories, railroads, the telegraph and telephone, electricity and running water in homes) started transporting the national way of life from rural areas to urban cities, that changed as clerical workers were needed everywhere. In 1880, 6,600 women held such jobs; by 1920, that number had swelled to 1.4 million.[13]

It didn't take long for women to start finding their footing in the workplace once canned foods and prebaked bread freed them from multiple chores. Certainly, it was more common for wives among the middle and wealthy classes to spend their days creating a warm and comfortable home for the breadwinner to return to each evening (and the role of childrearing can never be discounted—not then, not now), but being a housewife didn't appeal to all women (not then, not now).

Women not shackled by poverty found some space in which to pursue their interest in the betterment of society. Yes, wealth was growing in the country, but so was hardship, disease, immigration issues, and unemployment. The birth of social work in the United States arguably lies with the formation of the Charity Organization Society (COS) in the late 1870s, first in Buffalo, New York, and later in such cities as New Haven, Connecticut, and Philadelphia.[14] The organization's foundational ideas of "scientific charity" and "friendly visits" to the poor had good intentions, but ultimately, COS's approaches and attitudes led to more problems than solutions and met with much resistance.

To counter such resistance, several women stepped forward with their own ideas, better ideas. Jane Addams (1860–1935), one of the earliest and best-known social workers in U.S. history, made a profound impact in the field when she opened Hull House in 1889 with her friend Ellen Starr. Inspired by a settlement house she'd seen when touring Europe and then by the first one established in the States in 1886, the Neighborhood Guild in New York City, Addams's house in Chicago became the most famous settlement in America.

> Settlement houses reflected a different type of organizational response to the impact of industrialization and immigration and introduced an alternative model of a social service agency [as] a form of urban mission. . . . [S]ettlements focused on the environmental causes of poverty and expanding the working opportunities of the poor. They conducted research, helped establish the juvenile court system, created widows pension programs, promoted legislation prohibiting child labor, and introduced public health reforms and the concept of social insurance.[15]

By 1910, more than 400 settlement houses were in operation, and many of the early leaders and educators in social work had their start at Hull House, including Florence Kelley, Sophonisba Breckinridge, Edith and Grace Abbott, Julia Lathrop, and Frances Perkins. Now known as the "mother of social work," Addams cofounded the American Civil Liberties Union (ACLU) in 1920[16] and eventually won the Nobel Peace Prize in 1931 after decades of ardent dedication to community empowerment, social improvement, education, feminism, sanitary conditions, civic responsibility, and humanitarianism.[17] We still feel the ripples today of the tidal wave she created.

Another wave-maker was Mary Richmond (1861–1928), who worked for the COS in Baltimore, where she regularly witnessed deprivation and dire living conditions. She transformed her experience at COS into a method others could use to "investigate" the client's situation with an eye toward better assisting them. Getting to know the people she was visiting and their specific circumstances was a novel idea at the time, and it had lasting repercussions.

Richmond was one of the first social activists to push for the professionalization and standardization of social work, and the fundamentals for casework set forth in her 1917 book *Social Diagnosis* are still in use today. She was a firm believer in research in the field, instructing social workers on how to gather information with interview methodologies and by establishing contact and conducting conversations.

Throughout the course of her illustrious career, Richmond became a national advocate, lobbying for legislation to address housing, health, education, and labor. She was particularly concerned with issues concerning the welfare of children and women and founded numerous legal bodies that fought for the rights of the disempowered. And anyone with a master's in social work today can thank Richmond: in 1919, she established the first graduate school for social work at Columbia University.[18]

Meanwhile, scores of other female powerhouses in social work were picking—and fighting—their own chosen battles. Dorothea Dix (1802–1887) concentrated on getting the mentally ill out of the prison system and into their own mental hospitals. In her work for both the mentally ill and indigenous peoples, Dix "challenged nineteenth-century notions of reform and illness."[19]

Ida B. Wells (1862–1931) combined her passion for social justice and her journalism skills to fight for racial and gender equality. In contributing to the foundation of modern social work, she fiercely supported the right of African American women to vote, she was part of the founding of the NAACP and the Negro Fellowship League, and she exposed the horrors of lynching. She helped open settlement houses for Blacks migrating to the North from the South and worked to expand school access for Black children.[20]

By the time President Roosevelt named sociologist and workers' rights advocate Frances Perkins U.S. Secretary of Labor in 1933, women's role in advancing social causes couldn't be denied. The first woman appointed to the U.S. cabinet, Perkins actually began her career in social work before moving on to positions where she could actually enact policies to protect the people she saw victimized on factory floors. She was integral in the implementation of the New Deal and the Social Security Act, securing unemployment benefits, pensions for the elderly, and welfare for the poorest Americans. Her list of achievements runs broad and deep, which explains the "Golden Halo" posthumously awarded her in 2013.[21]

The list of females in highly influential helper roles in our nation's history goes on and on (it's really worth a deep dive into this topic), with so many pioneers working on behalf of so many societal problems, until health care, mental care, civil rights, women's rights, child protections, poverty relief, housing issues, and fair working conditions all blended together into one lump sum of "what needs fixing." And perhaps no single area of focus was more imperative—and more far-reaching—than education.

Whether you're talking nursing schools, flight schools, vocational schools, or nursery schools, education is the bedrock of any society's growth simply because it provides the citizenry with *opportunity*. There's a reason so many around-the-table games pose the question "Who was your favorite teacher and why?" and you'd be hard-pressed to find someone who doesn't have an answer. Teachers do far more than instruct, impart, guide, and grade; they nurture and nourish, shape and support, lead and, yes, love. In some cases, they give their students no less than the tools to *live*.

In 1850, however, most teachers were men. By 1900, a drastic shift had taken place and "teaching was essentially female."[22] Many variables contributed to this transition—a higher demand for teachers as school enrollment grew, westward expansion, better-paying job openings for men as industrialization blossomed, lower (much lower) pay rates for women—but it was during this time that "the image of the stern yet loving . . . female schoolteacher" took root and "primary and secondary teaching became a woman's occupation."[23]

They weren't just teaching more; they were learning more. Wesleyan became the first all-women's college in America in 1836, and by 1875, 50 more women's colleges had opened up. The coed Oberlin admitted the first females and Blacks in 1837, and in 1849, Elizabeth Blackwell became the first female doctor in the United States.[24]

Progress in gender equality in higher education definitely didn't happen overnight, but it did happen, slowly and steadily. It took a century, but by 1982, more females than males were enrolled in college and more earned their bachelor's degree. By 2019, women made up the majority of the U.S. college-educated workforce, and by the end of school year 2021–2022, close to 60 percent of all college students were female.[25]

Some of the gold-star educators who helped make all this happen include Alice Palmer, Mary McCleod Bethune, and Lucy Diggs Slowe,[26] in terms of advocating for education rights in general, and, in terms of advocating for women's educational rights in particular, Mary Wollstonecraft, Frances Wright, and Margaret Fuller.[27]

Though her crowning achievement may have been serving as president of Wellesley College, Palmer (1855–1902) is widely recognized for "raising academic standards and establishing a system of 15 preparatory schools" that paved the way for many to proceed to higher education.[28] Bethune (1875–1955) started a private school for African American students as part of her commitment to building better livelihoods through education and served as a national advisor to President Franklin D. Roosevelt on equal education. And Slowe (1835–1937), called "a catalyst for change," created the first junior high school in the District of Columbia and was selected as Howard University's first dean of women.

The British Wollstonecraft (1759–1797) argued that well-educated women would better contribute positively to society. The Scottish Wright (1795–1892) espoused universal equality in education. And New Englander Fuller (1810–1850) not only argued for "transcending" customary gender differentiations, but she's said to have been one of Susan B. Anthony's inspirations.

Those who stand on these women's shoulders today include psychology professor Alison Gopnik, one of the creators of "theory of mind" and a leading expert in the study of children's learning and development; Barbara

Snyder, president of Case Western Reserve University, who chairs the American Council on Education; and Professor Ayesha Jalal of Tufts, who emphasizes the importance of history in the study of nations.[29]

But you don't have to head a university or be appointed to a national committee to be an extraordinary teacher. It all starts on a child's first day of school, in the elementary school classroom—and for evidence of women's monumental impression there, you don't need facts and figures. Just look around you—in your local school district (where females comprise a full 76.5 percent of public school teachers[30]), at the faces smiling back you at PTA meetings, at your own kids. They all have a favorite teacher, and they all know why.

SO MUCH GOOD NEWS

Ever since women entered the workplace en masse during World War II as a direct result of the shortage of available male workers, there's been no stopping them. There were attempts: people tried to send them back to the kitchen when the men returned home . . . but there's no stopping a woman on a mission! And so, so, so many women have missions they feel compelled to fulfill.

They got the vote, they got education, they got women's lib, they got birth control, they got the freedom to live lives of their own choosing, they got same-sex marriage, they got top-echelon jobs—you know all that. This isn't a treatise on the *obvious* fact that women have *always* been equal in all ways to all other human beings.

Instead, this has just been a buildup to where things stand now, today, this very minute. To the state of the current American workforce and women's more-forceful-than-ever place in it, whether their dream is to run a local community garden or run their state's Department of Health and Human Services, whether they want to deliver supplies in the wake of international disasters, or deliver after-school child care.

And what's the status report here? It's pretty good. Not perfect, not limitless or barrier-less yet, but it's pretty damn good.

Just for perspective, consider the overall participation rate of women in the U.S. civilian labor force over a 50-year span: 34 percent in 1950; 38 percent in 1960; 43 percent in 1970; 52 percent in 1980; 58 percent in 1990; and a high of 60 percent by 2000.[31] (Keep in mind that this reflects all working women, aged 16 to 65 and older—the numbers for the prime working years are significantly higher.)

This isn't the same as the *percentage* of females versus males populating the civilian workforce, mind you—those figures are: 29.6 vs. 70.4 percent in 1950; 46.6 vs. 53.4 percent in 2000; and projected 47.7 vs. 52.3 percent in

2050.[32] The year 2020 marked a turning point, with just over half of all jobs in the United States held by women.[33]

These figures might not seem noteworthy, but they are. They point to clear and consistent remarkable growth that continues to level the playing field. For example, the percent change for women from 1950 to 2000? A whopping 257 percent compared to 72 percent for men. And though some might say it's atrocious that only 74 CEOs of Fortune 500 companies are women (15 percent),[34] others might say that's amazing, given that there were only seven 20 years ago.

See, there's strength in numbers, and no matter how you look at the data, the numbers are growing. And so much in life is a numbers game, isn't it? The more women there are in the workplace, the higher the chances are that they'll be the ones to get promoted to positions of leadership.

What else do the numbers tell us? They tell us that women have the stronghold in the helping professions. To take just a few examples: 74.3 percent of all health care practitioners and technical occupations are held by women; to get even more granular in health care, 95 percent of all speech-language pathologists and dental hygienists are female.[35] In nursing, of the 5.4 million nurses working in the field in 2022, 4.6 million (85 percent) of them were female.[36] Of the roughly 700,000 social workers in the United States at last count,[37] women predominate, at about 83 percent.[38] And in education, as mentioned above, women hold more than three-quarters of the teaching jobs in the public school system.[39] When the field is dominated by women, it's only a matter of time before women dominate the field.

But it's not just about quantity. It's about quality. Specifically, the qualities that women bring to their helping jobs.

MSW Online makes a superb argument that speaks to "why women make great social work leaders":

> Social workers in general, and women in particular, are well-suited for leadership positions. The core values of the social work profession . . . include service, social justice, dignity and worth of the person, importance of human relationships, integrity and competence.
>
> These are all excellent foundational values of great leaders—they focus on building relationships, recognize the value that each team member brings to the organization, continue to build their competencies and lead with integrity. Social workers have specialized skills in listening and communication, consensus building, recognizing power imbalances, and the ability to consider differing perspectives. As change agents, social workers are comfortable with ambiguity and even conflict, and in turn, work well on a team to creatively address barriers.[40]

And then *Forbes* takes it a step further: "Once women land leadership positions they excel—often surpassing men—because they have developed soft skills necessary for effective leadership. Traits like empathy, communication, and listening are qualities that serve women well when in management positions."[41]

Moreover, women leaders tend to be more collaborative than men and are more likely to reject inequity and promote fairness, thereby improving the culture of an organization.[42] Women have been ranked more effective than men in most qualities of leadership, like taking initiative; being resilient; displaying high integrity and honesty; developing, inspiring, and motivating others; championing change; and solving problems.[43]

In *She Thinks Like a Boss*, author Jemma Roedel cites a Pew Research Study stating that, compared to men, women have a stronger ability to create a respectful and safe working environment, are more likely to value people from different backgrounds, consider the impact of business decisions on society more, and provide more guidance to young employees (by large margins!).[44]

McKinsey concurs, praising women's ability to establish stronger rapport with employees: "Women managers are taking more consistent action to promote employee well-being—including checking in on their team members, helping them manage their workloads, and providing support for team members who are dealing with burnout or navigating work-life challenges."[45]

According to the *Harvard Business Review*, "Research has shown that firms with more women in senior positions are more profitable, more socially responsible, and provide safer, higher-quality customer experiences—among many other benefits." Women at the top also catalyze innovation. A study of 150 multinational corporations found that, after appointing female executives, "firms reported an average 1.1% increase in R&D investments—and the average total R&D investment of the companies in our sample was $6,538 million, so a 1.1% increase is substantial."[46]

How valuable are women? As it happens, researchers have put numbers on it. One study showed that companies with more women in management saw their stock price rise 64 percent over three years, compared to an industry average of 47 percent.[47] And the International Monetary Fund examined two million companies in Europe and determined that by adding a single woman to a company's senior management or board, its assets grew by 3 to 8 percent.[48] Just one. And last (because we have to put an end to this at some point, or the commendations for female leadership prowess would literally never end), Credit Suisse found that "where women account for the majority in the top management, the businesses show superior sales growth, high cash flow returns on investments, and lower leverage."[49]

Go, Team Women, go. Yeah, there are still realities that can't be avoided (proceed to the next section), but a hard-and-firm reality is that women are on the move. And they're climbing *fast*.

THE NOT-SO-GOOD NEWS

And yet, gender inequality exists. The "gender gap" is real. The glass ceiling has cracked, but it hasn't completely shattered just yet. Women are still judged by different standards at work than their male counterparts, and there are still preconceptions, perceptions, and expectations of women, simply on the basis of them being women, woven deeply into the fabric of our society. Not only that, but women still earn 82 cents for every dollar a man earns.[50] Though much progress has been made since the Equal Pay Act of 1963, rates have stalled around the 80–85 percent mark—and it's even worse for Black women, who earn 61 cents on the male dollar.[51]

We don't have to spend much time proving the point. We can just quickly revisit some stats above to show how the numbers can work both for and against women at the same time.

Remember all the masses of women in the workforce? Well, apparently, only 27 percent of them are managers and leaders.[52] And those 4.6 female million nurses? Evidently, only 33 percent of them are in management.[53] (And just 15 percent of CEOs in health care are women.[54]) In social work, disproportionately far more men are managers;[55] and even in education, where women thankfully represent 54 percent of school principals,[56] when it comes to district superintendents, only 27 percent (though at least this is double the rate from 2000).[57] In higher education, as well, women lag: they represent 44 percent of provosts and 33 percent of presidents on college campuses.[58]

We can't do anything about Bureau of Labor Statistics data that's already in black-and-white. Women can just continue to perform and shine and produce until the tide finally turns fully, until full parity is reached. But you know what women *can* do to help things along? They can stop being their own worst enemies.

In the aforementioned book *She Thinks Like a Boss*, the author devotes an entire chapter to "Stumbling Blocks for Female Leaders," and "lack of confidence" tops the list, which also includes pitfalls like "not speaking up" and "not knowing your leadership style." The "confidence gap," a term coined by Russ Harris in his book of the same name, refers to the phenomenon of women feeling less self-assured in their abilities than men, even when they outperform them.

Professionally speaking, this starts even before a woman enters the workforce. In a large-scale survey of college students in the United Kingdom, 41 percent of male business students perceived themselves as high performers compared to 34 percent of the female students, and male graduates expected to earn 12 percent more in salary than females did right out of the gate.[59]

Journalists Katty Kay and Claire Shipman did an in-depth analysis of women in the workforce for their 2009 book *Womenomics* and came to the conclusion that "there *is* a particular crisis for women—a vast confidence gap that separates the sexes. Compared with men, women don't consider themselves as ready for promotions, they predict they'll do worse on tests, and they generally underestimate their abilities."[60] In an *Atlantic* feature from 2014, these authors present a multitude of quotes and point to all kinds of ripple effects that emanate from this gap—fewer initiations of salary negotiations, lower raise amounts requested, reluctance to apply for promotions they aren't "100 percent qualified" for, assuming undue blame, a less competitive spirit, and so forth—and lots of other analyses (lots) echo such findings.

But what all these analyses also indicate (all of them) is that there is *no* evidence justifying the gap, *no* reason at all for anyone anywhere to believe that women's performance or abilities are lesser in any way than men's. So although the confidence gap is a very real phenomenon, it's not scientific fact, and it holds power over a woman only insofar as she lets it, due to psychological and societal conditioning. Furthermore, as well-documented and well-researched as this phenomenon has been since it was labeled, Dr. Harris's book was published in 2011. That's ancient history by today's standards, and fortunately, women have moved into modern times and are letting go of self-doubt more and more.

Far more pernicious nowadays is women's persisting reluctance to put themselves out there.[61] Or, as *Forbes* puts it, "Even when women know they've done as well as men, they still self-promote less."[62] As many studies as there are assessing gender inequality in the workplace? There's just as many showing that self-promotion is paramount to moving up: "Women who were the most proactive in making their achievements visible advanced further, had greater career satisfaction, and were more likely to attract sponsors. And making achievements known was the *only* career advancement strategy associated with pay increases."[63]

Lingering sexism and long-lasting but long-outmoded misconceptions aside, it's this—visibility, women making their impact be seen and felt in the workplace—that's blocking their upward mobility the most.

So what's the remedy? Well, if confidence is an issue, there are methods to bolster it. If you're reluctant to promote yourself, try taking some assertive steps toward doing so. If you're hesitant, be bolder. If you usually keep your hand down, raise it. Speak up. Show up. Stake your claim. Initiate. Know your worth.

There are still limits imposed on women, yes, but there is no limit on the number of seats at the table. Conditions and perceptions are changing, a little more each day—not because we're such an enlightened, egalitarian society, but because women just keep proving with their actions, deeds, and outcomes that they're up to the task at hand. Any task.

Hershey's CEO Michele Buck gives this advice: "Make an impact in every single assignment that you are given. Look at it as how can I take this to the next level. And be confident in yourself. I think women just don't have as much inherent confidence in themselves. They tend to be harsher critics of themselves than they need to be. So go for it."[64]

OPPORTUNITY AWAITS

It's been put forth that there are three kinds of capital.

The first is called "natural capital"—that's the kind that just exists in our environment that we don't have to make, like the gold that caused a mad rush to California's rivers, petroleum, wind, land.

The second kind is "physical capital"—the tools and devices we use to generate wealth, like the hoe and tractor on the farm, the motors that power modes of transportation, the windmills that produce electricity that runs computers, the solar panels that create power for the factory.

The third kind is "human capital"—it's the abilities of people, and this one is the real treasure: "The most important resource in any economy or organization is its human capital—that is, the collective knowledge, attributes, skills, experience, and health of the workforce."[65]

Over and over, time and time again, it's been shown that a woman's capital isn't worth a penny less than a man's. The confidence gap is a myth.[66] The glass ceiling is being dismantled as we speak. And there is no difference between male and female performance, so women should simply banish that suspicion from their minds. Once "blind auditions" were introduced in orchestras across the nation in the mid-twentieth century, female representation started climbing dramatically, and by the end of the century, it was approaching 50 percent.[67]

Similarly, when submitted résumés in male-dominated fields are stripped of any gender-identifying information, interview rates (and thus hire rates) surge.[68] Point being, there is no objective differential between the sexes when qualifications are on a par—any residual bias is purely subjective, in the eye of the beholder.

Sure, there are things you can do to level up your profile—to add reinforcements to your "prep kit" as you ready yourself to advance, like joining a female leadership program where you can benefit from collaborative info sharing, enrolling in a mentorship or sponsorship program that will actively promote your aptitudes, clearly communicating your goals to your superiors so they're aware of your interest to move up, joining or helping form your organization's ERG (employee resource group) or other internal policy-making committees. But who and what you already are—how you conduct yourself in professional settings and the effects that you bring about with your causes—is more than enough.

There may be only one Ketanji Brown Jackson, Jane Campion, or Gloria Allred, but there's only one you, too, and your power lies in your singularity. No one else in the world, not a one, can or would improve society exactly like you would. The same holds for men, of course, and that's why every single word of this book applies to all genders.

The obstacle course women have had to run throughout history to see their career aspirations realized cannot be denied. But it's also undeniable that right here, right now, in America, there has never been a better, more opportune time for women to lead. Women are in charge of big, important things all around us, in all domains, and you can be one of them. The opportunity is ripe, and it's time for you to pluck it.

So don't believe everything you read about the "bad news" out there for females—just set your focus on the overwhelming good news and believe in yourself. And if you don't think that your one voice can make a difference in today's crazy, complicated world, well, you're going to get an argument there. For it's not just the age of the female right now; it's also the age of the individual.

Chapter 3

Now Is the Time for Individuals to Make Their Mark

"What difference can one person make?" You hear it all the time, from all corners (especially around Election Day). It's a big hurdle that people face when they're weighing important life decisions and assessing future career paths. But is it perhaps a mental hurdle? Let's take a look at just one person's capacity to make a real and lasting impact in the present-day world.

Everyone knows that Kylie Jenner can determine the lip kit color of the year with one tweet, that Justin Bieber can make churchgoing cool with one post, that Taylor Swift can get the Grammys buzzing with one drop, and that Oprah Winfrey can turn the tide of a presidential race with one endorsement. But those people live in the stratosphere, not the real world, right? They're not like the rest of us. So let's do a reality check here.

Ever heard of Malala Yousafzai prior to 2012? Of course you didn't—she was just a Pakistani girl living in Mingora with her parents and two brothers. One day she was a bright, happy girl going to school, feeding her unquenchable thirst for knowledge, and the next, girls were no longer allowed to go to school when the Taliban gained control of her valley in 2007. By the end of the following year, hundreds of schools had been destroyed.

Luckily for Malala, her father was an educator who happened to run a school for girls, and she defied the Taliban by attending. In 2008, at the tender age of 11, Malala followed in the footsteps of her vocal social activist father by giving her first speech in Peshawar, where her father took her to protest school closings. Her speech, "How Dare the Taliban Take Away My Basic Right to Education," was picked up by the press and publicized throughout the country.

When it was announced that *all* girls' schools in the Swat Valley would be closed by early 2009, the BBC asked Malala's father if he knew anyone who'd be willing to blog for the network about the realities of living under the Taliban. There began Malala's diary, written under a pseudonym, 35 entries of which were published from January to March. Throughout 2009, Malala's presence grew as she made her first television appearance on a show called *Capital Talk* in February, was featured in two documentary films made by a *New York Times* reporter, and met with the U.S. special envoy to Pakistan to recruit his help in protecting the education rights of girls in her country.

All this coverage was amazing for her cause, but it blew Malala's cover as the BBC blogger. On the plus side, she was becoming recognized for her brave activism against tyrannical rule, nominated by Desmond Tutu for the International Children's Peace Prize in 2011 and awarded Pakistan's first National Youth Peace Prize that same year.[1] On the negative side, she was also drawing the attention of those who wanted to silence her voice—by any means necessary.

In October 2012, when Malala was riding the bus home from school, her textbooks hidden under her shawl, she was shot in the head by a Taliban gunman. She was 15 years old. The incident sparked an international outcry: condemnations of the attack came from the likes of President Obama, Laura Bush, Angelina Jolie, Hillary Clinton, and UN Secretary-General Ban Ki-moon; Madonna temporarily tattooed Malala's likeness on her back; Pakistan's president denounced the act and established a $10 million education fund in Malala's honor.

Overnight, Malala became known around the world, and her cause was taken up globally. More than two million Pakistanis signed a right to education petition, which ultimately led to the country's ratification of its first Right to Free and Compulsory Education Bill.[2]

And speaking of a teenager with a warrior's heart, what about Greta Thunberg? Did you know her name on August 18, 2018? Bet you didn't. But by August 19, 2018, she'd started a movement that would garner international attention. A mere 15 years old, and looking even younger in her blue hoodie, Greta inspired both headlines and a growing body of fans as she sat outside the Swedish Parliament in the chilly weather holding a sign: SCHOOL STRIKE FOR CLIMATE.

She came back the next day, and the day after that. With each passing day, she was joined by more and more people for the three weeks leading up to the Swedish election in September 2018. Even after the election, which was the impetus for her initial one-woman campaign to get her country's leaders to pay attention to her cause, she continued to skip school on Fridays for her "Fridays for Future" strike. Eventually, hundreds of thousands of students would participate, in Belgium, Canada, the United States, the United Kingdom, Finland, Denmark, France, and the Netherlands.[3]

Before long, Greta was being invited to speak around the word. Her gift for memorable utterance and her apparent immunity to criticism contributed to her popularity. By September 2019, the small action she'd taken in her own country had led to the millions-strong reaction (yes, *millions*) of protesters marching in climate strikes in more than 163 countries. Dubbed "undoubtedly the world's most notable climate activist today,"[4] Greta is perhaps the clearest modern-day example of one regular voice—a kid's, no less—being heard around the globe, carrying the potential to change the whole damn planet.

Here's a sample of that voice: "We can no longer let the people in power decide what is politically possible. We can no longer let the people in power decide what hope is. Hope is not passive. Hope is not blah, blah, blah. Hope is telling the truth. Hope is taking action. And hope always comes from the people."[5] In a little over a year, she'd gone from a solitary vigil to leading by example worldwide. She was named *Time*'s "Person of the Year" in 2019, and, aptly, a collection of her speeches published that same year is titled *No One Is Too Small to Make a Difference*.

One voice matters. One individual *can* change the world.

Take it from Greta.

Take it from the Dalai Lama: "If you think you are too small to make a difference, try sleeping with a mosquito."

Take it from Malala, a once-powerless girl who was living humbly and quietly more than 7,000 miles away from you and who later became the best-selling author of *I Am Malala: The Girl Who Stood Up for Education and Was Shot by the Taliban* (2013), one of *Time* magazine's "100 Most Influential People in the World" (2013), the youngest person to win Philadelphia's Liberty Medal (2014), and the youngest-ever Nobel Peace Prize laureate at 16 years old: "Some people only ask others to do something. I believe that why should I wait for someone else? Why don't I take a step and move forward. When the whole world is silent, even one voice becomes powerful."[6]

THE SEISMIC SHIFT OF SOCIAL MEDIA

Amplifying that "one voice" in today's radically new climate is, of course, the mega-phenomenon of social media—now an utterly ubiquitous, completely unstoppable, and totally mind-blowing force. When you throw "the media" in general into the mix to encompass the majority of the "news" that is now online and all of the streaming content that people watch on their screens, we live in a culture entirely imbued with, immersed in, and obsessed by digital social interaction, such that you can go from an ordinary Joe to an extraordinary Joe virtually overnight.

It's not uncommon to be "discovered" on YouTube; you can go "viral" with a product (*any* kind of product, even a dance) in the span of one day; you can launch an entire movement with a hashtag. You can become rich and famous (or infamous) for being a creepy zookeeper; you can get everyone (what literally seemed like *everyone* stuck at home) making a sourdough starter from one tutorial video; you can even help free an inmate if your posts get enough traction. One episode of *Shark Tank* can make you a millionaire, one reality-show competition win can make you a megastar, and one installment of *The Bachelor* can spark a national conversation at the watercooler the next day.

Just a few years back, you had to already be famous to hold a megaphone: think Al Gore instigating the discussion on climate change, Leonardo DiCaprio getting the green crusade marching, Michael J. Fox drawing unprecedented attention to Parkinson's disease, or Meghan Markle almost singlehandedly calling into question the actual firmness of the centuries-old "Firm."

But now you can be anybody and get heard—which has its downsides, of course, but also its upsides:

- In February 2022, 20-year-old Ukrainian Marta Vasyuta happened to be in the United Kingdom visiting friends. She liked sharing her lip-syncing and nights-on-the-town videos on TikTok. But one night she received the news that bombs had begun falling on Kyiv, and she was able to access videos of Russia invading her country. She went to sleep with a few hundred followers; she woke up to nine million views. Within a month, she had 200,000 followers and 17 million likes. *A lot* of people have been exposed to crucial footage through Marta's account.[7]
- In 2022, the number one TikTokker in the world was Charli D'Amelio (born in 2004), with, at last count, roughly 150 million followers. (It's really hard to grasp the implications of such numbers; so, by comparison, note that the *Los Angeles Times* reached peak circulation in 1990 with 1.5 million subscribers on Sunday.)[8] She posted her very first dance video in 2019 and has been a sensation ever since. But one year later, she used her enormous popularity for enormous good. When COVID-19 broke out, too few young people in Ohio were social distancing and Governor Mike DeVine didn't know how to reach them. But Charli did. On March 24, 2020, the 16-year-old posted a video with the hashtag #distancedance; it not only garnered 192 million views (more than the number of residents of England), but Charli demanded that a charitable component be added to her campaign, a demand met by Cincinnati-based Procter & Gamble. Who knows how many lives she may have saved?[9]
- Teacher Vicki Davis posts suggestions for good books and teaching tools to her 167,800 followers. She keeps abreast of podcasts to recommend, like "How to Teach AI with Experiments & Ethics" and one on graphic design for educators. She also shares parts of herself with her audience, as in this tweet: "Mistakes can be masterful teaching moments. So I

save the mistakes—the evidence of things gone wrong. I do not hide faults, problems, and crazy missteps but instead use them to teach the next generation how to do better—and how to learn from their own mistakes as well."
- Many teachers have found a sense of community online. High school Spanish teacher Trevor Boffone, for example, with 249,000 Instagram followers as well as a presence on Facebook, TikTok, Twitter, and YouTube, is known for his online dancing. Amber Harper offers aid for burned-out instructors. And Alice Keeler uses Instagram, Facebook, and YouTube to help teachers get comfortable with instructional technology.[10]
- Nurses are also taking advantage of the platform social media affords them. "At present, there are numerous Instagram accounts that exclusively feature content related to the nursing profession that has amassed sizable followings of more than 10,000 users, arguably pushing them toward microcelebrity status on Instagram."[11] Content ranges from offering advice, passing on learning opportunities, describing how they've met challenges, and conveying their feelings to like-minded colleagues.
- Some examples: Alexis Nicole's YouTube channel "The Nurse Nook" has 263,000 followers. Crystal the IV Queen is tracked by some 150,000 people on Instagram. Brittney Wilson, "The Nerdy Nurse," posts questions to spark dialogue among her 35,000 followers. And here's a sample tweet from nurse educator Kati Kleber: "Compassion and empathy are tough for nurses to have boundaries around. We dive deep into empathy and do all we can to alleviate suffering practically. It's difficult not to get lost in [our patients'] pain."

These are leaders and helpers all. Unlimited numbers of individuals like Marta and Vicki and Kati have something to say, something they want to accomplish, and they're using the tools of the day to do so. In the process, they are advancing conversations, posing important questions, and moving the needle. And they're all doing it just by being themselves—by engaging with others about topics and themes that matter to them, in ways that feel comfortable to them, and by sharing their ideas about how to remedy or redress challenges in their areas of interest.

You don't need to be famous anymore to influence and impact. You don't even need to leverage social media (hey, it's not for everyone). But we all have a chance at the mic now . . . so we can all drop the mic when we've made our splash!

A NEW BREED OF HERO

But we're not just talking about the radical change of social media and the worldwide stage that has been given to individual voices, individual dreams, and individual missions in today's culture because of it. We're also talking about a shift in the collective mindset as well, in the zeitgeist of our cultural identity. Ever since 9/11, Americans no longer live in a bubble of contented protection, feeling invulnerable, invincible, and indomitable. It's like the heinousness of that one devasting attack shocked our eyes open, and now we can't close them.

We can't close them to the series of calamities that have ensued in the first quarter of the twenty-first century, seemingly one after the other, on our own soil and abroad: the mass shootings, the school shootings, the terrorism, the kidnappings, the civil wars, the displacement and refugee crises that result from them, the famine, the poverty, the brutality. Then there are the natural disasters that are threatening the human race just as much as the human race is threatening itself: the diseases and viruses, the droughts, the floods, the hurricanes, mudslides, sinkholes, earthquakes, and fires. We can't *not* see all the tragedies, and we can't look away. We shouldn't. We must look.

Some people do more than look. They act.

When a condominium tower in Miami just collapsed to the ground in the middle of the night in June 2021, Nicholas Balboa was out walking his dog. When he heard a cry for help, he could have walked on, he could have begun filming the scene on his phone, he could have just called 911. Instead, he rushed over toward the sound of the voice and was responsible for saving the life of a 15-year-old boy when 98 others perished around him.[12]

When Hurricane Maria devastated Puerto Rico in the fall of 2017, chef José Andrés took it upon himself to basically feed the entire island.

During the massacre in Las Vegas that same season, in lieu of fleeing to safety, concertgoer Jonathan Smith raced back toward the danger to help 20 or so strangers. His explanation? "I just did what anybody would do."[13] Um, not necessarily.

And at the 2022 mass shooting in Highland Park, Illinois, during a Fourth of July parade, even though the sniper was still on the loose, anesthesiologist Wendy Rush and bystander Bobby Shapiro attended to the victims instead of seeking shelter.

This is just a very small sample of the *big* things people do for one another when the opportunity emerges. The acts of astronomical bravery and selflessness on 9/11 are another shining example, and the sheer outpouring of loving-kindness displayed, the ways in which people devised means and methods to creatively and compassionately lift and help others during the COVID-19 pandemic, was altogether breathtaking.

Even amid the bleakest of times, beams of light surmount the darkness and serve as beacons of hope to all of us. Those beams of light are no longer buildings or monuments, edifices or entities, politicians or world leaders. They are everyday, regular people, one individual at a time, who are leading by showing us a way forward through crises some of us never even imagined.

It's often a frontline worker, yes—the firefighter, police officer, paramedic, or ER nurse—who grabs the reins and gains control of a spiraling situation. But solutions can also come in the form of a community gardener toiling to counter supply-chain fractures, a virtual teacher who finds a way to grab the attention of restless students, an anti-gun activist willing to take a stand, a striker outside a closed reproductive rights clinic, a small-town mayor who entices a company to open a plant to employ the impoverished citizens of his dying town, a church volunteer who finds housing placements for incoming immigrants.

All of this adds up to a new reality. In our current climate, a "science nerd" like Anthony Fauci or Neil deGrasse Tyson can become a household name, even a sex symbol! In our current climate, a young boy like Jaylen Arnold can do more to combat bullying than the U.S. Department of Education, and a young girl like Marley Dias can do more to get culturally diverse books on bookshelves than all the librarians in America.

In our current climate, in other words, our definition of "hero" has evolved. And with it, our society's traditionally held notions about who should lead have been totally upended. In this new reality, it's possible for the individual voice to be louder than a whole corporation's, and it's possible for a single individual to hold more power than an entire industry.

Congresswoman Maxine Waters speaks for a lot of people when she says, "You know what I'm told? I'm told that there are so many people out there who believe they don't have power, that they don't have influence, and what they have to say doesn't make a difference. I would like, in the best way possible, to support people being able to think of themselves as people with influence and power."[14] Let's support *ourselves* as people with influence and power. Let's believe that we have it, because we do.

There's no better time in the history of humankind for one "ordinary" individual—and helping professionals indeed think of ourselves this way, don't we?—to make a resounding mark where and how you want to. You don't have to be some kind of remarkable, perfect person.

A woman who was once so destitute that she lived in her car ended up writing a seven-part fantasy book series that rocked the world. A college dropout on the spectrum became the richest man in the world in 2021[15] and just sent a rocket into space. And a young Florida-born woman who was selling fax machines door-to-door in her early twenties had already come up with the idea for an industry-revolutionizing hosiery line by her late twenties; she became the youngest self-made billionaire in history and was the first female signatory of the Giving Pledge.[16]

You don't need to be J. K. Rowling, Elon Musk, or Sara Blakely. You just need to be your own one person, with your own personal mission. Do you have one? Are you ready to set it in motion? If so, what have you got packed in your personality suitcase to help you get there?

Chapter 4

Putting Your Personality Traits to Work for You

The concept of "servant leadership" encompasses helpers' approach to their work. As envisioned by the man who invented the term in an essay in 1970, Robert K. Greenleaf, it is defined as "a non-traditional leadership philosophy, embedded in a set of behaviors and practices that place the primary emphasis on the well-being of those being served."[1] Extensive research has shown the value of this holistic approach, which "engages followers in multiple dimensions (e.g., relational, ethical, emotional, spiritual), such that they are empowered to grow into what they are capable of becoming. It seeks first and foremost to develop followers on the basis of leaders' altruistic and ethical orientation."[2]

The companion "servant leader" label is also an apt descriptor of helpers themselves: "A servant-leader focuses primarily on the growth and well-being of people and the communities to which they belong. While traditional leadership generally involves the accumulation and exercise of power by one at the 'top of the pyramid,' servant leadership is different. The servant-leader shares power, puts the needs of others first and helps people develop and perform as highly as possible."[3]

According to the Center for Servant Leadership, this philosophy begins with a "natural feeling" of wanting to serve above all else, and, interestingly, this desire to serve precedes the aspiration to lead and yet is the driving force behind this aspiration.

This "natural feeling"—that's what this chapter is about. For there is a way of being in the world—both in one's approach to life and to their work—that is just innate to the helping professional. And it seems to grow out of a set of characteristics or traits that helpers inherently possess. What are these personality traits, why have they worked to your advantage thus far, and how can they help you become a servant leader of exceptional magnitude in the future?

PERSONALITY CHARACTERISTIC #1: WARMTH

Helpers just emanate goodwill. The attribute of warmth brings to mind visions of coziness, affection, caring, and kind-heartedness—the kind of connection that hugs bring. Yes, your warmth is like a hug to the people who meet you.

But warmth has almost-magical qualities as well. A genuinely warm person has a sort of radiance about them that puts others at ease, draws them in, makes them feel secure and attended to. They can tell you are sensitive to their needs, and you feel accessible and approachable enough to come to you with those needs. You're the kind of person others feel comfortable asking a favor of—a ride to the airport, feeding their cat while they're away—because you give off the message that you like to help, that you want to make the world a little bit better every day.

You wear your good intentions like clothes, and so people clearly see them. And being warm comes easy to you, it takes no effort at all; if you tried to be standoffish and distant, you would feel like you were betraying yourself. That's because your warmth is just organic to you, a part of your very fabric. Your warmth beats within you. It exudes from your pores because you've got heart. And people can sense that right away.

Applying Warmth in a Leadership Role

The fundraising committee was in a meeting, and it was Samantha's turn to present her slideshow on the theme for this year's gala. But she had trouble getting the file to open, and even when she did, the work didn't seem complete—the presentation was lacking some details she'd been tasked with and there were noticeable errors in her text.

Her supervisor, Jason, was on the verge of being annoyed—they were really up against a tight deadline and the board needed a final venue and budget, like, yesterday. But Jason did one of those instantaneous mental sweeps of what he knew about Samantha—how together she always was, how prepared and dependably efficient—and so instead of questioning her on the missing information in front of the group, he simply thanked her quickly and moved on to the next item on the agenda, saying they'd circle back to finalize the gala theme later in the week.

After the meeting, Jason visited Sam in her cubicle. He startled her, and when she turned to face him, he saw tears brimming in her eyes. Her cell phone was in her lap with her text message window open, and he noticed that her normally sleek hair was quite disheveled. He immediately abandoned his plans to ask his subordinate when he could expect the completion of her assignment and turned his focus to the human being in front of him who was in visible pain. He could tell in the meeting that she was in need of something, he just didn't know what, and now he asked her what was wrong in the hopes of being able to support her.

It turns out she'd just learned the night before that the adoption she and her partner were planning on had fallen through—she was so sorry her distraction had affected the quality of her work. Jason slid from leaning on her desk to a chair directly in front of her, rested his elbows on his knees, then looked up to meet her gaze straight in the eye. The slideshow could wait—he'd get Chad to help her finish her research. All that mattered right now was how she was feeling. "What can I do to help?" The second the question was out of his mouth, Samantha's trembling lips turned up into a small smile and she breathed an audible sigh of relief.

What Warmth Looks Like in Practice

Warmth is one of the most valuable soft skills there is—it comes so naturally to you that it doesn't seem like a skill, but it's both a quality and an aptitude. Among nurses, for example, patients named communication, trust, cordiality, listening skills, kindness, and gentle treatment as attributes that mattered the most to them in satisfaction surveys. But warmth was the most important of all.[4]

It can make all the difference in leadership. Workplace experiments have shown that just small gestures like smiles and nods convey warmth to employees, helping the leader bond with them and displaying empathy with them. As a helper, you likely don't need to practice or develop what's an inborn characteristic for you, but be aware of its strength, applicable to any field at all—even an early incarnation of "reality TV"!

Bob Ross, for example, was not one of the great artists of the twentieth century, but he certainly was an engaging one. As the host of the PBS show *The Joy of Painting*, which premiered in 1983 and ran for 11 years, he built a loyal following on the basis of his "loveable hippie persona . . . and intimate speaking voice that made the viewer feel as if [each episode] were a personal, one-on-one painting lesson."[5] His soft voice and kind smile, paired with his almost-joyous halo of frizzy hair, endeared him to viewers as he painted "happy little trees."

In a recent Netflix documentary on him, the director said, "Despite how difficult things got at times, he just had this unbelievable ability to connect with whoever was watching."[6] That's what warmth does. It connects.

PERSONALITY CHARACTERISTIC #2: EMOTIONAL INTELLIGENCE

This term has pretty much become commonplace in our lexicon since the publication of Daniel Goleman's 1995 bestseller *Emotional Intelligence: Why It Can Matter More Than IQ*, but like "servant leadership," the qualities and values that the concept of "emotional intelligence" (EI) embody long predate any label assigned to it. Emotional intelligence (aka emotional intelligence quotient, or EQ) refers to "the ability to perceive, interpret, demonstrate, control, evaluate, and use emotions to communicate with and relate to others effectively and constructively."[7]

It's the kind of smarts you learn from living in the world in relation to others, not the kind you get from books or technical training. Only helpers don't usually need to "learn" EI at all; they usually come into any situation already able to sense how others are feeling, to relate to and empathize with those feelings, to understand the deep importance of self-acceptance, and to be able to keep their own and others' emotions in check at challenging times.

Goleman's particular brand of EQ consists of four components: (1) self-awareness, (2) self-management, (3) social awareness, and (4) relationship management. The first two contribute to "personal competence" and the latter two to "social competence."[8]

The self-aware individual is able to accurately identify their own emotions; in turn, they're able to accept their feelings, reflect on why an emotion has arisen, consider the impact of their mood or emotion on others, and then take appropriate actions to deal with the emotion. Interestingly, self-awareness is linked to self-confidence, as people who recognize their own strengths and weaknesses and have insight into their own behaviors have greater self-esteem.

Self-management follows closely on the heels of self-awareness, as it allows one to keep a handle on disruptive emotions and impulses, act in alignment with one's values, adapt well to change, and carry on pursuing objectives in spite of setbacks encountered. Because of these advantages, self-regulators are skilled at bringing about desired outcomes and have a firm sense of well-being and self-efficacy.

Next, social awareness makes one adept at picking up on others' moods, at truly hearing what others are saying, and using that capacity to enlarge empathy. The socially aware individual is great at "reading the room," and because of that, others feel seen and heard and personal connection is facilitated. Being socially in tune has also been linked to organizational awareness and service-mindedness.

Last, relationship management is precisely what it sounds like: having an aptitude for managing relationships successfully, with all that that entails, like teamwork, initiation, problem solving/conflict resolution (*not* conflict avoidance), inspiring and motivating others, and bolstering others through helpful feedback and mentoring. It is the sum total of the other EI components, the natural outgrowth of the other three, and has sometimes been called "friendliness with a purpose." Talented relationship managers are able to catalyze change and to influence those around them to make positive decisions for the group.

When you put these four dispositions together, you get someone who thinks before reacting, is highly motivated by their work, is greatly empathetic to others, has exceptional social skills, takes accountability for themselves, gives others the benefit of the doubt, collaborates well, and displays open-minded agility in different scenarios ... someone like you.

And although IQ still counts (as it should and always will), EQ can be a more accurate indicator of leadership ability. In the words of the popularizer of emotional intelligence himself, "it is the sine qua non of leadership. Without it, a person can have the best training in the world, an incisive, analytical mind, and an endless supply of smart ideas, but [they] still won't make a great leader."[9] According to Goleman, it becomes more and more vital as people rise in organizations,[10] which is very good news for you as you rise higher and higher!

Applying Emotional Intelligence in a Leadership Role

Keiko was in charge of overseeing the new off-site communications network that her organization was putting in place so that her team of 35 caseworkers could automate intakes, interventions, and referrals when they were out in the field. The idea was to expedite data collection, optimize real-time data entry, and immediately initiate outreach to resources from the employees' tablets so that they didn't have to come back to the office between field visits to activate cases through the primary database.

But the way the IT department representatives assigned to the project were talking to the team about signal speeds, encryption languages, full-stack requirements, and application programming interfaces just sounded like a foreign language to the caseworkers. IT was asking them what kind of "capacities" and "functionalities" they needed, and the social services workers themselves, who Keiko could see were growing increasingly impatient with the loss of precious time, only wanted to know how quickly and accurately they could populate the screen to turn each "interview occurrence" into a serviceable needs assessment and personal profile for a real person.

Both sides were frustrated and very little progress had been made all morning, so Keiko stepped in to "translate." Instead of working from the back-end to the front-end, she suggested, why not demonstrate to IT exactly what the caseworkers needed the interface to be able to do in real time? She organized a role-play that involved the majority of the people in the room and that spanned the entire client encounter, from the moment the caseworker logged arrival time at the site from their car until they returned to their vehicle to continue on to their next appointment.

No, a facility name and address field alone wouldn't do—there also had to be a place to enter the type and size of the facility, the services provided there, the number of staff, the hours the doors were open. No, a diagnostic code and date were insufficient—there needed to be additional drop-down menu options for comorbidities, a rating scale for severity levels, subfields for the name and credentials of the professional who made the diagnosis, a notes area of unlimited length for initial observations about each diagnosis. Did the person have a roommate? What medications were they on, in what doses, and for how long? What family members were involved in the patient's care plan and how?

Before long, the IT folks were happily taking extensive notes about what they needed to build to fulfill the caseworkers' needs, and the caseworkers were excitedly piping up with more and more details that would customize the new system to accommodate all kinds of variables and variations. By end of day, a solid foundational structure was in place and everyone went home feeling like they understood next steps.

What Emotional Intelligence Looks Like in Practice

A good example of a leader who opted to use emotional intelligence instead of intimidation or admonishment in the face of adversity is Satya Nadella, who became Microsoft's CEO in 2014. He'd been with the company for decades as a low-profile computer scientist and not only had big shoes to fill but a lot to prove. When he'd accomplished that, leading the software giant to an annual revenue to the tune of $85 million, he turned his attention to new and somewhat risky emerging technologies, like the launch of a Twitter bot named Tay intended to advance the communication of artificial intelligence. However, the experiment went horribly wrong, and in less than a day's time, the hacked technology started posting racist and profane tweets, which obviously led to an immediate shutdown and the need for a public apology.

Nadella may have had cause to blame or berate the bot's engineering team; instead, he sent them an email encouraging them to "keep pushing, and know that I am with you. . . . [The] key is to keep learning and improving." To help ease their shame, he advised the team to view the criticism they were receiving with a healthy perspective while simultaneously showing "deep empathy for anyone hurt by Tay."

Later, in a *USA Today* interview, Nadella commented that it's essential for leaders "not to freak people out but to give them air cover to solve the real problem. If people are doing things out of fear, it's hard or impossible to actually drive any innovation." Nadella's EI successfully navigated this failure and led the company to ever greater successes in its future.[11]

PERSONALITY CHARACTERISTIC #3: ACTIVE LISTENING

Lots of occupations require listening. Students must listen to their instructors if they hope to pass the class. Sound engineers must listen to the myriad elements all contributing in different measure to one track. New military recruits have to listen to their drill sergeants—to the letter—if they want to make it past boot camp. Just the act of listening holds enormous value in virtually all social encounters; in fact, Virgin Group founder Richard Branson has been widely quoted as saying the secret to his success is to "listen more than you talk," and no one argues with the Greek philosopher Epictetus's adage, "We have two ears and one mouth so that we can listen twice as much as we speak."

But we're not talking about basic listening here, not even close listening; we're talking about a *caliber* of listening that gets to the heart of matters and shows the person you're conversing with that they, beyond a shadow of a doubt, matter to you. "Active listening is the highest and most effective level of listening. . . . It is based on complete attention to what a person is saying, listening carefully while showing interest and not interrupting. AL requires listening for the content, intent, and feeling of the speaker. . . . [It] generally does not occur in hurried communications between two people."[12]

Actual techniques are involved here, such as:

- Being fully present in the conversation
- Making steady eye contact to show interest
- Noticing and using nonverbal cues
- Asking open-ended questions to elicit further responses
- Paraphrasing and reflecting back what has been said
- Listening to understand rather than to respond
- Withholding judgment and advice[13]

At this level, real progress can be made with people and with situations, because your goal is to comprehend before you can cure, to take in that full picture we talked about in chapter 1 instead of zeroing in on only the aspects that will allow you to make a snap decision.

Is it too much to expect an organizational leader to listen with such depth of concern? Jean East, author of *Transformational Leadership for the Helping Professions*, doesn't think so: "Deep listening and reflection are what happens in the conversation that follows critical questioning. Deep listening requires that we have empathy and that we truly have a desire to hear what another is saying not just in words, but in heart and spirit."[14]

But you know all this, don't you? You know, because you carry this degree of listening with you. If you didn't, you wouldn't get through to one kid, you wouldn't make inroads with the couple you're counseling, you wouldn't be trusted with confidential or sensitive information. But you do and you are. You get people to open up because they viscerally *feel* your open ears. And when you're truly listening to the problem, you can devise the right solution.

Applying Active Listening in a Leadership Role

It was 3:20 p.m., and Lyle was in a hurry to pick his daughter up and take her to soccer practice. But just as he opened the door to his principal's office, briefcase in hand, his admin sent in 12-year-old Audrey. There'd been a physical altercation between her and Marlon in the bus line that had resulted in Marlon's bloody nose and the reddening welts Lyle could see forming on Audrey's arm.

Now, Audrey had gotten in scuffles before—Lyle was aware of her history of short-temperedness, and they'd discussed it multiple times in this very office. He'd explained to her the standard disciplinary actions prescribed by the district and the consequences she could face for continued episodes. As he looked at her now, clutching her bookbag to her chest, mouth set in a hard line, he saw defiance and defensiveness in her face, but he also saw that she was terrified.

He sat her down next to him and asked her to explain what had happened, and he listened, he *really* listened, gently prompting her for more details when appropriate. He was careful not to accuse, not to lead, not to jump to conclusions. He didn't look at his watch, he didn't check his phone when it pinged, he just attended to Audrey's words and movements as she told her side of the story, which seemed quite valid to him. "Okay, Audrey, I think I understand. Since you already missed the bus, can you call one of your parents to come pick you up?"

"Do I have to sit here and wait? Are you going to put me on detention or expel me when they get here?"

"No. We're not going to do anything right now. You can wait with Eileen until your ride comes—for now, I just wanted to understand what happened, and I thank you for sharing that with me."

On his way to pick up his own daughter from school, Lyle figured out exactly what he would say to Audrey's and Marlon's parents and exactly what he would propose to fairly rectify the situation.

What Active Listening Looks Like in Practice

David Abney was only 19 years old when he joined the team at UPS, loading packages onto brown trucks at a local depot. Forty years later, when he became CEO, one of his first acts was to go on "a worldwide listening tour" so that he could hear firsthand what the company's customers and 480,000+ employees thought UPS should focus on going forward. Here's what one employee said about Abney's mission to "listen intentionally" to his staff: "When David issued a call for ideas, many of which were actually implemented, it was almost earth-shattering. We couldn't believe leadership was finally listening and taking action on our recommendations."

Angela Ahrendts, one-time senior VP at Apple with 137,000 employees under her, got to the point even more succinctly: When asked by ABC Radio, "What advice would you give to a new chief executive?" she had a one-word answer: "Listen."

"And what is the greatest mistake a leader can make?"

"Not listening."[15]

'Nuff said.

PERSONALITY CHARACTERISTIC #4: GRIT

Many people first became familiar with the then-uncommon word "grit" from the 1969 movie *True Grit*, starring John Wayne as the boozy, gruff lawman Rooster Cogburn. It's the story of a 14-year-old girl named Mattie Ross who is intent on avenging her father's murder. She knows enough to the seek the help of a guide on her journey through dangerous territory where they will encounter who knows what, but other than that, she has a sole, unwavering focus, and she's committed to it at any cost—including (in the original novel and the 2010 remake) the loss of an arm. Fans of Westerns might assume that John Wayne is the hero of this story, but it's actually Mattie to which the film's title refers. She has a resolute goal, she will stop at nothing to achieve it, and because of her fierce determination, she succeeds.

You obviously don't have to lose a limb to display grit in your role; you don't have to lose anything, really, quite the opposite, you get to hold on to your integrity. For grit means going after what you want with all the resources you have at your disposal with a steady perseverance that does not falter in the face of resistance and impediments. It means you're willing to get your hands dirty to uncover what you want and you're self-disciplined enough to keep digging until you do. It means you're scrappy enough to devise creative workarounds when things get in your way and you'll stay the course of that way forward.

And although it's not necessarily an uncommon personality trait—every single doctor and every single nurse who showed up every single day during the pandemic despite all the death and devastation around them displayed their grit in spades—it's an uncommonly valuable one.

Angela Duckworth, psychology professor and bestselling author of *Grit: The Power of Passion and Perseverance,* goes so far as to posit that grit, which she defines as "sticking with your future, day in and day out, and not just for the week, not just for the month, but years," is the defining factor between those who succeed and those who fail. Additionally, "Grittier people are dramatically more motivated than others to seek a meaningful, other-centered life."[16]

It's not a coincidence that that's what helping people do too: in seeking meaning beyond the self's desires, the helper as leader can embrace their grit to keep hope alive when it's fading, to stay in alignment with your purpose when you're at risk of veering, and to get mentally tough when things get rough in your quest. When you think about it, quest stories are all about grit. If you're on a quest (and almost all helpers are)—if you're mapping out your own journey toward your goal like Mattie Ross—then your grit will help you get there in no small part.

Applying Grit in a Leadership Role

The stockroom was a complete mess from the massive influx of food that kept pouring in beyond the donation deadline, and the kitchen wasn't nearly ready to begin preparing the holiday meal that would feed hundreds in only two days. The floor supervisor put in a call to the shelter's director to alert her that two volunteers were out sick, one was stuck out of town due to a snowstorm, the delivery of green beans wasn't coming at all, and the heater was on the fritz. Maybe they should post a limit to how many people they could feed on the website? Given all these unforeseen obstacles, maybe they should just redirect everyone to all the churches around town also hosting Thanksgiving dinner?

"No, no," Helen responded quietly. "We'll figure this out. Let's figure this out. I'll be right there—we're not going to scale back or let down our community unless absolutely necessary."

Ten minutes later, Helen entered the soup kitchen, direct from a board meeting, in her fancy suit and shoes. After gathering the information she needed, she immediately started organizing the staff into groups and began verbally formulating an ad hoc plan, all the while rolling up her sleeves, donning an apron, and trading in her heels for a pair of waterproof clogs she found in the pantry.

The first step was to finalize the menu: Green beans were out, but there was a surplus of carrots? Good, fine, that's the main vegetable now. Not enough russets came in, but they were swimming in yams—then mashed sweet potatoes it is. Group A was set to work peeling and slicing. Group B was assigned to the stockroom, pulling out only what was needed for this meal, storing reserves for later. Group C did the same thing in the kitchen: prepping only the pans and utensils that would be used in the final menu, everything else could wait.

As for extra hands, did anyone have friends or family they could call on? And Tomás, who knew the electrician personally, could he call him about the heater, promising a special holiday bonus if he'd make an emergency "house call" today?

By afternoon, everyone was covered in foodstuffs, splattered with sink water, and achy from lifting and hauling. But they were laughing. They were dancing to music. They were enjoying the pizza lunch Helen had ordered in. They were one big exhausted team, working in unison together, with their coach right alongside them.

Only hours earlier, the staff had been feeling pretty dejected. But Helen's enthusiasm and can-do determination had rejuvenated their energy and shown them what was possible. They worked until 8 p.m., until all the donation crates were empty, the stockroom shelves were in order, and the tables were set in the dining hall. They'd pull tomorrow night off after all.

What Grit Looks Like in Practice

Grit lies in the crevices nearly everywhere you find accomplishment, even if it isn't conspicuous to the eye. Basically all pro athletes know grit up close and personal—they couldn't put themselves through the grueling physical exertions they do without it. Kobe Bryant and Ted Williams come to mind, the latter of whom was known to go out into the forest to pick the wood for his bats. Walt Disney, too, was known for his grit, having resorted to eating dog food to survive before starting his first animation company (which went bankrupt).[17]

A study done on West Point cadets showed that a "grit questionnaire" proved the best predictor of who would graduate, more than SAT scores, class rank, or leadership skills.[18] Another study done on novice teachers found that grit was the primary indicator of future effectiveness and retention.[19] And even among National Spelling Bee contestants, "Grit predicts success over and beyond talent."[20]

Grit sustained Anne Frank and Victor Frankl through the Holocaust; it fed Nelson Mandela's soul through 27 years in jail. We couldn't see what they were going through in their imprisonments, but we now know what they were made of.

As internal as grit can be, sometimes it is just entirely out in the open. Mahatma Gandhi wasn't bluffing when he vowed not to eat in his lifelong crusade for India's freedom via nonviolent means. Through the course of many hunger strikes and acceptance of, even the welcoming of, a life of extreme poverty, he remained true to his overarching mission: "Even if all the United Nations opposes me, even if the whole of India forsakes me, I will say, 'You are wrong. India will wrench with nonviolence her liberty from unwilling hands.' I will go ahead not for India's sake alone but for the sake of the world. Even if my eyes close before there is freedom, nonviolence will not end."[21] Gandhi inspired people worldwide, he's *still* inspiring people worldwide, and in the end, India did wrench its liberty from unwilling hands.

PERSONALITY CHARACTERISTIC #5: RESILIENCE

Grit is what keeps you standing through all kinds of storms and perils, but resilience is what gets you back up when the winds of life knock you down. If you're out there fighting the good fight and striving for a better future for all, you *will* get knocked down. It just comes with the territory of being a helper. When it's your job to help other people, in any kind of capacity, there's no way you can bat a thousand every time. There's no way you haven't experienced some hard knocks, some dilemmas you couldn't resolve, some people you just couldn't save.

What also comes with the territory, however, is that hard kernel of fortitude you have inside you that refuses to stay down when you get down. It's more than the strength to persevere—it's picking yourself up and dusting yourself off when you've taken a fall; it's the ability to handle the difficulties that beset you without letting them overwhelm you; and, most of all, it's bouncing back when you've been deflated, somehow finding a way to recast adversities into opportunities for growth and progress.

Resiliency both fortifies your strength and affords you elasticity when it's time "to surrender to the rollercoaster ride of life."[22] To roll with the tide instead of futilely thrashing against it, trusting that you'll end up on the shore where you need to be to carry on.

That's a pretty potent characteristic to have, wouldn't you say? It doesn't mean you're tougher than anyone else, it just means you'll keep trying longer and harder than most anyone else. Usually, in the case of the helper, because the struggle is for someone else. There's a nobility in that that you shouldn't underestimate and that any organization should be honored to have on its leadership team.

Applying Resilience in a Leadership Role

Santana was really close to the young men in his detention center. He knew they had criminal backgrounds, knew they could be dangerous, had seen their rage on multiple occasions, had been the object of their menacing stares on far more. But he'd also seen their vulnerability. He knew most of them were just scared little boys under their coarse exteriors, wanting to fit in, to find a group to call their own, to find a place of belonging. He was committed to making their stay as productive as possible and to easing the shame and discomfort of their incarceration for them in the small ways he could.

What they wanted now, they told him, was the cool kicks all the kids were wearing. It didn't matter that they were locked up where no one would see them or that all they'd have to pair them with was their uniforms. They wanted them. Bad. And Santana wanted these boys he'd grown to love to have something, anything, they wanted, not just needed for basic survival. They were expensive. They were a total indulgence. There was absolutely no use for them inside the center. Santana didn't care. He cared about his boys—making them feel like they were important enough to ask for something, to deserve something.

He started with his immediate superiors. Immediate no. He'd have to go higher up in the chain. So he did. He appealed to every officer and director in the Department of Corrections, filling their in-boxes and voicemails with messages of all types—formal, informal, humorous, heartfelt. Some responded tersely; some responded apologetically; some didn't respond at all. He contacted bureau chiefs, mayors, district representatives, congresspeople. He reached out to the city, the county, the state. But the answer was always no—it wasn't within their authority, it wasn't in the budget, it wasn't . . . well, it just wasn't *done*.

Finally, eventually, Santana received a reply he could work with: if he was able to raise the money himself, the boys could have the shoes. He'd have the support of the State Department of Juvenile Justice, he could use office supplies and resources to launch a fundraising campaign; the system just couldn't fund the purchase directly.

So Santana went to work with the local community—with the boys' families, places of worship, and youth and outreach centers—devising an ingenious plan, based on pledges for young people's good behavior, to collect the thousands of dollars needed. Four months after he'd placed his first phone call, Santana had enough to buy all 73 pairs of designer sneakers. The chief of police in the county was so impressed with Santana's efforts that his department matched the funds to purchase new sporting and recreational equipment for the facility as well.

What Resilience Looks Like in Practice

Did you know that Michael Jordan was cut from his high school varsity basketball team? Arguably the best basketball player of all time may never have lit up the NBA if he hadn't rebounded from that blow. "Whenever I was working out and got tired and figured I ought to stop, I'd close my eyes and see that list in the locker room without my name on it. That usually got me going again."[23]

Thomas Edison failed as many as 10,000 times before he made the lightbulb practical. Stephen King's first novel, *Carrie*, got rejected 30 times before it was finally picked up; now, he's one of the highest-selling authors of all time, with 350 million copies of his books sold. And Bethany Hamilton is nothing but the epitome of resiliency, returning to the waves on her surfboard only one month after she lost her arm to a shark attack at age 13, taking first place at the Explorer Women's Division of the NSSA National Championships within two years.[24]

Tiger Woods has also shown impressive resiliency, first bouncing back from a series of unfortunate personal scandals and physical ailments in 2009 to win the Masters in 2019 and, more recently, returning to the links after a life-threatening automobile accident in 2021.

As for Martha Stewart, she "totally rebranded herself" after her five-month stint in federal prison in 2004 for financial misconduct, which required her to step down from the board of her own company. These days, she's more famous and successful than ever, with forays into writing, multimedia projects, a cannabis company, a retail food line, and a seemingly unlikely friendship with Snoop Dogg that's garnered her loads of publicity. Having been featured on the cover of *Fortune* magazine declaring, "I cannot be destroyed," Martha Stewart just might be the greatest comeback queen of our times.[25]

Another remarkable, weightier comeback owing to personal resiliency belongs to Benjamin Netanyahu. In a political career that has spanned close to 35 years, Netanyahu is Israel's longest-serving leader, having won a record five elections, more than any other prime minister in the country's 74-year history. But the road has been rocky at times, including the death of his beloved brother, much political opposition, several lost elections, a resignation in protest, a suspected coup, allegations of criminal activity, and an ousting from office in June 2021.[26]

But now Netanyahu is back, promising "a national government that will look after everyone" and pledging to heal the divisions in Israeli society in a country that "respects all its citizens."[27] Whether or not you support his stances and whether you think "Bibi" is a brilliant leader or a threat to democracy, Netanyahu's tenacity cannot be denied. He isn't giving up, and he isn't going away. As a central player on the global stage since the 1980s, he's a patent example of staying in the ring despite numerous knockouts, holding fast to his place and his case as he aims to impact and influence the world.

PERSONALITY CHARACTERISTIC # 6: PASSION

"Passion," "having a calling"—we've all heard this so much when talking about professional development that it's become a cliché, right? But here's the thing about clichés: they arise out of universal truths. If people didn't have callings, there'd be no religious leaders, there'd be no Doctors without Borders or war correspondents, there'd be no teachers. Heck, there'd be no parents.

Passion is supremely important—and odds are, if it weren't deeply rooted in you, you wouldn't have chosen your profession. Instead, comments like this (aptly from teachers) probably resonate fully with you:

> [Passion] says that what you do can't be separated from who you are. Your gut tells you what you must do, not some pro-con list. Work-life balance is not about disconnecting from work but pursuing all the things that generate inspiration for your work. A true teacher never turns off. For a teacher, it means you couldn't imagine doing anything else. It means that everything in your life—relationships, hobbies, you name it—feeds your teaching mind and winds up in your lessons.[28]

Or this, from an interviewer, "Teaching is a calling, something they must do to feed their souls. When I asked a first-grade teacher in Minnesota why she chose teaching, she paused and said, 'I think teaching chose me.'"[29]

Doing something you're passionate about brings a profound sense of gratification, an almost-spiritual awareness that you're doing what you were meant to do. It also carries practical benefits. According to psychologist Patricia Chen, "When employees are passionate about their work in an adaptive manner, they tend to experience more positive emotions and fulfillment when working, which buffer them from many of the stressors and strain that they might otherwise bring home."[30] In other words, passion yields improved health and shields against burnout. When our insides are taken care of, our outsides respond.

You'd think that passion is so sublime, it can't be quantified, but *Forbes* has taken a crack at it with a list of indicators that passion is present in your occupational calling:

1. Your actions further your plans, even if they are ambitious and distant. You follow your passion naturally. It's your destiny.
2. You regularly find yourself in flow. You're highly engaged in the task at hand, with your thoughts streaming freely; when you check the time, you're surprised at how much has passed.
3. You don't halt or stop what you're doing. You stay on the path until circumstances force you off, and then you can't wait to get back on.
4. You're confident you have strong tailwinds propelling you toward the future.
5. You're highly productive—"in the zone," as they say—intent on doing the best you can to both apply your abilities and augment them.
6. You make progress. Noticeable progress.
7. You love what you're doing—it nourishes you soul-deep. You can't imagine being happy doing anything else.[31]

Does any of this ring true for you? Do you know you've found your calling? If so, you're fortunate, as not everyone does, and, interestingly, those who leave a calling unanswered are actually far unhappier than those with no calling at all.[32] It isn't always an automatic process, though—hefty decisions and sacrifices sometimes have to be made to get to that place; but when that readily accessible passion inside you is what drives the process, it's far easier to get there.

To paraphrase an eloquent summation, a calling resides at the intersection of three things: doing something you're good at, feeling appreciated, and believing your work is making people's lives better. "When those three things line up, it's like lightning."[33]

Applying Passion in a Leadership Role

The whole team at the teletherapy company was gathered in the conference room for their monthly meeting, and the owner of the company threw out a question for consideration: "What else can we sell to our market?" The owner was looking to expand the service line—find other ways to generate income beyond direct treatment sessions with their speech, occupational, and physical therapy patients.

The head of the accounting department instantly offered up, "Whatever makes the most money," which earned a little chuckle. But Preeti quickly countered with, "No, that wouldn't feel right to me, especially with our service-based orientation. It would have to be something I could believe in and get behind."

The owner agreed. She didn't want her team to "sell" something just for the sake of selling—she wanted to add value to both the company's service menu and its clients. "I have an idea." She left the room quickly and returned with a big box of matches they stored in the kitchen and a stack of plain envelopes. "I want to know what would rev you up—what you'd be excited to promote and what you think our brand *should* be promoting."

She instructed everyone to write *What Lights My Fire* on the outside of their envelope, then come up with at least five things they were passionate about in their lives. For each thing, place a match in the envelope and name what that match represents on the back.

Daniel was a bit confused. "You mean, like, music? I'm passionate about music, but I don't see how in the world that relates to my job." But he went along with the others and completed the exercise, mostly because it was enjoyable.

And something like joy is what resulted. When everyone had shared their "matchsticks" and the group brainstormed about how to translate those passions into revenue, they came up with offering music lessons to their physical therapy patients, outings to the local trampoline park for the occupational therapy patients (in line with Fabian's love of gymnastics), and evening classes to demo specialty recipes for their patients with swallowing issues (amateur chef Gillian's idea). It was the best meeting they'd had in a year.

What Passion Looks Like in Practice

The matchbook exercise is about identifying your passions so you can start incorporating them into your daily life as much as possible. "Living with passion is about paying attention to and following what makes you come alive inside."[34] When people are passionate about their vocations, they give more of themselves willingly. They'll work longer hours. They'll volunteer for nonmandatory tasks.

And they approach their assigned tasks with far more creativity and vigor. Once they find that path that brings them joy and fulfillment, they have much greater job satisfaction, their productivity increases, and employers retain them longer. That's really key—an employee who relishes their job is a rare find.

As much as Americans are working nowadays, a growing number of companies are financially supporting their team members' passions *outside of* work. The clothing company Betabrand, for instance, pays for its employees to travel to an international destination of their dreams. The software company FullContact offers a "paid paid vacation," which includes $7,500 on top of paid vacation time that employees can use for anything they want, as long as it's *not* work related.[35] These programs easily pay for themselves through the added motivation and commitment that employees bring to work in return.

Isn't this fantastic? This recognition of the igniting force of passion and actually valuing that now in the workplace?

It's hard to talk about passion in the workplace without thinking of Herb Kelleher, cofounder and later president, CEO, and chair of Southwest Airlines. Kelleher was all about people first and profits second (understanding that the former will create the latter), building a standout culture based on passion for work, respect for employees, fun, and love. Yes, love. Southwest was branded "the love airline," with tickets issued from "love machines," in-flight drinks labeled "love potions," and snacks served as "love bites."[36] Kelleher savored getting his people excited about his vision, considering Southwest "a cause or a crusade," not a faceless corporation.

Their mutual adoration—Kelleher's for his team and his team's for him—led to an astounding array of awards over the years (like the airline being named the Best Place to Work in America in 1998 and Kelleher earning the title of CEO of the Century from one publication),[37] industry-revolutionizing innovations, enviable profit margins, extraordinary retention rates, and, unbelievably, not one furlough on his watch. This is a man and model to study in depth. "If you're crazy enough to do what you love for a living," he said, "then you're bound to create a life that matters."[38]

This list of personality traits certainly isn't exhaustive. Others have proffered their own takes on what characteristics contribute the most to leadership potential—to take just one example, *Kelly Vana's Nursing Leadership and Management*,[39] which adds such entries to those above as integrity, daring, curiosity, sociability. But the underlying premise is that there *is* a generally agreed-upon personality profile that makes for an exceptionally talented leader. And the underlying premise here, in this book, is that this profile is reflected in a helping professional's constitution uncommonly well.

Whatever your leadership style may be now or in the future, your innate traits that have been further refined throughout your career to date transfer wonderfully to all sorts of leadership spheres with all kinds of populations. Let's take a look at some of those now and some of the lessons you can glean from each.

Chapter 5

Learn as You Go

Those who rise in their fields have no choice but to learn as they go along, for each new role brings with it new experiences, new colleagues and bosses, new challenges. Typically, one masters, or at least becomes sufficiently proficient in, each job duty before taking on or being given more functions, and with each additional responsibility you assume, another layer of experience is draped over you, another color and texture of thread is woven into your personal and professional fabric.

Sometimes people get so consumed by the "moving up" part of their career—maybe because they have financial pressures on them, maybe because they put the pressure on themselves to seek promotion after promotion—that they rush through the "now" to get to the "then," perhaps missing some of the incredibly worthwhile learning to be accrued along the way, which can then be intelligently and strategically applied later. There's learning to be had at every level, at every tier of every career's progression, even those at the very beginning.

There's also a direct connection between learning and leadership. John F. Kennedy knew it 60 years ago: "Leadership and learning are indispensable to each other." And motivational speaker and professional development coach Brian Tracy knows it today: "Continuous learning is the minimum requirement for success in any field."

So no matter what rung of the ladder you're currently on and no matter how high you want to go, pay attention to what the position is teaching you—what lessons you can take from it in return for all the effort you've devoted to it. This will serve you in your current role, it will serve you in all future roles, it will serve you in life. And what is life, really, if not an ongoing learning process? In the poetic words of George Whitman, "All the world is my school, and all humanity is my teacher." The value of continual learning is inestimable—you're never done, and it never runs out. What else delivers that kind of return on investment?

LESSONS LEARNED WHEN YOU'RE STARTING OUT

When helpers are first starting out in their careers, their early exposure and education often come in the form of unpaid work, like volunteer positions, trainee programs, and school-assigned internships. Even once they've completed the formal education needed to embark on a career in their chosen fields, initial jobs are commonly high-exertion, low-paying affairs that send you home at night with just enough energy to veg out on the couch until bedtime. But don't mistake a paucity of financial compensation for a lack of growth opportunity. There's a tremendous amount of knowledge and personal insight that can be amassed in the early steps of one's helping career.

Volunteer Work Crystallizes Your Purpose

Money might make the world go round, but it's time—our most precious commodity—that people yearn for when they're being serviced by a charitable organization. Donations are necessary to fund the operation, sure; but without feet on the ground walking the walk and hands outstretched to deliver goods and services, the donations would never make it to the intended recipients.

When you're one of those volunteers giving your time freely, you'll no doubt find that you get far more than you give. It doesn't matter if you try your hand at planning a bake sale for a church, working the register at a thrift shop, driving people to doctor's appointments, coaching Little League, or building a house for Habitat for Humanity, you'll feel instantly rewarded just by doing something selfless and outward-focused. And the "trying your hand at" part is very important: the more ways you volunteer, the clearer you'll get on what area of need appeals to your sensibilities the most.

Tamara's mother was a nurse and her role model, and she couldn't wait to turn 16 so she could become a junior volunteer (what they used to call "candy stripers") at the hospital. On day two, she discovered she had an almost-allergic reaction to the sight of needles and blood. She wouldn't be following in her mother's footsteps after all.

Viktor was an English major and loved words above all else, so he was excited to become a literacy volunteer. But he found himself very surprisingly but very genuinely irritated at the middle schooler he was tutoring when she just wouldn't do the homework he assigned her. She just wouldn't put in the effort on her own. When he heard that the office needed someone to compose the monthly newsletter, he volunteered for that instead.

Both Tamara and Viktor had to pivot—and that's okay. In discovering what they were not cut out to do, they were one step closer to finding what they were cut out for. In this way, volunteering is kind of like going shopping for jeans. You can't really know which pair you'll want to buy until you try on enough to find just the right fit. Volunteering lets you "try on" a variety of roles—usually of your own choosing and on your own schedule—and in the process, it's a particularly useful means of pinpointing where and how you want to dedicate your time and effort.

Volunteering is far more than a "means" to an end, of course! It's a win-win circle of enrichment all around, with well-documented benefits for everyone involved. But that doesn't mean it can't also be an extremely enlightening learning tool. And to get the enlightenment? All you have to do is show up.

Internships Provide an Essential Foundation

Learning from the bottom up just might be the most prized form of learning there is. Why? Because when you're a part of mixing the cement for the foundation, you know exactly what that base can hold, what it was built to withstand, and what underpins the entire structure. Participating in an organization at its ground level, which is often where interns are placed, not only contributes to an understanding of the organization as a whole as you observe the fundamental and inner workings of the day-to-day operations, but it gives you an excellent view of the way up.

Since most internships are assigned by the future helper's college or training program based on availability, need, and existing partnerships with the agencies or establishments offering the internships, you often don't have much say or choice at all as to where you'll be placed. You might love it or you might hate it, but you're stuck with it for the term of the internship, so you might as well use your time wisely.

You're literally the boss of nothing and no one, and you have to do what anybody and everybody tells you to do, which is usually what nobody else wants to do, like clean the bathrooms, empty the garbage, collate a thousand copies of a manual, go clean up that guy who vomited on himself. On it and on it.

You learn humility from that. You learn how to do small tasks with great pride. You learn how to treat others who will be in the same position later in your career.

But being in a low-ranking position carries some advantages too. The employees aren't trying to impress you or hide anything from you, so you'll get a good feel for what makes the place tick—you'll see who's really pulling the strings, and on what or whom the service organization actually relies. And because you're not a paid employee who's expected to perform skillfully yet, you get some leeway to experiment by trial and error, you have the freedom to try things out without worrying about getting demoted or fired. You're there only to learn, and the people guiding you know that. So not only are mistakes and missteps easily pardoned, but they're beneficial opportunities for those mentoring you to show you how to do things correctly.

You know what an internship is? It's pure, unadulterated experience in a jar. Years, even decades, later, you'll look at that experience through the glass and still remember how you got it. You'll never forget the first time a client or patient or student screamed at you. Or was clearly upset by or disappointed in you. Or cried in your arms. Good. Don't forget. No one drives forward without regular glances in the rearview mirror that illuminate those first steps of hands-on learning that paved the road for all the steps taken afterward.

Starter Positions Point You in the Right Direction

Kiva felt so lucky when she landed her first job just two weeks after graduating with her MSW. As an associate counselor at a clinic providing family services, she'd be working one-on-one with young children aged three to six, also leading a small-group session with the kids twice weekly. Her first couple of weeks didn't go so well. She came home unsettled and frustrated, knowing she wasn't making a connection, feeling like she hadn't made any significant strides with a single child since she'd started. When the next few months didn't get any better, Kiva went to her supervisor and admitted that she just didn't feel effective—somebody else would be better at this than she was.

Her supervisor had noticed Kiva seemed uncomfortable with the youngest kids there but had wanted to give her time to acclimate. Now, since Kiva had been the one to request a change, her supervisor suggested she try working with older kids—there was a higher level of comprehension with them, more advanced dialogues that could be had, and Kiva's supervisor suspected she'd be more comfortable with that. So Kiva started working with the middle school kids instead, and although things got a little better, they didn't improve enough for Kiva to want to extend her contract beyond the one-year commitment she'd made.

She took a position at an assisted living facility working with geriatric patients, and almost immediately, the tenseness left her chest and her spirits rose. She blossomed in the company of her thoughtful and serene clients, who seemed to accept and appreciate everything she did. Her heart lifted every time she made a resident laugh or smile. She felt useful and productive and proficient.

Kiva always knew she wanted to do work that carried a high level of client interface—that was her goal straight out of school and that hadn't changed; she just realized she related much better to individuals of a certain age. When a friend caught up with Kiva four years later, she'd been appointed the assistant director of the facility and told her friend she absolutely loved going to work every day.

This happens a lot: first jobs (or even second or third) aren't always the right jobs in which a new helper will thrive—but learning that, getting rerouted onto a more suitable path, the earlier the better, is the bright side of what seems like a cloudy start. Jin never would have discovered that he shone in the office, in a controlled setting with his colleagues nearby, if he hadn't attempted a job that entailed solely home visits; and Lauren never would have shifted her focus from grief counseling to hospice care if she hadn't taken that earlier job at the cancer center—being with people at the end of their life just felt like where she wanted to be more so than with those mourning the end of life.

Either way, whether your initial experiences feel far afield or close to the target but not quite there, when you're in a job that doesn't feel like home, move. You'll find your place. You'll find your people. And the jobs you take early in your career are what will point your way there.

LESSONS LEARNED IN THE FIELD

Those of us who actually go into the community to do our work—visiting speech-language pathologists (SLPs), roaming BCBAs, social workers, home health aides, early interventionists, rehab specialists—know that "field experience" is its own brand of experience. There's nothing quite like seeing the people you serve in their own environments instead of yours, among their own families unknown to you, walking into a place you've never been and having no idea what to expect.

What you *can* expect is to learn *a lot* from observing people on their own turf and then discovering how to apply all the know-how and "street smarts" you pick up across other places and people.

What You Can Learn Working with Underprivileged and Underserved Populations

Many helping jobs—not all, but most—serve populations in need. They may be in need of financial resources, employment, housing, health care, mental health services, social services, legal services, or education/training. Whatever the need, it has created some form of lack in their lives, and the helper is there to fill it.

It's not always easy to work off-site with people who are struggling with something—all you want to do is make it better for them, blink your eyes like a genie and make their problems or issues go away . . . but you can't. All you can do is your job. But you can do your job with the utmost kindness, tenderness, understanding, diligence, and grace you can muster.

You will hear stories of inequity and bias—racism, ageism, sexism, classism. Listen with those awesome active listening skills of yours and make sure the speakers feel heard. You will see living conditions that make you feel equal parts guilty and grateful for your own. Ease those conditions directly whenever you can through the resources of your organization, then do your best to teach your clients what they can do to improve their own environment. You will see hardship and pain, whether in the eyes of an adolescent with a stutter, an adult with advanced diabetes, or a parent whose child has been taken away.

In all cases, lead with compassion, guide with patience, and preserve dignity no matter what. And keep your composure—the people you're treating, teaching, or helping are looking to you to keep them balanced and hopeful, so train yourself to maintain your own equilibrium and optimism. In the field, you will learn how to do all of this, and more.

At their core, the helping professions are about serving other people. That's it. It's that basic. So when you encounter individuals who are clearly being underserved, serve them. Serve them with your heart and soul, serve them with your expertise and resourcefulness. You will learn that you can make a difference in every single life you touch. You already have.

The Importance of Mentors

No one just lands a job in the helping professions and knows how to perform their role perfectly right of the gate. With your helper's mindset, the ways your heart and brain influence you are huge advantages, it's true, but there's only so much you can know going into any new endeavor and there's only so much you can learn on your own.

That's where a mentor comes in. Find one. Get one.

Where would Rocky Balboa be without Mickey? The Karate Kid without Mr. Miyagi? Nowhere, that's where. Even when there's plenty of natural raw talent and gumption, having a veteran on hand and on call to share their knowledge with you and help you make career-defining decisions is indispensable.

Even the very biggest names in business, the most successful of all success stories out there, had mentors. Mark Zuckerberg learned from Steve Jobs, Warren Buffet advised Bill Gates, Oprah Winfrey relied on the wisdom of Maya Angelou. And get this: even Mother Teresa had a mentor. *Mother Teresa.* An actual *saint*, who devoted her entire life to the most impoverished peoples on the planet, even she sought guidance from Father Michael van der Peet.[1]

It can be at any point in your career, but this is a case of earlier is better, because as you make a go of it, you won't have to go it alone. Bryan had to admit he was proud of himself when he was promoted to team supervisor after only 18 months on the job, but inside, he wasn't feeling as confident as his smile suggested on the outside. When Francine took him under her wing, though, things shifted significantly for him.

She believed in him before he ever believed in himself—in fact, he learned that she was the one who'd recommended him for the promotion. She invited him to accompany her when the organization's various vice presidents met monthly so he could get a preview of how things were run at an upper echelon, and she even scheduled mentoring sessions with him every other week—prodding him to consider where he wanted to go in future and then helping him develop a plan to get there. Having Francine in his corner made all the difference for Bryan, and she remained an active contributor and his biggest champion throughout his career.

And keep this very important point in mind: mentoring goes both ways. A helping professional will develop in multiple ways with their own personal guide showing them the ropes and how to avoid pitfalls; but in your role, you're serving as a mentor too, particularly with the young people you meet. Any gain you can induce for each individual has a far-reaching ripple effect.

One research study put it this way: "Mentored youth are likely to have fewer absences from school, better attitudes towards school, fewer incidents of hitting others, less drug and alcohol use, more positive attitudes toward their elders and toward helping in general, and improved relationships with their parents."[2] If every person mentored one kid in need, just imagine the massive sea change that would create in society.

Whatever you learn from your mentor? Pay it forward. Think of your clients as mentees, approaching them as such when appropriate, and watch them—and you—prosper with the effort.

If You Want to Lead, Learn How to Follow

It's a simple idea, really, but it's not always easy to execute. Similar to the song lyric in Aerosmith's "Dream On"—"You got to lose to know how to win"—you can't really be an exemplary leader if you don't also know how to follow. And when you're out in the field, where "everyone's got their dues in life to pay" (still Aerosmith), it's the prime time to take a look around and see where and how following someone else's lead can work to your own advantage and to those you serve.

Don't mistake "follower" as a subservient or inferior role. Rather, says Professor Greg Shea from Wharton's Center of Leadership and Change Management, the leader-follower dynamic must be *relational* to exist. In other words, one can't even be a leader without requisite followers, just like there is no great teacher without students, no great novelist without readers.

"Fluidity" between the borders of both functions is optimal, Shea continues, "so work on your leadership and your followership, transitioning as needed between the roles. The best results come when you identify and leverage everyone's strengths, not just your own."[3] He gives the terrific example of explorer Ernest Shackleton, who never would have made it out alive with his crew when the *Endurance* was immobilized by Arctic ice in 1915 without heeding the expertise of the ship's carpenter on the soundness of wooden ships and deferring to the ship's navigator for direction.

When you, too, are out there captaining the waters of your career, you will play both roles, so you'll want to absorb and remember what being the follower feels like when you become the leader. There are two reasons for this.

First, no one wants to follow a "my way or the highway" kind of boss—not only does that make you a difficult person to work for and with, but your way won't always be right, it's just not statistically possible. "There's real value in followership," claims *Fast Company*, arguing that "the best followers make the best leaders" because "leadership isn't about expecting those around you to cater to your every need. It's about identifying your team's potential, and maximizing them as you work toward a shared goal together."[4] When you learn to take direction graciously, you can learn to give direction diplomatically.

Second, any good leader must delegate—you're not going to get very far without it. Nothing in the helping professions is a solo act, no accomplishment is going to be had by just one individual, no matter how devoted or bright they may be. Effective delegating rests on learning where you're weaker and where someone else is stronger so you can let them take the lead, *as their leader*, trusting them to do the job better than you could.

So discover the areas where you don't shine so brightly when you're doing your fieldwork, as this will markedly inform and enhance your subsequent work. Knowing when to turn the reins over to someone more skilled than you in this or that area just might be the strongest display of leadership.

LESSONS LEARNED IN THE OFFICE

Once you're in a management position—any level of management position—that means you're now leading people and not just directly delivering services. It's a whole new ballgame now, where you suddenly find yourself coaching the team and calling the shots instead of out there in the field with the other players. It's different to sit behind a desk and direct—to be in charge of orchestrating plans and strategizing initiatives. It can be edifying and empowering, too, but it's still different.

And yet what remains the same for a helper—what marvelously and thankfully always seems to stay the same—is the focus on people, the concentration on human capital and what that's capable of doing to improve the quality of life for other humans. So it should come as no surprise that some of the most decisive lessons you can learn when you transition to an office setting (whatever that looks like for you in today's rapidly changing remote workforce) apply to your staff more than your services. When you prioritize their growth and efficacy, the services your organization provides will grow in kind.

Leadership Is a Balancing Act

One of the biggest things leaders figure out when they first start to lead is that leadership is a balancing act. There's never just one approach that will work all the time, one "script" that all your employees will respond to uniformly. Management is more like a seesaw on which you have to continually keep multiple facets of your goals in parity, sometimes in differing quotas for differing circumstances on a sliding basis, to create a harmonious whole that is both pliant and firm, adaptable but consistent.

Here are a few dichotomies you will encounter frequently. When you learn to employ them in tandem, occupying each seat of the seesaw in equal measure but at varying intervals as the situation calls for one or the other, you will achieve a well-balanced and agreeably symmetrical workplace in which you will be admired by your people for your fairness and your people will feel steadily respected.

Pair Empathy with Accountability

Empathy, as you know, is being sensitive to another's feelings, the ability to put yourself in their shoes and understand where they're coming from and why. Accountability, on the other hand, is holding someone responsible for what they've been entrusted to do—expecting them to act, speak, and behave in ways commensurate with their job description such that the objectives of that description are attained. One is all about emotions, the other is all about outcomes. You *can* lead with one but not the other, but you shouldn't. As with all the contrasts we'll cover in this chapter, a balanced blend of both will prove a far more potent methodology to attain desired ends.

Empathy comes far more naturally to the helping professional, like Ethan. Ethan ran a vocational training program for young adults with disabilities, and his whole staff genuinely liked him. He was liberal with his compliments, loose with his encouragement, and always supportive of whatever they were going through at work and at home. But Desiree had grown frustrated with him as her boss, eventually confiding to him, "You're great with the students, holding them accountable for their performance, but you don't do that with the staff." Half of her colleagues were self-motivated and effectual, she told him, but the other half were slacking, not putting in the same time and effort and not following directives. As a result, Desiree was losing trust in his leadership ability, and he was losing control of the staff.

"You're a nice guy, Ethan—if I were having a party, I'd invite you. But I don't really care anymore that you're nice. I want a boss who can see the distinction between my output and that of others and rewards us differently on the basis of that." This was a big wake-up call to Ethan; he thought he'd created such a congenial, understanding work environment, but Desiree made him realize that he may have done so at the expense of losing his best people. With empathy alone, you may be held in high regard but not necessarily in high esteem.

With accountability added to the mix, however, justice and decency are reestablished, as you hold all team members to the same standards, you clearly communicate their roles and responsibilities, and you expect all to make their contribution to the overall group mission. Feedback is based on actual performance and merit matters. Without holding people sufficiently to account, the best and the worst get similar treatment. This causes incentive to fade, productivity to flounder, and turnover to spike.

As a leader, it's part of your job to keep others responsible for doing theirs. You can still do this with the affinity and awareness intrinsic to your instinctual empathy, but neglecting to enforce accountability across your whole staff in the interests of being well-liked will eventually breed resentment and dissatisfaction. Finding the sweet spot between the two that will best motivate each individual employee will lead to spot-on results.

Show Strength and Compassion

It's not just one or the other—it's both. You already have both within you, and a leadership role calls for you to exhibit both: the firm resolve and stamina that's needed to get things done and the warm-heartedness that you'll always want to preserve when it's people, vulnerable and flawed real people, you're depending on to get those things done. Being strong and being compassionate seem like antithetical qualities that do not go hand in hand, but when you conjoin the two, the result is a much more powerful sum: compassionate strength.

When people make mistakes (which they inevitably will), when difficult conversations must be had (which they often must), and when you need to accomplish a task that cannot be done without your team's cooperation (which is frequently the case), displaying compassionate strength will get you much farther much faster than either strength or compassion alone. The one can be too hard and demanding; the other can be too gentle and forgiving. But comingling the two is like hitting upon Goldilocks's "just right" formula.

Compassion is akin to empathy, but whereas empathy entails the capacity to share one's emotional experience, compassion is a bit more active, incorporating a desire to want to *do* something to alleviate one's distress—you don't actually have to pick up on the other's feelings to respond with concern and care for them. Gallup research indicates that compassionate leadership makes employees feel like they *matter*; consequently, their productivity, profitability, customer ratings, retention, attendance, and even safety all rise.[5] Similarly, the *Harvard Business Review* states that compassion "improves collaboration, raises levels of trust, and enhances loyalty."[6]

All of this is great, no doubt about it, and the fact that helpers have an organic bent toward compassion means they don't even have to train themselves to get in better touch with it. However, just acting in ways that show you care about your staff and recognizing them as the most critical and meaningful resource you have isn't going to maintain the budget, generate the annual report, or meet the quarterly mileposts.

Strength of purpose and focus is a prerequisite for any organization's success, and it's a leader's obligation to embody a certain amount of toughness to keep the train on the tracks. This means having to be the responsible adult in the room. This means being decisive. This means doling out constructive criticism when warranted, not just the praise you'd prefer to give.

There are ways to practice a well-proportioned amalgamation of strength + compassion:

- **Use the "reverse Oreo" technique:** Whenever you need to deliver some "bad news" to someone, encase the hard bit on both sides with "good news" for counterbalance. "Simon, you're such an exceptional worker, and even though I have to ask you to redo the proposal because it didn't include all of the grant parameters, I have full confidence that you can do it in time because of your full understanding of what's at stake here and your proven drive to always meet your objectives."
- **Follow the one-in-ten rule:** For every negative comment you need to transmit to an employee, relay ten positive comments about them in an adjacent span of time.
- **Gain commitment:** People like to feel that their viewpoint counts, so give them choice and agency whenever you can. As you assign Pamela the white paper, ask *her* to name a manageable "by-when" date to show consideration for her schedule and workload. When she answers, "By four o'clock on Thursday," she has been given the authority to set her

own deadline, and it will become a matter of conscience to her to fulfill her promise to you.
- **Be sympathetic but direct:** When you have to tell someone something you know they won't want to hear, getting right to the point is actually far kinder than beating around the bush. "Hey, Jerry, I know this might sting a little, and I'm sorry for that—I remember how it felt when the same thing happened to me—but we're going to have to replace you on the Smithson case with Bradley at the client's request. It just wasn't the best fit for either of you, so we'll find you a better one next time."
- **Go private, not public:** Calling someone out for a misstep or slip in judgment in front of their coworkers isn't just a no-no, it's entirely avoidable. When you need to reprimand someone in any way, do so in private, behind closed doors. Publicly embarrassing or belittling an employee isn't strength-based, it isn't "setting an example"; it's mean-spirited.
- **Replace "but" with "and":** A pet guideline in popular psychology, this tactic nevertheless works. Would you rather hear from your spouse, "You're such a loyal and loving partner, but I simply cannot tolerate your sloppiness anymore" or "You're such a loyal and loving partner, and I'm asking you to keep the bathroom neater so we can spend less time arguing about the towels on the floor and more time enjoying each other's company"?
- **Give immediate, specific feedback:** "Your performance just hasn't been up to snuff lately, Violet" is vague, pejorative, and, thus, useless. It's far better to be completely clear about what you need to say and to say it while the incident is still timely: "In yesterday's log, Violet, I noticed you haven't gotten to your assigned follow-up steps yet. Did you encounter some kind of obstacle I might be able to help you with?"
- **Conduct trainings with your staff:** Last, you can't expect people to know how to do something if they've never done it. If you're under pressure to meet a target or launch a program, you can't will it into existence on the strength of your commitment to the project or by subtly bullying your staff to produce. But you can teach them what to do instead of just assuming they'll figure it out on their own. Remember, compassion has an active element to it—your willingness to improve a situation you can improve—and equipping people with the tools they need to do their jobs at the highest possible level so that you can do yours at the same level is an act of compassionate strength.

Be Tough on Results, Soft on People

Human beings weren't meant to withstand gale-force winds, torrential downpours, or (despite what your parents or grandparents might have told you) walking four miles to school through mountains of icy snow in zero-degree weather. Each way. They *can* survive the severe hardships of life, we know, but when at all possible, they shouldn't have to. Instead, throughout the history of our race, we have perpetually sought shelter, sustenance, protection, and safety. As Earth became easier to inhabit, we were free to go in search of ever more convenient creature comforts.

We are warm-hearted, thin-skinned, well-meaning creatures who respond *so* much better to encouragement, positivity, and caring than to intimidation, negativity, and coercion. With your helper's nature, you hardly need to be told to lead with a benevolent hand, but when there's a ton of top-down pressure on you or you're in the midst of a crisis situation, you might be surprised at how that stress can sometimes pour out and roll onto others. Leading by fear might get you what you need in the short term, but the minute an employee becomes frightened of you, they'll be running for the hills looking for a warmer, more welcoming clime.

And yet the results that are utterly necessary for an enterprise to continue operating are an entirely different matter altogether. Results are not animate, sentient, sensitive, or subjective like people are. You can stay on them like glue and they're not going to get hurt. So you can and should be tough when it comes to adamantly adhering to what must get gone, but that doesn't equate to being tough on the people who are going to make it happen for you.

In fact, the softer, warmer, more understanding, and more magnanimous you are toward them, the harder they will work for you—the more they'll be willing to go all in when the chips are down. This does not translate to forgoing the accountability and strength of leadership just discussed above, but it does mean that there are times when the internal state of your people must take precedence over external results, even when the results are nonnegotiable. You simply won't get the latter if you don't nurture the former—afford your people the shelter, sustenance, protection, and safety our race is programmed to seek.

How do you do this? Well, you *separate* the people from the product in all your communications with the staff, along these lines: "The district has mandated that we achieve a pass rate of at least 80 percent. If we don't hit this mark by the end of next quarter, our funding will be cut, and we'll be at risk of losing the contract. So we need to make this happen. We *can* make this happen. All of us as a group, each of us doing our part. I'll need all hands on deck, each of you contributing your own ingredient to our special sauce in the way only you can. I have some ideas to get us started. When we all meet next week, I'd love to hear your ideas too."

You make it crystal clear that your employees are not personally at fault for any shortcomings in the organization, that they are not and never will be alone in the pursuit of the necessary results that must be achieved at this time. Rather, you are a team, a united front, with a leader who is willing to go to bat for them. "What do you need to help me make this happen, Kevin?" "What can I take off your plate right now, Serena, so that you can allocate more time to this project?"

When your people come to you with stress, you acknowledge it and try to assuage it. When they ask for a mental health day, you grant it. When they request a part-time admin to help free up time in the office, you find a way to send one. And when they break down, you bolster them back up. You let them know that it's okay that they're not indomitable and invulnerable, that you're not either. When you feed your people with kindness and transparent appreciation for the singular contribution they make to the larger whole, they'll go the ends of the earth for you to make you—and themselves—proud.

Don't Mistake Kindness for Weakness

Speaking of kindness . . . It's not that you can be *too* kind at work—kindness is one of those things that there's no limit on; it's that sometimes people will misjudge your extreme likability for extreme leniency. When and if that happens, you'll need to set the record straight—not overtly, with words, but subtly, with a pattern of actions and behaviors that demonstrate over time that you may be very, very nice, but you're also very, very committed to skillfully fulfilling your leadership duties, even when those duties require taking a firm hand or making a firm stand.

Effective organizations don't run themselves—they need deep-thinking, quick-acting conductors at the controls who are ready, willing, and able to make decisive calls, judiciously weigh options, spur growth, and properly and professionally manage teams. You can do all these things kindly, but you cannot do them weakly. Being wishy-washy, enacting things willy-nilly, hemming and hawing too much, tiptoeing around budding issues—these are all signs of anemic management that will slowly erode your employees' belief in you.

It's not that different than parenthood. With your kids, you want to be kind, of course you want to be kind—you want to be their hero and their savior to boot. But it's of greater importance to provide them with the proper direction and guidance that will equip them with the solid footing and internal compass they'll need to successfully make their way in the world. When it comes to their safety and well-being, you're not tentative or hesitant—you're their parent first and their friend second.

The same holds at work. Avoid allowing your kindness to manifest as reluctance or uncertainty to evade stepping on toes or perhaps rubbing some people the wrong way at times. Your kindness is of central importance to your self-identity; but as a leader, you'll want to keep an eye on making sure that it doesn't detract you from what you're there to do. In letting your people see that you'll always be good to them and do right by them and *still* steadfastly hold the line in the name of the company's best interests, your kindness will shine all the more.

Model Your Own Expectations

This one is rather self-explanatory, but it's nevertheless worth a brief discussion, because without "being the change you want to see in the world," leadership is a nonstarter. So:

- If you want punctual employees, be punctual yourself.
- If you expect employees to work overtime as needed, don't cut out at 5 p.m.
- If you expect your people to meet their deadlines, meet yours. Come prepared to meetings, deliver what you say you're going to deliver, and follow up on responses you promise to provide.
- You want a friendly, supportive workplace that's also proficient and ethical. Then be equally personable and professional yourself.
- You want to create a courteous, democratic environment. Then request rather than demand, give feedback not orders, and ask for feedback in return.
- Own up to your own mistakes so your team members aren't afraid to own up to theirs.
- If you want your staff to keep challenging themselves, keep challenging yourself.

It's simple, really: be the employee you want your employees to be . . . and then watch them follow the leader!

The Business Model Needs to Flex with the Times

As much as we've talked about the people side of doing business (because that's the side you stand on and hopefully always will), there is, of course, a business side of business underpinning the entire organization. Your organizational resources need to be taken into consideration as much as your human resources.

Just like you must learn to be flexible and responsive with the people you lead based on what the situation calls for, you'll also learn that the business plan that drives your organization is going to have to adapt to changing circumstances as well. Mike Tyson is famous for saying, "Everyone's got a plan until they get punched in the mouth," and that applies to basically any arena in life you can think of.

Within the "win-lose" paradigm that characterizes most industries, when a loss or multiple losses start threatening to interfere with your winning formula, it's necessary to rewrite that formula with new integers and variables, no matter how long it's been in place and how well it's served your people and your mission thus far. And whatever you add or subtract to reinstate an actual or theoretical "profit margin" should be based on what's happening in the real world around you right now. The world is changing much faster than it used to; your business practices have to change with it.

Music downloads have replaced purchased CDs. Netflix and other streaming services have replaced Blockbuster. Amazon is poised to potentially replace almost all brick-and-mortar retail shopping. These are extreme examples of industries that have experienced complete upheavals in the span of a single generation, but not all longstanding entities need to go down with the ship if they can figure out a way to ride the tide and leverage the direction of the trade winds.

The Yellow Pages in the United Kingdom successfully transitioned to Yell.com—they stayed true to their value proposition, but to continue delivering that value, they shifted to the online platform required by the modern marketplace. LEGO has been a household brand for close to a century, but to stay current with the market, they started innovating (after a few false starts at *over*innovating that almost sent them into bankruptcy) by collaborating with the likes of the Harry Potter and Star Wars brands and by making movies starring LEGO characters to continue to see the steady profits they'd become accustomed to.[7]

So let your business model guide you, yes, but don't get so stuck on it, so dictated by it purely because it's been mapped out (think Blackberry, RadioShack, Yahoo!, Sears), that you can't find detours and workarounds when you hit newly erected roadblocks. If you add a product or service, don't stray so far from your mission statement that the novelty will seem foreign and unrecognizable to your client base. If you need to subtract a product or service for profitability, don't sacrifice something that's essential to your company identity even if it isn't your biggest draw any longer. And make sure you have people around you who will tell you the truth—who will advise you on economic and financial matters beyond your realm of knowledge and who understand the consequences of business decisions for which you're going to have to answer.

You've been charged with keeping an organization or a division of an organization sound and afloat through any kind of waters. To do so most effectively, you'll still want to prioritize your team—without a skilled crew, your ship is just a bobbing mass on the sea—but you can never lose sight of your ultimate destination either, of getting there as quickly and smoothly as possible, not regardless of the weather, but building the weather forecast into your plan so you're prepared to reinforce your structure if cracks or leaks form.

Helping professionals are not immune to economic forces—the helping professions are buffeted about by the state of the economy as much as any other kind of profession. But when you learn to roll with the punches, taking your business model along with you to keep up with the times, you'll stay standing.

LESSONS LEARNED OUTSIDE THE OFFICE

As you advance in your helping career, there's much to be learned when you're not at work as well, but still working on your own personal development. There are many avenues you can take to expand your skill set and enhance your competencies beyond the confines of your job, and each offers its own lessons and dividends.

Teaching Is a Learning Experience

It's not uncommon for helpers to fall into some kind of teaching role—it's just a natural fit to find yourself instructing, guiding, or mentoring an individual, small group, or whole auditorium full of people based on your inherent communication skills, empathy, patience, and affinity to problem solve with open ears and an open mind. When you're a teacher of any sort, you have a somewhat rare podium to *imprint*, to make a real, lasting impression on others—something for which your helper's mindset is particularly ripe.

But whether you take on training a group of colleagues at work on a new program or initiative, demonstrating to a group of youngsters how to acquire a new skill or hone an ability, or instructing a college-level class in one of your specialty areas, it's pretty much guaranteed that you'll learn as much as you teach.

You will learn what holds (or doesn't hold) people's attention. You will learn what your students consider valuable as opposed to throwaway information so you can refine your instructional materials for next time. You will learn if you're putting too much or too little time into your preparation. When you read their papers or hear their proposals or listen to their oral presentations, you'll see what sunk in, what went over their heads, and what their biggest takeaways were.

You'll learn to accommodate different learning styles. You will gain a richer understanding of your subject simply by virtue of examining it so closely. Interestingly, you'll learn what *not* to say as much as what *to* say—like leaving your personal opinions at the door, keeping your religious or philosophical beliefs outside what should be objective tutorials, and checking any biases you discover you have. When you offend people, even completely inadvertently, you lose their belief in your expertise.

If you can find an opportunity to teach, do it. If you get an invitation to instruct, accept it. If you're looking for a way to learn, coach learners. Your personal and professional development portfolio will grow in unexpected ways, and the better the teacher you become, the better the student you will remain.

What You Pick Up as a Presenter

Presenting is different than teaching an ongoing course because it's a onetime shot. You have one chance to impress people with your own style of conveying information, one chance to prove why you were the key pick to deliver the keynote address, one chance to connect on the same level as your audience and, at the very same time, position yourself as an expert who has something actually advantageous to impart to them . . . usually in far under an hour. It's a tall order, but it delivers statuesque rewards.

These rewards include things like partaking in incredibly interesting and enlightening discussions you never could have anticipated. (The Q&A portion of presenting is by far the most educational part.) Like being asked questions that stimulate your critical thinking and heighten your ingenuity as you're challenged to respond helpfully and intelligently. (When you come up with an on-the-spot answer that you can tell sticks the landing, it's invigorating!) Like training yourself not to get riled, to stay neutral and professional at all times, even when publicly triggered. Hitting upon touchy issues will develop your tact.

And as mentioned in chapter 1 in reference to your adept communication skills, you'll become even more well-versed in presenting complex concepts through simplified language. In the words of Nobel Prize–winning physicist Richard Feynman, "If you cannot explain something in simple terms, you don't understand it. . . . The ultimate test of your knowledge is your ability to convey it to another."

Because you'll be presenting to people older than you, younger than you, smarter than you, and more or less experienced than you, you'll get a crash course in sharpening your delivery skills. The first time you see glazed-over eyes, bored yawns, and people shuffling the papers in their lap instead of looking at you, you'll be taking mental notes on how to avoid such disengagement at all costs in future. But you'll also be exposed to a wonderful array of folks who will enlarge your perspective and enrich your outlook on your own subject matter with *their* commentary in response to yours. And continually efforting to reach them all will make you an even better helping professional than you already are.

Presenting gets you in front of a wide variety of people in a relatively controlled atmosphere with clear parameters, time limits, and expectations. As such, it's excellent training ground for taking what you learn back to your people at work as you simultaneously relate to them and resonate with them more than ever.

Continue to Engage in Continued Education

In the helping professions especially, professional development programs and advanced certifications are both highly emphasized and highly valued. The more sensitive and attuned you can become to the nuances of your profession, the more impactful you'll be. The more initials you can add after your name, the more you increase your chances of being the first in line for promotions and advancements.

When Lydia was sent by her company to the Advanced Management Program at Dartmouth College's Tuck School of Business, she really didn't want to go at first. She didn't want to take two weeks away from work right when things were heating up, and she told her superiors she'd much prefer to allocate the cost of the program to her team's professional development instead of hers. But once she settled into the program a few days in, she felt this welcome wave of freshness and invigoration she hadn't realized she'd been missing.

She was animated by the units that concentrated on areas she didn't focus on much in her role, like strategy and branding, and she was greatly inspired by all the different voices and viewpoints she was exposed to during the interactive workshops with other executives who'd been complete strangers only days before. She came back to work a much stronger leader who did indeed apply the cost of her tuition to her team by passing on to them so much of the knowledge and excitement she'd gained.

Aaron had been looking for a certification he could pursue that wouldn't require too much of a time and financial commitment but would augment his clinical training with a very focused specialty. His agency was expanding its trauma division in light of the recent school shooting in the area, and when he read about eye movement desensitization and reprocessing (EMDR), he was intrigued by the psychotherapy treatment designed to attend to traumatic memories.

He was able to complete the 50-hour basic training program on his own time over the course of several months, and he'd relished the new challenge so much, he'd signed up for the advanced accreditation course next year. When he shared his news with the director of clinical services at his agency, they scheduled a lunch to talk about launching a new support program Aaron would lead for individuals with PTSD, anxiety, and panic disorder.

It's a given that continuing education is nothing but a boon to you and to everyone in your circle. It keeps you open to change, up-to-date in your field, and constantly upskilling in your career. From it, you gain visibility and agility, and you increase your relevance and confidence.[8] It enhances your networking, your interests, your innovation, and your mental health. It's a personal investment in your own personal growth, and you'd be hard-pressed to find someone who has made or is making this investment who doesn't think it's worth every penny and every drop of sweat equity.

What underpins the desire to continually learn, it's commonly agreed upon, is curiosity—a priceless trait both personally and professionally. *New York Times* journalist Adam Bryant ended his "Corner Office" column after a decade of interviewing CEOs by citing a few qualities common to them. One was their "applied curiosity": "They tend to question everything. They want to know how things work, and wonder how they can be made to work better. They're curious about people and their back stories."[9]

Keeping your curiosity always simmering on the back burner will work to your tremendous advantage throughout your career, and engaging in postsecondary learning is a particularly effectual away to feed that flame.

All this said, it's time for a reality check. Maintaining work-life balance is just as important, if not more so, than pushing yourself to continue learning. There will be times in your life when you just can't swing another commitment, when your family needs to be the sole focus of your off time, when your job alone fills your schedule to the brim and just the thought of taking on more—another course or another certification—is overwhelming.

We helping professionals may want to be and try to be superheroes . . . but we're not. We have the same 24 hours a day that everyone else has, and we have the same obligations and responsibilities outside of work as anyone else, no matter how big our hearts and aspirations. So keep this in mind: It is not necessary to return to school to progress in your career. It is not necessary to keep accumulating accreditations to advance. But if you do set your sights on doing so, allow yourself a realistic and manageable timeline that will preserve an acceptable work-life balance—whatever that balance looks like for you. If you feel drained instead of energized by continued education, if it feels too much like a drudge and not enough like an impetus, hold off until you have the bandwidth to emotionally and mentally accommodate an added learning component. It's absolutely worth taking your time earning that extra degree or credential if a slower pace adds to the quality of your life at that particular point in your life.

So do what you can reasonably and responsibly do. Follow this piece of advice from Albert Einstein, but do it in ways that work for your own lifestyle, schedule, and personal circumstances: "Commit yourself to lifelong learning. The most valuable asset you will ever have is your mind and what you put into it."

LESSONS LEARNED IN THE BOARDROOM

Things can get kind of complicated at the highest tiers of organizational management. Well, not necessarily more complicated, but usually more impersonal in nature, which can often feel contradictory to a helper's identity. But the learning doesn't stop (the learning should never stop) even if you advance to the highest position in your organization, if and when you're in charge of the whole shebang.

It is here, in fact, where your education can broaden in truly unanticipated ways, because it's the business side of your intellect that's being challenged more than the well-developed service side that got you where you are. You'll want to be as prepared as possible for the types of goings-on you'll encounter in a boardroom environment.

Your Board Wants You to Lead

Say you're the head honcho (or one of the head honchos) of an organization overseen by a board of directors. The board has ultimate control and final say over the large decisions and overall direction of the organization, but there's still a management structure in place that runs the day-to-day operations, maintains the company culture, plans the company's growth, and is thus responsible for the actual success of the enterprise. (In other words, you're still accountable for results, you're just not always the one setting those bars!)

At first, it can be intimidating to walk into a boardroom and take a seat with all those suits at the table with their Ivy League degrees. (Yep, it's not just in the movies—board members typically wear awfully nice suits and have awfully impressive credentials.) And even though you're all on the same team, they still have the power to reassign, demote, or fire you. So when you're first getting acclimated to standing in front of a board to speak your piece, you'll likely experience a mixture of nervousness, insecurity, possessiveness over the ground you hold, and a huge dose of approval seeking.

Here's the thing, though: The board wants you to succeed. Very much so. The board is on your side. Not only that, but the board is looking to you for your expertise—they want *you* to lead *them* when it comes to what your client base needs, what your employees want, what will benefit the business, and, of course, what will maximize profits. (Even nonprofits want to maximize revenue to bolster the budget and keep the organization financially sound.)

Sure, you may encounter some arrogance, some off-putting self-righteousness, some preconceptions you wish you could set straight. Loudly. But most board members have other full-time jobs and may sit on several boards. They don't have the time, desire, or even the inside knowledge to lead you. They're depending on you to do your job and want to be able to follow your guidance.

So give them what they want. Have a plan B ready if plan A doesn't work for them, and a plan C after that. Show them you're the right person for the job by always coming prepared with your two cents and open to the two cents they'll want to give in kind. Prove the smarts they're hoping you have and respect theirs in return. Share your ideas and welcome theirs. And you know what? Some of their ideas can be very good. It's a partnership, not an oligarchy. So just follow your natural helper's instinct to be a collaborative partner, and odds are extremely good that your board will soon become your ally.

A Merger Is a Mirage

Okay, this is not always the case, but it usually is. There are some merger unicorns wherein two different entities indeed come together in equal measure and retain equal footing. But if you're faced with a merger at any point in your career, you'll likely find that it's a tug-of-war (albeit an unspoken one) in which one side will eventually overpower the other.

If the merger is managed adroitly, deliberately, and impartially, it's possible that the two parts can coexist harmoniously and equitably while also creating a much stronger, richer whole when combined. Otherwise, sorry to say, a merger is really just an acquisition in which one half emerges the controlling party (even if it's a 51 versus 49 percent split) and the other becomes its subsidiary. And it's usually been planned that way by the "powers that be" (even when you thought you were one of those powers).

More often than not, however, a merger happens between one clearly larger company and a clearly smaller company. Just by using the term "merger" instead of "takeover," the smaller company is meant to feel more secure—and the larger company may even respect and retain some of the values of the smaller—but it's generally assumed by all that the smaller company will fall in line with the bigger. It doesn't have to be a hostile takeover, but it's a takeover nonetheless.

Unfortunately, on average, it seems that around half of all mergers fail (with some studies suggesting well over two-thirds).[10] They continue to persist on the basis of the rationale mentioned above—that one part strong in this area plus one part strong in that area will create an even stronger sum—but it's harder than it sounds to pull off a viable merger due to all kinds of issues, ranging from human resources problems to synergy incompatibilities to clashing cultures.

A well-known example is the 2016 "vertical merger" of AT&T and Time Warner. It seemed like a surefire triumph for a "content distributor" to acquire a "content producer,"[11] forming a far more commanding whole together, but the deal went completely south by 2021, largely because of competing business strategies.

If two media giants cooperating on a deal worth billions of dollars can't pull it off with some of the sharpest business minds at the helm, what chance in hell does your modest service-based helping organization have if a merger is imminent? What can do you do about a merger that's really a takeover in disguise, and what can you learn from this initially disruptive and disorienting development?

Well, once again, you can look to your human capital first when lots of monetary capital is on the line. You can champion your people and yourself, clearly communicating the highly valuable experience and highly informed perspectives you're bringing to the mix, backing up your claims with evidentiary data.

Assuming you're the "smaller" company in this transaction, you'll want to showcase the profitable contracts your team has in place and the established trust your service providers have built in your market. Your brand has recognition clout—if it didn't, you wouldn't be party to this M&A—so you must use all means at your disposal to wield that clout and project the consequences that would result if your brand reputation were underestimated, marginalized, or even erased.

Make it your business to learn the other business so that you can pitch new divisions and lines of service that make sense for the new umbrella organization. Exhibit your nimbleness to organizational shifts and restructuring. Propose solutions for the inevitable friction that will result from the merger, which will illustrate your forethought and your intimate knowledge of your company's culture and staff dynamics. And keep your people informed every step of the way; if you stand by them, they will stand by you.

You must accept that the bigger entity is now in control, yes, and you'll want to acknowledge the redundancies that you realize will be eliminated, but your principal role in an M&A is to fight for your people because you know that it's your people who make your business. Fight like the dickens to preserve as much of your "winning formula" and "special sauce" as you can, broadcasting loud and clear the unique talents and skills your best people possess and the key relationships they have in place with clients, customers, vendors, and even subordinates.[12]

If you are part of a merger, you will learn that you don't have control over all that much. However, when you take the reins over what you still *do* have control over—advocacy for your people, the knowledge required to preserve your organization's standing in the market, and your own unflinching dignity and ethical code—you will come out all right. You might even come out ahead.

A Buyout Doesn't Have to be Bad

There may come a point in the evolution of your organization when an outside entity wants to buy it, which is a good indicator of the company's successful track record. Unlike a merger, wherein the terms can get blurry, a buyout is pretty clear-cut. Most often, a private equity firm does its homework on your organization, likes what it sees, purchases a controlling share in the company, improves the bottom line for a handful of years, then plans to sell it for a profit. The firm doesn't have to specialize in your industry or market, it doesn't have to have any personal stake in the acquisition at all—you just look like a promising investment that has payoff potential in the near future.

If this happens on your watch, there are things to consider and things to know. First, you don't want to sell to an outfit that has just enough money to buy your operation—if so, it won't have the funds to invest in improving your organization, and why sell if it's not going to reap (considerable) rewards for the organization's future? Second, you'll want to find out if the bidder plans to keep the company intact, as in your business model *and* your staff, acknowledging your deeper knowledge of the industry. Does the buyer value your service line and the leadership team that's administering it? Or are you actually looking at a significant overhaul of practices and people?

When contemplating a purchase offer, you'll want to weigh the pros and cons, of course, examining both subjective and objective aspects of the sale. An example of subjective considerations would be the effect on morale and the emotion attached to a loss of control, whereas objective concerns include the need for an influx of cash and the potential to grow the business much larger and much faster than would otherwise be possible. Will you dread or welcome a call from your new owner at the end of the day? Does it feel like good news or bad news to share this proposition with your team?

Before your leadership cadre makes a decision, when you still have a great deal of leveraging power, prioritize transparency. Now is the time to ask a slew of questions, to get clarity on the buyer's intentions and timeline, to analyze what-ifs and discover ramifications of unmet expectations.

Be honest about your own plans too. If you're thinking about transitioning out, the new ownership needs to know that; if you need a commitment that they'll keep you on, they need to know that as well. Who will you be reporting to and how might that affect your role and standing with your people? You may find that you're fine with what you learn. They may want to add a business development person to the team or a business development structure to your approach, and that can be fine as well. Just learn as much as you can about what you're getting into.

The truth is, a buyout is neither good nor bad. It can seem very advantageous at the start and then take a downward turn; or it can feel disheartening at first and then become very positive. But a buyout in and of itself can be a neutral undertaking—just an investment and not an appropriation in any other way. It's the aftermath that can become emotionally charged. So if the buyer doesn't plan on changing anything, great. It's business as usua. But if changes are afoot, you must tell your people that. You've got to be candid with your team, and you've got to be candid with yourself.

Private equity's goal is to invest only what they must up front to make the asset as fiscally attractive as possible, then reap a percentage of the final sale, after which partners split a profit among themselves in an event called a "waterfall." Your goal is to keep the organization alive and well, benefiting as much as possible from the buyer's involvement, such as their business acuity, their resources, their marketing strategies, and their recommendations to bolster the financial health of the company.

If new ownership comes in and cuts staff or quality just to raise profits, then it's a problem. But if their presence allows for more growth, more opportunities, and more sites to do more and better work, then it's the opposite of a problem—it's the prime objective of any business endeavor. When a buyout adds value like this, everyone can win—it isn't a given, but it can be good thing. For you, your people, and your organization.

The Challenges of Launching a Start-Up

Another scenario you might be confronted with in your career trajectory as a leader in the helping professions is being approached (or assigned) by a board or a company's ownership to launch an entirely new venture. It might be your own company that entrusts a start-up to you, which will give you a leg up purely on the basis of your familiarity with the organizational milieu, or it could be a different company that recruits you or that you seek out on your own.

Hopefully, it will be related to the company's current offerings (perhaps an offshoot or spin-off in the form of a new growth asset), and it will likely be right up the alley of your field of expertise (which is why you were chosen for the job), but we're talking about building something from scratch this time. And you're the builder.

Actually, to be more accurate, you're the contractor—because you will learn from the get-go that it's going to take a whole lot of people to erect this new structure, and although you won't be performing all the individual tasks yourself, you will be overseeing every single person doing every little thing to hit your launch date. You might be opening a brand-new school in another region of the country. You might be creating a digital platform for a service that has thus far been provided in person. You may be founding a training institute or designing a new agency or implementing a new program that just received government funding.

But no matter the specific start-up project you're tasked with, you're in charge of planning this menu from soup to nuts—and taking on this feat of engineering can be both terrifying and exhilarating. This is your chance to take everything you've learned thus far and apply it to a blueprint of your own making—no footsteps you have to follow, no on-site boss you have to report to, no business plan already in place. You *are* the business plan.

Here's just a taste of what you'll learn to do when starting up a new enterprise. You will learn about either online protocols or building codes. (Just because you know all about running a nursing training center doesn't mean you know how to properly and legally set up a leased property for this new training center.) You'll learn to set meetings with city officials, health inspectors, boards of education—anyone and everyone required to sign off on your new space in a new place.

You'll possibly have to learn about property taxes or sales tax in your state of operation. You will interview more people than you've ever interviewed in your life (and not the usual helpers you're used to recruiting—now you'll need folks like graphic designers, a marketing or PR firm, carpenters, welders, webmasters), and you'll have to devise a system for deciding who to contract or hire.

Long before you ever get to actually running this business according to your own business model and with your own staff in place, you will learn how to set up payroll. If you haven't already, you will learn to manage accounts receivable and accounts payable. You'll need to figure out how to get all the requisite social media accounts up and running. Will you need an employee manual composed? Independent contractor agreements drawn up? Who will clean and maintain your brick-and-mortar location or safeguard, gatekeep, and update your online location? Most importantly, where will the coffee come from?

This list goes on and on depending on the nature of the project, of course, but did you ever imagine yourself immersed in all this when you first set out to be a helper? It's amazing where your skills can take you, and once again, it's your helper's people skills that will get you the farthest the fastest.

Granted, yours may not be a completely nascent start-up with absolutely no legs to stand on—the company you work for may already have certain systems and personnel in place that you'll be utilizing, like an accounting office, an IT department, a legal team, a supplies provider, or an already up-and-running website for your new branch. Even so, 90 percent of start-ups fail, 10 percent of them before they ever reach their second year, and 70 percent within years two through five.[13] (Lucky for us, in the business sector labeled "Education and Health," the failure rate is only 44 percent within four years.)

Whether you were given adequate funding or a shoestring budget, whether you were allotted assistants or had to find your own, and whether you're very familiar or only partially familiar with the service commencing under your guardianship, getting a new business arm or division off the ground is a challenging undertaking that you may or may not take to. At various junctures along the way, there are some rules of the road you can refer to (or destination points mapped out for you by the ownership), but you must be comfortable when there are no rules.

And at the end of the ramp-up—when you're ready to go live, press the start button, cut the ribbon, or turn the key—you might just find that you loved being the one in the driver's seat, making the whole thing go.

LESSONS LEARNED THROUGH SELF-EMPLOYMENT

Finally, there may come a time in your career when you've had your fill of managing a large group of people or a collection of sites, when the C-suite just doesn't taste as sweet anymore, or when you just don't want to report every morning to someone else's company, working under someone else's shingle, meeting someone else's goals. You want to create something of your very own. You want to be your own boss.

Yeah, there's no more salary and benefits package, no more paid vacation, no more annual retreats, company computer, office breakroom, and water-cooler camaraderie, but there's also no more commute, no more required travel, no more board meetings, performance reviews, and HR politics. If you've never been a CEO before, you can become one now, instantly, overnight. It's a lot of work—you've got to do *all the stuff* just covered above for a start-up and then some—but now you're doing it for yourself. Pretty cool, huh? Cool, yes. But it can also be super hard, super stressful, and super risky.

The great thing about your own entrepreneurial venture, though, is that it can be as elaborate or as streamlined as you want. You can take a bank loan to start a multifaceted operation, or you can drastically mitigate risk by starting with virtually no investment of cash. Either way, you're the visionary and every single thing in your sight line is at your sole discretion. You can start with a fully formed business plan that you began composing in your head years ago, or you can start with just one incredible idea, like Jeanine Patten-Coble did.

In 2009, when Jeanine learned she had breast cancer, she had an epiphany on a beach in the Outer Banks: "I realized, 'You've got to create a place like this where cancer patients can relax.'" By 2010, following her chemotherapy and radiation treatment, Jeanine, a former history teacher, launched Little Pink Houses of Hope by talking property managers and homeowners into donating residences for free weeklong retreats. Her nonprofit, which runs on a network of volunteers, has since gifted more than 2,000 families with all-expenses-paid vacations, including food and activities. She's currently working on securing free transportation to the getaways, the one expense not yet covered.[14] Jeanine didn't need money or a staff or an office space. Jeanine only needed her dream.

Here's some of the fun stuff you'll learn to do when you start your own business: Come up with a fab and fitting name. Pick a great-looking logo and branding color palette. Choose your own website design. Write a pithy tagline. Decorate your office. Set your World's Greatest Boss mug on your desk. Appoint your kids your first interns, your spouse your VP, and your friends your first mock clients.

Here's some of the not-so-fun stuff you'll have to do: Mop the floors. Get the broken pipe fixed. Pay the bills . . . *all* of the bills, *all* of the time. Talk people into working for you for less than they're currently making—praying but not guaranteeing that you'll make it up to them later. Fire some of those people who just don't work out. Set up a legal business entity, including such things as separate bank accounts and utility accounts. Secure all the types of insurance you'll need: health, liability, workers' comp, disability. Tally every expense, down to the last staple. Make sure the bathroom *never* runs out of toilet paper.

In all seriousness, branching out on your own is a momentous decision that carries significant implications for your future. A few dos and don'ts can be helpful starting points:

- Do start with a sound and specific business plan that includes step-by-step procedures for running operations and a clearly marked roadmap for strategic growth.
- Do study your market, do your research, and scrutinize your competition—closely.

- Do investigate and set a timeline to scale manageably and responsibly—you don't want to expand too fast, but you also don't want to be caught unprepared when an exciting opportunity arises. Bud and Nancy were utterly thrilled when they landed three multiyear contracts within their first two years of business; when the unexpected offer of a fourth came along, they were equally dismayed to have to pass on it because they just didn't have sufficient resources and manpower in place.
- Do expect delays. If you're launching a product, piloting a program, or outfitting a workspace, build in extra time for inevitable interruptions. There's plenty of anecdotal evidence on the web about enterprises derailed by timing issues.
- Do put in place a small starter team of key players you hand select and believe in wholeheartedly. At the very least, you'll want to be able to call on a business development expert, a lawyer, an IT professional, a marketing professional, and a financial professional. You don't have to hire them all; you just need to have specialty consultants on hand to help you handle the business aspects outside your wheelhouse.
- Do seek advice and input from your personal network of supportive, encouraging contacts and connections who can offer insights you don't necessarily see about yourself and your business model. Likewise, invite feedback from your more cynical, naysaying contacts who will challenge questionable ideas or play devil's advocate to your overly rosy outlook.
- Do invest in a smart and snazzy website—it's often the first encounter you'll have with a potential client, and if it doesn't impress, it will likely be the last.
- Do thoughtfully plan out your social media presence and content—you can hardly do business today without it.
- Do hire a payroll company—this isn't something you'll want to be spending your time doing.

- Don't ignore anything—not the smallest detail. Whatever you neglect could come back to bite you later. You're in charge of *everything*. So take charge.
- Don't fall into the trap of taking mishaps personally. Your business is separate from your selfhood, so when snafus happen, as they will, deal with them professionally instead of internalizing them as personal failures.
- Don't let yourself get caught up in analysis paralysis too often. It's scary to put yourself and your career out there on the line, but trust the instincts that got you where you are and the expertise and business savvy you've worked so hard to accumulate. When your heart and your head

are in conflict, your gut will tell you what to do. This doesn't mean you shouldn't deliberate over decisions of import, just don't take so much time assessing and debating that a window of opportunity closes.
- Don't let your expectations exceed your reality. There's hardly anything worse than luring good people away from good jobs and having to let them go a year or two later because you couldn't deliver on the promises you made them.
- Don't use money you need for life to fund the operation—you can use your own money, just not sums you cannot afford to lose. You'll make calmer, more objective decisions when you know you can pay the mortgage.

And while we're on the subject of money. Depending on the nature of your business, you may or may not have to find funding. You may or may not have to beg for funding. If you fund yourself, that's wildly different than being responsible for a corporate budget. If you go the venture capital route, you're entering a whole new sphere of pressure and accountability, but it's sometimes the best and most viable option if you think you have a really big idea that warrants a big investment.

All of this suggests that when you own your own business, the weight of responsibility is both more and less. No longer having to answer to anyone—there's far less responsibility in that. But you're much more responsible for yourself and for every outcome your business generates.

As a business owner, you will be humbled. Regularly. You will routinely face down frustration and exasperation. You will experience disappointments galore, setbacks aplenty, and unforeseen pitfalls that trip you up far too often. But you know what accompanies all that? Immense pride, intense fulfillment, extreme gratification, and a jubilant sense of freedom. You'll see. You'll learn.

And so, we're right back where we started from—with learning lying at the core of any occupational endeavor worth pursuing. Every job you take and every day you spend in it will imbue you with more and more learning. It has a cumulative effect. It builds upon itself naturally and automatically. It is the single most valuable acquisition you will make as you progress in your career, equally essential to personal achievement and to professional advancement. "The ability to learn is the most important quality a leader can have," says Sheryl Sandberg.

Lifelong learners show more interest in their surroundings and their society and are more interesting people to be around. Making a conscious effort to continue learning as you go—wherever you go—will not only fortify your leadership potential and prowess, it will make you a more resilient, inspiring, and impactful human being.

As you grow, so do others around you. It's one of the few win-win scenarios you can count on in life, so engage in ongoing learning as often as you can, enjoying its bountiful rewards. It's meant to be absorbed. Then it's meant to be shared. There's no better gift you can give someone than sharing what you learn along the way to make the world a better place.

Isn't that what you're here for? Yes, that's what helpers were built for.

Chapter 6

A Spotlight on Leadership in Education

Education is one of the biggest businesses in America. In fiscal year 2021, $754 billion was spent on defense (11 percent of the federal budget).[1] In comparison, transportation accounts for approximately 2 percent of government spending (or $132 billion, per 2022 statistics) and the Department of Agriculture is allocated around 4 percent (or $245 billion).[2] Education? In 2019–2020, almost $795 billion was spent on public elementary and secondary education, when you combine agency spending at the local, state, and federal levels,[3] and that figure doesn't even include postsecondary degree-granting institutions.

That's big bucks, big stakes, big stakeholders. But even with a national average of ~$14,000 spent on each general education student each year (and that's just the average; the range is about $8,000 to $23,000, depending on what state you're in), we've got big problems in America's 130,930 public and private K–12 schools.[4] Daunting, truly distressing problems.

Problems like a massive shortage of qualified teachers who are fleeing the field because they feel their needs to teach effectively aren't being met; an even larger dearth of school counselors to aid the ever-growing number of students with mental health challenges; violence in schools; an ongoing bullying crisis (now including cyberbullying as well), despite *years* of aggressive on-campus antibullying campaigns; habitual absenteeism; a dropout rate hovering at around 5 percent (which might not sound that startling until you consider that 5 out of every 100 students sitting in an auditorium will never graduate from high school); overcrowded classrooms; an overemphasis on standardized testing; and, of course, the inequity of education funding (and therefore of access to technology and advanced curriculums like STEM) between economically advantaged states and economically disadvantaged states.

It's inescapable that the behemoth of education would be fraught with difficulties—*any* colossal system is, like health care, Social Security, the FAA, and the USPS. The U.S. government itself is the biggest culprit of all. It's impossible that a national system of such labyrinthine expansiveness with feelers that extend into virtually every American household isn't going to work to the benefit of some far more than others, isn't going to push some people to the margins for all those it enfolds.

Nothing as gargantuan as the U.S. education system is going to get stellar ratings from the majority of participants. It's the nature of the beast. We're a democratic society that believes in justice for all, but we're still a long way from justice for all.

What's so alarming about the persisting, even worsening problems in education, though, is that we're also a society that values education enormously. We *care* about education. We set store by it, lionize it, and grant it the glory and gravity it deserves. Parents the country over are willing to go to the mat to secure a quality education for their children—and they're willing to pay for it too, out of their tax dollars and their savings accounts.

Everyone wants it to work. *Everyone* has a claim in it. Even the parents who aren't as involved as they could be (another of education's chronic issues) want their children to get a good education so they can have a good life. *Everyone* profits from its success. *Everyone.*

At least with health care, another mammoth system that seems to work against so many of the people it purports to serve, we can blame the insurance and pharmaceutical companies for all the quagmires, exorbitant costs, and obstructions. But in education, *no one* profits from the system's barriers, *no one* wants low test scores or borderline illiteracy or neglected children or the need for on-campus security guards. *No one.*

Given the sheer ubiquity of education as a central talking point in American culture, it should come as no surprise that it's been written about and theorized upon endlessly and encyclopedically. Commentary, complaints, opinions, and proposed solutions rampantly abound from every Tom, Dick, and Harriet in blogs, articles, essays, lectures, podcasts, and books.

That's why this book, this chapter, isn't going to even *attempt* to "cover" the current state of education in America. No regurgitating of what others have already ably argued; no explanations of how we got here or pontifications about what programs we must enact or policies we must eradicate to turn this whole bus around.

Rather, this discussion is going to zero in on just three very basic but crucial needs that are calling for our immediate collective attention. For there to even be a road for the school bus to continue to travel, certain prerequisites need to be in place. At this point in time in the evolution of the American education system—early in the second decade of the twenty-first century—if we could adequately attend to these three commonsensical essentials, we've got a fighting chance . . . specially when helpers are the ones leading the charge, helpers who never give up the good fight.

BUT FIRST: WHAT MAKES EDUCATION SO DISTINCTIVE?

In the Jewish faith at the Passover seder, the question is asked, "What makes this night different from all other nights?" The same can be asked of education: What makes this component of our society so seminal and singular among all the other parts that comprise the whole?

Well, education is a business that needs to be run effectively to produce desired outcomes (6 percent of our GDP is allocated to it, after all),[5] but it is *also* a service provided to people and it is *also* a helping profession. It is a global necessity, not an option, for our species to progress in its development (of *any* kind), and it is therefore the most vital and critical helping profession there is.

It's not an exaggeration to deem education the bedrock of society (as worded earlier), for without it, there would be no civilized society at all, anywhere. Humankind would not and could not advance even the tiniest step without first learning to walk (or learning to make fire or invent the wheel or grow crops). And "learning" is the verb form of the noun "education."

When you think about it, basically *all* of the helping professions have learning at their core. Counseling and all forms of therapy teach coping skills. Rehabilitation, both physical and in the criminal justice system, teaches people how to redirect their energies and efforts to self-promoting actions and behaviors that are going to advance their goals. Social and human services teach people how to live better in the world with the assistance and resources available to them. Every time a nurse does an intake or questions a patient, they're doing so to learn what the medical issue is by listening and watching so that the proper treatment plan can be implemented.

Education is everywhere. It's the basis of everything, and societies that do not promote and promulgate it exist in the dark. When it's denied to a citizenry or part of a citizenry, they remain in the dark.

Education is unique in other ways as well that warrant all the attention it gets:

It's mandated. No nation compels you to buy a car or do yoga. But ever since Massachusetts started the ball rolling in 1852 by becoming the first state to enact a compulsory education law,[6] it's actually illegal in this country to not educate a child (homeschooling counts) of a certain age span, for a certain length of time, with very few exceptions (e.g., the Amish after eighth grade).

It's legislated. Say what you will about some of the laws on the books that might actually stymie instead of stimulate growth (No Child Left Behind, for example, is highly contentious), but the United States—thankfully, mercifully—indeed has laws on the books that guarantee a "free public education" (and a "free and appropriate public education, FAPE, for students with special needs), including the Fourteenth Amendment of the U.S. Constitution, the Equal Education Opportunities Act of 1974, the Individuals with Disabilities Education Act, numerous antidiscriminatory measures, and multiple Supreme Court decisions. Legislation isn't a cure-all remedy for sectors beset with formidable complexities, but in the words of an eloquent NAFSA blogger, the United States recognizes that "education is fundamental to the fabric of society and key to ensuring people are equipped to lead economically productive lives to the benefit of everyone"[7] and, thus, protects it dearly.

It cultivates centers of economy. Cities evolve and thrive when an educated populace inhabits them. There should always be a place for rural lifestyles and the agrarian communities that built this nation, but it's the urban metropolis and the research hubs that now serve as the wheels that make our modern world go round, thus fueling the economy. Scholar Edward Glaeser says that cities that have the revenue to invest in schools in turn attract better-educated parents and produce students with more skills, both of which increase productivity. "Education doesn't just improve a region's economic prospects," he writes "it also helps create a more just society" through civic engagement.[8]

It propels innovation. All of the products and industries that make our day-to-day life flow so fluidly now—computers, app development, Wi-Fi, online and streaming services, cell towers, biotech, Fitbits—they all needed an educated workforce to get them working.

It's a child's first gateway. A child's first exposure to the world they live in beyond their family home is usually school. It is here that they will learn the ABCs that will fill their lives with the richness of literature, the 123s that later become bank accounts and grocery bills and the language of coders and scientists. It is here that they learn to interact with peers, socialize in groups, make friends, respect authority, and ride the bus. Education opens doors for children, and school is their portal to the panorama of everything there is to explore in life!

It's a second home. Students are in school for six waking hours straight, longer if they participate in after-hours enrichment programs and extracurriculars. For some, it's a cherished respite from a less-than-ideal home situation, and for others, it's their childhood job that they simply have to report to; but while they are there, they are fed and warm, they are attended to and guided, they are seen and heard, they matter. Not every school has the capability to fully serve this role for every child, it's true—but that's the dream, that's what we're all working so hard toward: for school to be the inner home many children crave.

It's a common experience. Our culture has never been more diverse, variegated, colorful, and flavorful than it is now, and it will hopefully become even more so. But the very foundation of the acceptance that will allow us to continue celebrating our individuality is composed of, ironically, all the things we share in common that remind us, that infuse us with an understanding of, our shared experiences. School is one of those experiences that almost everyone can relate to: sitting at a desk, listening to a teacher, raising our hand, dreading gym class, recess in the courtyard—education gives us this common ground on which, ideally, all of us can stand equally.

It's a universal good—it just is. With education, you might learn something you wish you didn't know, about the environment or a disease or world hunger statistics, but learning is *always* the preferred path for all people. Ignorance might be bliss, but knowledge is power.

For all these reasons and many more, education is like no other asset under the sun. It is a treasure available to us at no cost. It is the means by which we forge a meaningful, purposeful life. It is the key that unlocks the secrets of the universe. It is the ultimate form of liberty. It's not just our way forward—it's our only way forward.

THE BIG THREE: THE URGENT NEEDS IN EDUCATION

If you've spent any amount of time working in a school for grades K–12, even just a semester, you will witness a multitude of scenes that make your heart soar: one student voluntarily helping another with something they're struggling with, faces full of wide-eyed wonder during an awesome chemistry experiment, teachers who clearly connect with their kids so much, they might as well be family. You will also see things that make your heart ache: the abject look of despair of a girl who knows she's fallen too far behind, a boy being physically harassed just because of how he looks or dresses, supply cabinets lacking supplies, technology in the classroom not even turned on because it no longer works or hasn't been kept up-to-date.

Education is a business *and* a service *and* a helping profession that needs fixing in many ways and many places, but there are no easy answers on how to do that. Throwing more money at it hasn't solved the problems. Earnest efforts to recruit and retain the best of the best teachers haven't solved the problems. Shaming the American school system by comparing its statistics to those of other countries hasn't solved the problems. State education departments narrowing their focus on individual districts and individual schools hasn't fixed the problems. And instituting nationwide curriculum standards certainly hasn't solved the problems.

Though it's impossible to pinpoint what *will* solve the problems, what *can* solve the problems is strong leadership—not of the one, but of the many: administrators, superintendents, supervisors, department heads, principals, vice principals, and entire instructional staffs working in concert within a framework of distributed leadership in the best interests of the students over the schools. School leaders cannot force students to learn or undo their pasts; they cannot order teachers to teach better or override government regulations or coerce cooperation and agreement.

As author and TED Talk sensation Sir Ken Robinson sees it, "The real role of leadership in education . . . is not and should not be command and control. The real role of leadership is climate control, creating a climate of possibility."[9] Likening educators to farmers, Robinson reasons that farmers cannot *make* plants grow; instead, their job is to create optimal conditions for growth.

Education expert Pedro Noguera echoes that sentiment in comparing educators to gardeners, who cannot control external forces. "But educators do have the power to create the conditions that will make it more likely for [a] child to feel supported so that she can learn and thrive. By focusing upon the conditions that they can control, educators are more likely to make a difference."[10]

Taking the analogy one step further, plants need three things to grow: fertile soil, sunlight, and water—those are the conditions. So what three conditions will create a "climate of possibility" in America's schools?

1. Safe Schools
2. Quality Schools
3. Equality in Schools

These are the three most pressing educational issues we must attend to now. If we start here, with these necessities, we can work our way from the ground up from there.

Safe Schools

Safety is a primordial need. It's nonnegotiable. Abraham Maslow knew it when he mapped out his famous hierarchy of needs in 1943, ranking safety second only to the physiological necessities of survival. Cave people knew it when they devised ways to stay alive in the most hazardous living conditions imaginable. Babies know it straight out of the womb, when swaddling is what soothes them. Nothing else can be undertaken or achieved until safety concerns are first satisfied.

And yet we're in the midst of the biggest threat to safety in our schools that our nation has ever seen (scarily, this seems to be a particularly American problem). The duck-and-cover drills of the 1950s were a response to escalating fears in the Cold War era—to the theoretical possibility that Russia could launch an atomic attack that could reach the United States. Even with the enemy thousands of miles away and the danger only a speculative one, these exercises were traumatic for schoolchildren and left lifelong scars. Today? When the threat is not at all hypothetical but only too real? When the "enemy" is your own neighbor, *your own classmate*? Yeah, Bert the Turtle isn't going to make a dent anymore.

Statistics vary based on differing definitions of "school shootings" and gun-related violence, but Sandy Hook Promise cites 948 school shootings between December 2012 and June 2022[11] (with BBC News clarifying that in that same ten-year span, 189 of those shootings resulted in at least one fatality).[12] *U.S. News* laments the worst year on record as 2020–2021, with 93 school shootings that entailed causalities.[13] And then K–12 Dive reports even worse news for calendar year 2022, with a total of 300 shooting incidents on school grounds before year's end.[14] Tragically, Columbine, Parkland, Uvalde—these are no longer geographical places in the American lexicon; they're shorthand for mass murder. Even more tragically, all of these figures need to be qualified with "and still counting."

This isn't a school issue. This isn't a partisan political debate. This can't be blamed on eroding family values or teenage bullying or societal rage. It's a public health epidemic that marries a deepening mental health crisis and a gun control problem.

There are measures that can be taken—of course there are measures that could control access to firearms, particularly to young people. There's a growing industry of products like Kevlar inserts for backpacks, bulletproof film for windows, and door shields. There are things we can do on campuses to stave off or ward off incidents, like installing cameras as a deterrent to violent behavior, never leaving students unchaperoned, controlling building and room access with specialty locks, doing locker and backpack checks, instituting metal detectors, and hiring professional security guards. We already have lots of this in place at many schools, and we're already conducting lockdown drills and reverse evacuation exercises and shelter-in-place trainings.

But the situation isn't likely to improve until we start chipping away at the *root* of the problem instead of treating and reacting to the symptoms and aftereffects following an incident. Educators cannot do this alone—even the greatest government in the world cannot do this alone. And even though the actual chance of a student getting killed at school by a gun is often cited as just 1 in 614,000,000,[15] schools don't *feel* safe to kids (to the tune of 57 percent of them)[16] or to their parents (with a minimum of one-third fearing for their children's safety at school and many sources reporting significantly higher numbers).[17]

Most of the time (in four out of five cases, in fact), someone knows of the attacker's intention; most of the time (a whopping 75 percent of the time), the attacker displays clear warning signs.[18] This indicates that we need to get to the shooters before the shooters get to the weapons, intercept their plans before they can enact their plans. There *is* a prototypical profile to refer to, and some pretty reliable common traits psychologists and sociologists have identified.

So here is where we need to concentrate our efforts. Here is where we need to bolster all our mental health resources: on teaching people to look and act, not look away and hope for the best when they have knowledge of an impending threat, on removing the stigma still attached to admitting your child or someone you care about may be seriously ill. Here is where our education, political, public health, and youth leaders need to dedicate our time and money. Here is the root of the weeds we must pluck from the dirt so that safety in schools can be reinstated and learning can recommence in full.

And let's be clear: extreme violence of the sort we've been discussing is not the only menace to safety in schools. Money can take care of external structural perils, like lead, asbestos, and dilapidation. But the more covert and insidious damage schoolchildren do to one another with verbal and emotional abuse in and outside of school—a level of bullying so far removed from the typical playground taunting of days of yore this is the more regular occurrence that is terrifying some of our children far more than the irregularity of a gun-related incident on campus. It's this climate that must be metamorphosed for anything to grow on school grounds. It's this soil that leaders must till.

We cannot guarantee safety at school anymore. Maybe we never could. We cannot promise parents that their children will never be in harm's way when they are in our care. But we can make a promise to ourselves to direct our efforts, en masse, to getting *in front of* the problem before it gains even a sliver more traction. In the long game of chess that is the healing of the fractures of our education system, this is our opening move.

Quality Schools

"Quality" here refers to a two-columned approach to school management that rests equally on (1) an excellent program and (2) an excellent staff. To strive for quality in schools means to strive for *excellence* in schools, and although this lofty goal cannot be achieved overnight, there's no better goalpost to run toward, no better way to counteract the mediocrity that has crept into so many American systems than to consciously choose superiority over acceptability and then map out steps to approach it.

Any school district in the country is only as good as its weakest school. We have a tendency to showcase the blue-ribbon schools when reporting on performance, but that simply is not an accurate representation of the larger whole, and it does a disservice to the schools that need more assistance—to hide them behind the pretty curtain of the fewer number that are exceeding expectations. Besides, even in the star schools that can tout impressive test scores, GPAs, and college entrance exam results (and kudos to them, by the way, not trying to downplay their triumphs *at all*), that's just not where the emphasis is being directed today.

The old paradigm gauged success by report cards, standardized test performance, and SAT scores. The new paradigm's barometer of success is looking to applications of experiential learning—learning by doing—that will *prepare students for life*.

This equates to numeracy and financial literacy (things like responsible banking and personal accounting, knowing how to calculate the interest on a home mortgage) over memorization of the multiplication table; to a demonstration of the supply-demand chain in the economic system rather than a textbook chapter on the history of the railroad system; to an outdoor unit on gardening for sustainable nutrition instead of a lesson on the Battle of Hastings.

We might lose some things in the process (kids *should* know all the U.S. presidents, all the geological eras), but what we gain, the thinking goes, will prove more worthwhile to them in the long run; namely, meaningful outcomes in such areas as critical thinking, reflective decision making, problem solving, conflict resolution, and productive group dynamics. More social-emotional intelligence, too, more life learning in lieu of short-term, rote learning.

To carry out this maturing conceptualization of quality education, however, requires more than just espousing all the catchphrases of the day—twenty-first-century learning, blended learning, differentiated learning, student-centered approaches—in our marketing materials and on our websites. To approximate excellence in the education system as a whole, we are called to actually embrace and absorb the intentions and objectives of these methodologies. Are they just terms in an operational statement—more lip-service demands being placed on schools and teachers from on high—or are they being put into useful and strategic operation daily in the classroom?

Now, there are *great* schools doing *great* work to the *great* benefit of their students all over the country. We should look to them for inspiration and insight—in truth, where there's already an exceptional recipe being cooked up, shouldn't we all try a taste? And there are other things we can do to dial up the quality in our schools, like (here comes the potentially controversial part) perhaps adding a healthy dose of competition to the mix.

If educational leadership borrowed some pages out of the business and financial leadership book, it could be somewhat polarizing, yes, but it could also be incredibly motivating. Furthermore, it could dilute some of the paralyzing subjectivity that comes with the territory of running the business of education with some much-needed objectivity.

For example, Jack Welch, the famous (or infamous) CEO of General Electric, fired the lowest-performing 10 percent of his workforce every year—what he called the "C players." The A players (20 percent), the biggest energizers and most passionate and productive staffers, earned hefty raises; and the B players (70 percent), "the heart of the company" critical to operational success, earned solid increases and ongoing coaching so they could move to A status. Welch believed that cutting the C team was actually the opposite of brutality because it's just "false kindness" to keep "people around who aren't going to grow and prosper" in their careers.[19]

The point here isn't to argue the kindness or cruelty of Welch's technique. It's to ask: If you were a C player, wouldn't you work much harder all year to get on the B team?

Or take a more relatable example: Bettina was the principal of Grenville Regional, and Sanford was the principal of Grenville Memorial. At the annual district awards ceremony, Bettina received hearty praise, a personal bonus, and two new interactive white boards for her middle school based on year-end performance metrics. Instead of begrudging Bettina her accomplishments, Sanford was inspired by them. He invited her to lunch so he could talk to her about her initiatives and learn how to implement them in his school. Interestingly, one of the new ideas she'd tried in the past year was bringing in a business leader to host a professional development workshop for her staff instead of the usual education leader.

Competition can be collegial in nature too. In a district with six schools that are lagging and four that are doing well, it makes sense—business sense, common sense, just plain good sense—to bring the leaders of the latter schools into the former schools to advise on effective processes and procedures and share knowledge with their colleagues. If raising the bar of educational quality is what we're all here to do, then we need practitioners to clear the bar, right? The bar alone means nothing if team members aren't vying to hurdle it.

Think of it this way: If your performance were splashed all over the news Monday morning the way the media does with professional athletes, would you be doing your job any differently? If teachers were being filmed in their classrooms for a documentary, would they be instructing any differently? Holding education a bit more accountable, like business, unveils both the strengths and the weaknesses. Some competitive spirit can be a good thing. It's good to want to excel, to want to be the best. We urge our kids to do it in the classroom, so why demand any less of ourselves—at each individual school, each in its own way?

Never underestimate the power of just one school to move the needle. There are so many pressures on schools these days, so many directives and mandates; but even within the confines of what's permissible, there's room for autonomy and authority. In the never-ending public debate over education, says *The Age*:

> What is too often left out is the level of influence an individual school can have on its students and how they perform. While every school must provide a teaching and learning program that follows the state's curriculum, there is a surprising amount of flexibility in how each school can implement that program. The influence of an effective principal, or a motivated group of teachers, or a particular approach to student welfare can have an enormous impact.[20]

And that leads us right to the enormous impact—the integral, invaluable, irreplaceable role—of teachers. To quote Ken Robinson again, "There is no . . . school in the country that is better than its teachers. Teachers are the lifeblood of the success of schools."[21] This is a given, this is a known fact. But the degree to which they are able to contribute to the type of school quality we're discussing depends in large part on their leadership—their talent and dedication will take them only so far; their leaders have to take them the rest of the way.

Some are better than others—that's a fact too—and treating the exceptional teachers the same way you treat subpar teachers will only lead to losing the good ones. We're not talking about veterans versus newbies here—we need an incoming pool of new teachers each and every year, and we need to give them adequate time to actualize their potential. But it is critical to recognize, reward, and retain that higher echelon of instructors because they are the ones forming that second column of excellence upon which the whole future of our education system rests.

Do you know why everyone is moved to tears by the heroic teachers in movies: Hilary Swank's role in *Freedom Writers*, Edward James Olmos in

Stand and Deliver, Michele Pfeiffer in *Dangerous Minds*, Morgan Freeman in *Lean on Me*, Paula Patton in *Precious*, Robin Williams in *Dead Poets Society* and *Good Will Hunting*? Because they're based on real people! Not all of those characters were real, but their stories are—they play out in real-life classrooms every day, and they show us just how vital teachers are and the difference they make in *all* our lives.

The exceptional teacher finds a way (the active verb is important here; gifted teachers just don't wake up and don a magic wand that shapes their students) to inspire and engage students, to get them interested in the subject matter and invested in their own education. They make boring topics fun, and they make complicated concepts clear. They pique curiosity, they birth scholars, and they get results. To teach kids, you first have to reach kids. That alone deserves a Medal of Honor, every damn morning.

They teach you pedagogy, curriculum, instructional approaches, and educational theory in school; they can't teach you how to *care*, how to *ride or die*, how to *show up*. Like the chemistry teacher who taught her subject by making lollipops. The physics teacher who brought his students to an amusement park to see the laws of motion in action. The math teacher who took her kids to a clearance sale so they could configure percentage discounts.

What's so captivating about teachers is the individuality with which they approach their work. Coders all speak in zeros and ones. Bank tellers all perform the same functions. Police officers and firefighters must all follow the same procedures. Even creative chefs all expertly chop onions and garlic the exact same way (you've noticed that too, right?).

But teachers? Walk into any classroom in any city anywhere and you're going to witness a one-of-a-kind style and sensitivity to student needs. Unlike many professions that ask you to leave your personality at the door, teaching invites teachers to incorporate all aspects of themselves at the head of the room—their humor, their flair, their artistry, their originality.

Yes, there's a curriculum in place that most have to follow and they're all so inundated with responsibilities by day that they must take work home by night, but the way in which they opt to apply their ingenuity to the curriculum and their lesson plans is mostly left to their discretion. That's why school leaders need to give them as much leeway as possible to use that discretion, to not tie their hands or their minds, to celebrate their individuality, and to rejoice in the passion they somehow manage to keep blazing day in and day out.

In this way—when teachers are allowed the freedom to perform their calling to their own high standards, when they're extolled for doing so and supported in doing so—they will be inspired by their leaders the way they inspire their students. In this way, they will discover, develop, and deploy their excellence.

Equality in Schools

A fascinating (if sometimes confusing) discourse has arisen rather recently about the difference between "equality" and "equity" in education. The finer points of that discourse are beyond the scope of this discussion, but it's nevertheless necessary to at least summarily distinguish them.

Equality means what it sounds like: everything is equal, with every student having the same rights, opportunities, and resources. This kid gets a model XYZ laptop, that kid gets a model XYZ laptop, every kid gets a model XYZ laptop.

Equity is more complicated because it's based in fairness, in justice, in giving each child what they need to succeed per their specific circumstances once they already have equal access to everything the child sitting next to them has. But because students often come to us later in their development—as in the case of middle or high school—equity is trickier to achieve across the primary and secondary education continuum when disparities in early education are already existent and since *un*fairness, *in*justice, has a cumulative effect as an individual ages.

In other words, Tommy and Tammy both have model XYZ laptops from school, but when they're doing their homework in their bedrooms at night, Tommy is at an advantage because of his home's higher-quality internet service and Tammy is at a disadvantage because of her home's lower-quality connection. Or Tommy and Tammy have both been assigned the same novel by the same wonderful English teacher who gives them the same amount of attention, but Tommy's preexisting reading deficit that has not yet been fully resolved blocks him from engaging with the material as deeply as Tammy can.

There's a visual that lots of publications reproduce that *perfectly* captures the distinction. Picture this: On the left side is an illustration of three schoolboys—one very tall, one average, one very short—peering over the fence at a baseball game. They are all standing on a block of the exact same height, meaning the tall boy (the most advantaged) towers above the top of the fence, with a clear, unobstructed view of the action; the middle boy has to crane his neck just a tad to see over the top; but the short boy (the most disadvantaged) doesn't even come close to the top—if he's lucky, he can get a glimpse of what's going on through the cracks.

On the right side is a same-sized illustration of the same three boys; this time, however, the tallest boy isn't on a block at all—doesn't matter, he's a head taller than the fence and can still easily watch the game. The middle boy is on the same-height block as before, thus with the same view. But the shortest boy has now been given two blocks to stand on, and now he, too, can enjoy the game like his peers.

Clearly, equity is the ultimate end goal, and there are a lot of revolutionary educators doing remarkable things in this area, like the aforementioned former classroom teacher Pedro Noguera and Muhammad Khalifa, one-time science teacher and district administrator for Detroit Public Schools.[22] We need both equality and equity, however, not one or the other, and both ideals are unquestionably worth our maximum exertion—no one is arguing otherwise.

But in the context of this chapter's proposed framework that offers just three immediate-need focus points for consideration, let's stick with equality to start. Because equity is harder to attain and requires more in-depth, long-term work, let's start with what seems more manageable and doable in the near-term future.

Why is equality more obtainable? Because equality in schools—sameness, if you will—is largely a matter of money. That's good news and it's bad news. It's bad news because (a) we're a long ways off from every single like school getting the same amount of funding, every single student being allotted the same per-pupil expenditure, and (b) even if we were closer to full financial parity, we're totally reliant on local, state, and federal revenue to provide the funding. Budgeted money for education per state just doesn't fall to the jurisdiction of State Departments of Education.

But it's good news because of this really simple but life-altering saying: If something can be solved with money, it isn't really a problem, it's an expense. If "equality" can be bought at a price—and theoretically, in education, it can—it comes down to amending fiscal policy. And that's a helluva lot more likely than altering attitudes, belief systems, ethical codes, and long-standing inequities. It's like the idea of a flat tax: hard to get passed, hard to enact, but a really sound, viable, *equitable* measure.

(Actually, from a linguistic point of view, "equitable" education might be what we're all really after since it means "dealing fairly *and* equally with all concerned"—emphasis added—at least according to *Webster's*. Just sayin.')

We cannot control what goes on at home and outside of school, we're *never* going to be able to control what goes on outside of school. But we *can* control equality in school—we can ensure that every single schoolchild receives the same rights, opportunities, and resources. That every single student at Middlebury Elementary is equipped with the same instructional materials, library access, and lunch tray. That every single schoolchild at Thomasville High has the same scientific calculator, access to after-school tutoring, and amount of time with the college counselor.

Equality is not foreign or new territory in America's schools. We've been working for it for a *long* time, and we've made tremendous strides in its name. But just because all the kids at Thomasville High in Ohio get the same scientific calculator, that doesn't mean their counterparts at Chesterton High in Utah received scientific calculators. That's where the discrepancy, the inequality, still lies. Lower-income, more tax-disadvantaged regions still get far less than higher-income, tax-advantaged regions—even in the same state.

In Connecticut, for instance, one of the wealthiest states in the nation, high-income towns such as Greenwich and Darien enjoy the latest texts, sufficient numbers of counselors and psychologists, and personal laptops. Elsewhere in the state, though, poorer towns such as Bridgeport and New Britain lack these resources. All the schools get their funding from city property taxes, which amount to much more in one place than the other. According to one lawsuit, Greenwich spends $6,000 more per pupil each year than Bridgeport.[23] Where funding is uneven, you can pretty much bet that school quality is too.

This is why equality can't just be trumped by equity in today's climate. We must get a handle on equal funding—at least get all students on the same playing field—before we can ever expect to start properly and adequately equipping them with a left-handed mitt there, a heavier bat here, cleated athletic shoes for this one, the grade-A sun visor for that one. Let's get *all* the boys and girls lined up at that fence at the ballgame—the exact same arm's-reach distance away. When they're treated uniformly, we'll have much more means at our disposal to start custom-tailoring their uniforms.

A NOTE ON SPECIAL EDUCATION

A child with special needs is far more alike than different to any other child. General education and special education students both fear being ostracized. They dread being bullied, feeling outcast, and seen as "other." They all want to learn, they just resist it at times, afraid of failing or embarrassment. They all wither from neglect, recoil from criticism, and blossom with attention and affection. They actually have the same needs—all the needs we've been discussing.

Special needs kids just need *more* of them. More safety in their school environment, more quality in their educational programming and instructional precision, more equal access to any and all accommodations and adjustments that will maximize their learning potential.

Some people liken special education to the song "New York, New York": if you can make it here, you can make it anywhere. It can be tough. Special educators can face some tough, tough situations.

But general educators and special educators are more alike than different as well. They all love their kids, they really do—they wouldn't have signed up for the gig if their hearts weren't dedicated to the cause. And the cause is the *same* for all educators: guiding and encouraging young people toward the fuller, richer, better lives education can afford them; opening their minds to the opportunities that await them with the acquisition of knowledge and self-belief, whatever those opportunities may be.

Safety, quality, equality—all the fundamental needs are the same, just with the volume turned up, up, up here. And here is where equity *really* comes into play. Here is where individualized, differentiated instruction isn't just an idealized goal, it's a right and a mandated requirement.

It can't be stressed enough that consistency, routine, and reliability are paramount to the special needs child's ability to learn; so safe schools are required for them *even more*. But here, safety translates more to structure and security than to freedom from gun-violence worries.

In the special education sphere, students can still be perfectly abled; they just have some form of disability. Not all kids with a diagnosis have intensive needs, but some do, and the behavioral eligibilities are particularly challenging. Sometimes there's a need for solo time in the reflection room. Sometimes there's the need for restraints.

But just like a quality program and a talented teacher in general education will find a way to reach a child, a special educator will stop at nothing to do so. The special educator learns not to show fear of the student. To respond in a way that they don't anticipate. They're expecting you to push back, to get defensive, to reprimand and punish. Instead, you side with them. You say, "I'm not leaving no matter what. You can call me all the names in the book. I'm going to be here. I care about you. I'm here." All kids want that, all kids long for that.

With a little time and built-up trust, even the most challenging of students start to feel safe enough to let go of their bravado and actually show signs of interest in their education. At that point, they have the capacity to learn as well as anyone else. Yes, specialized instructional materials might be called for. The previously mentioned accommodations are common. So you specialize and you accommodate. That's your job. That's your mission.

The point in all of this isn't to try to make general education and special education sound the same—in some ways, they're entirely different animals, and a teacher can do wonderfully in one domain and poorly in the other. The general ed teacher leads a class of 25, 35 students; the special ed teacher has 8 or 10. The special ed teacher is trained what to do if a student physically attacks them; the general ed teacher is trained what to do if a student has some kind of physical attack in the classroom.

No, they're not the same. But they're *same enough*. The goals are the same. The call for excellence is the same. The teacher's dedication is the same. And the students want and need the same things. Whenever student needs are put at the forefront of the education system's efforts, the system works.

Safe schools, quality schools, and equality in schools. . . . These are not solutions to all our systemic ills in education. These are not answers to all the hard questions being posed in our present-day educational environment. But they are three areas upon which to focus our lens at this time, starting points from which to tackle the myriad challenges detracting from the magnificent, if marred, institution of the American education system. These are the seeds that need to be watered the most in order to flourish the most on the long and arduous, but possible and passable, road to revitalizing a lush and fertile educational landscape for our children and our children's children.

Chapter 7

What Did COVID-19 Teach Us about Getting through Crises?

The last chapter talked about some problems and perils in one helping profession. But as the world learned, starting early in the spring of 2020, for most of us, a crisis of magnitude can arise at any time—the kind of largely unforeseen, or at least unexpected, calamity that has the potential to interrupt market forces, decimate hardest-hit industries, halt the entire global economy, devastate families the world over. When the power goes out for one day—for one hour!—how does it affect your job, your productivity, your place of business, your household? With the coronavirus pandemic, we all got a very unpleasant taste of what it means for our societal "power" to be temporaily turned off.

If and when something like this happens again (and all kinds of experts from all kinds of fields concur that it is surely a matter of "when") to either stop a helping profession in its tracks or, on the flip side, overstrain it to its breaking point, what did we learn from the last crisis that might help us better manage the next crisis?

WHO SHOULD TAKE THE LEAD?

Before COVID-19, most people just assumed that any national crisis would be adequately handled by our federal government, first and foremost, supported by the corporate bigwigs and powerful industry leaders who most influence the federal government—the movers and shakers who seem to run everything in this country anyway. With all their money, cachet, educational pedigrees, and sway, they can come up with better solutions than we can, right? They'll have all the answers the rest of us lack.

Can they? Will they? Not to unfairly criticize or unjustly demonize any individual governing body or entity in a situation no one really had much experience with—to be fair, we were all sort of shooting blind into the fog, just hoping and praying we'd hit some targets to relieve the most painful pressure points in what everyone was labeling "uncharted territory"—but just because someone sits behind a desk and directs policy for an entire government department or committee or subcommittee, that doesn't mean they know better or know how to do better. They don't have a crystal ball either. There weren't any obvious answers to the COVID-19 crisis, and there won't be any obvious answers to the next one. We learned this.

The same holds for local governments. They adequately manage troubles like snowstorms, road closures, and felled trees, but what about when entire communities are at risk of collapse? The comptroller isn't the one who has to distribute masks to vulnerable populations. The governor isn't the one seeing students struggling with remote learning on the other side of the computer screen. The senator isn't the one counseling the fresh hordes of people dealing with depression and suicidality in the wake of a societal catastrophe.

COVID made us all rethink who we want in the driver's seat when traffic is backed up for miles or a crash seems imminent, and both factual and anecdotal evidence is pointing to the conclusion that crisis management authority should fall to the actual folks dispensing supplies and services on the ground, at the site, and to the people in need. If our next crisis is in the meat-packing industry, for example, then the meat-packing sector should take charge of doing what they know how to do better than anyone else could. If our next crisis is psychological in nature, then psychologists should call the shots. If it's another public health emergency, then public health officials should be appointed first in the line of ascendancy.

(Do you know why TV viewers looked more to Anthony Fauci and Deborah Birx than to President Trump and his cabinet during press conferences? Because Fauci and Birx are both medical doctors with infectious disease and immunoregulation expertise! Because President Trump isn't a public health expert!)

Certainly, we need oversight by systems that protect the public (in the instances above, for example, the USDA and the APA); but crisis management is best left to the hands, hearts, and heads that are best equipped, educated, and experienced in the specific area of crisis. When the crisis falls within the domain of the helping professions, then helping professionals should take the lead. With COVID-19, the helping professionals saved us.

HELPERS WON'T STOP HELPING

Another thing we learned is that helpers will just keep on helping—that they are dedicated and dutiful models of resilience and perseverance whom we should all emulate. No one helping profession proved this more than the medical community. Medical professionals were scared, some terrified, sometimes even more than the rest of us because they know better than the rest of us what contagions like AIDS, Ebola, SARS, or MERS can do to ravage a body—many have seen it firsthand, have treated it.

Benjamin, an infectious disease doctor, had to wear a hazmat suit to treat his patients, and his wife worked in the same hospital. When they came home after their overtime shifts, they slept in different beds, they quarantined from their own children who were cared for by the nanny they hired when schools and daycares shut down. Still, they got up every day to return to the combat zone—they never even questioned doing otherwise. Yes, doctors and nurses sign up for the job; yes, they take the Hippocratic Oath or the Nightingale Pledge. But you can walk out, you can quit. They didn't. And neither did millions like them (including all the support staff behind them, by the way, the clerical workers, repair people, technicians, and cleanup crews who kept the facilities running while the practitioners were practicing).

Ivy was only two years into her physician's assistant career when COVID hit. What frightened her even more than the sick patients she was seeing all around her were the frazzled, stressed-out, overtaxed providers around her who were opting to leave their jobs. If the reports of one in five health care workers resigning are accurate,[1] that's a full 20 percent who left due to burnout, overly long hours, personal safety concerns, and other COVID–related issues.

But that also means 80 percent—the vast majority—remained, still remain (not to mention the large number of who stayed in the field, just moved to another setting). Ivy considered following on the heels of some of her superiors; in the end, she's so glad she didn't: "I wasn't sure I wanted to be around so much sickness, so much risk. I'm so young, just starting out. What if this virus killed me or I brought it home and it killed someone I love?" she recalls. "Now, looking back, it was just so great to be there for people. It felt *so* great. I made things better. I helped people survive."

The health care community was bent, severely bent . . . but it didn't break. COVID-19 proved that during times of crisis, the caretakers keep right on caring, the aides keep right on aiding, the teachers keep right on teaching, the counselors keep right on counseling. We do not know what lies ahead or what systems we will have to depend upon the most in future; but as to whom we can rely on—we do know that our helping professionals will *always* be there to help.

THE POPULACE WILL SUPPORT THE HELPING PROFESSIONS

While the helpers ceaselessly go on helping, you can pretty much bet on the fact that the masses will buttress, not block, their efforts. This is important to recognize about crises: that the public *wants* to be led through them, they *want* to be told what to do to make things better. We want proposed solutions we can back, leaders brave enough to fight at the front line while the rest of us hold the forts down at home, heroes we can root for.

What a beautiful display of support it was when, throughout the spring of 2020, cities all over the world picked a designated time each day to make some noise to voice their appreciation and gratitude for all their compatriots who were still showing up for their jobs throughout worldwide lockdowns. New York's highly publicized #ClapBecauseWeCare movement was blasted all over the media, not only to encourage essential workers to keep doing the hard, hard work that was rescuing us all from complete despair, but to extol the virtues of human beings coming together in a common cause.

Writing for CNBC, Adam Jeffrey said, "We scream, we clap, we bang pots and pans, we make music" every night at 7 p.m. "My kids and I look forward to these two minutes every day because in this moment there are no negative headlines, there are no sirens blaring. There are just New Yorkers united together to see this through."[2]

When people feel like the appropriate individuals are on the case instituting appropriate measures, you'll create a cheerleading squad like no other.

MENTAL HEALTH NEEDS TO TAKE TOP PRIORITY

Crisis situations induce panic, worsen depression, and send anxiety levels skyrocketing. During COVID-19, mental health alarms bells were sounding everywhere, with no populations invulnerable. In a *Washington Post* poll asking readers to sum up 2020 in a word, the most common replies included "exhausting," "lost," "chaotic," and "relentless."[3] New York psychiatrist Valentine Raiteri could barely handle his caseload and couldn't refer patients to colleagues because none had the capacity to take on new patients.[4]

Before COVID-19, about one per dozen U.S. adults were suffering from depression. In 2020, the rate had risen to one in four; and by 2021, it climbed higher still, to one in three.[5] Of all races, Blacks saw the largest increase in anxiety during the pandemic; of those who voluntary took an online screening in 2021, 39 percent reported suicidual ideation; and that same screening pool was found to be struggling the most with loneliness and isolation.[6]

Low-income populations were, and are, especially susceptible to crisis-activated mental health challenges, largely on the basis of added economic pressures, lessened access to health supplies, and lower-quality health care. Per usual, the people who need help the most are often the farthest from its reach.

Pediatric mental health proved especially concerning, for although otherwise-healthy young people were the least at risk for contracting the virus (especially with complications), they were actually impacted the hardest in terms of their emotional stability, keenly feeling the unprecedented interruptions to their educational and social lives. Keeping in mind that these statistics are based only on filed health claims (and thus do not take into account God-knows-how-many undocumented cases), anxiety increased 93.6 percent, depression increased 83.9 percent, substance use disorder rose by 62.7 percent, and incidents of intentional self-harm catapulted a staggering 334 percent in the 13–18 age group year over year from 2019 to 2020.[7]

ER visit records show a one-third jump from 2019 to 2020 in suspected suicide attempts among youth, with girls aged 12–17 affected most in this area.[8] All in all, just in 2021, 37 percent of high school students reported experiencing poor mental health throughout the pandemic, and 44 percent admitted to feeling "persistently sad or hopeless."[9]

We could go on citing statistics all day—literally, *all* day, and studies continue to pour in—but the point is clear. We were a nation in trauma—and in many ways, we still are. Because of the acute immediate effects of trauma and then the longer-term aftershocks that continue to destabilize society when a crisis has abated, mental health simply must be a paramount focal point in any future crisis, second only to keeping people alive. In many cases, mental health treatment *is* about keeping people alive, and we can all be taking steps now to curtail the side effects on the horizon.

More money needs to be (and is being) budgeted for mental health reform—for more outreach and education. We need to open up Medicare and Medicaid coverage for mental health treatment.[10] We need to maximize "school connectedness" for our youth, even during times of disconnection, and take aggressive measures to prevent drug use and high-risk sexual behaviors in young people.[11] Most of all, we need to expand capacity to mental health providers who will be in dire need, beyond psychiatrists, psychologists, and social workers to perhaps peer specialists and community health workers.[12]

Every single mental health worker is a helping professional. When our next crisis hits, we will need every single one of them at the ready.

CRISIS THEORY SHOULD INFORM OUR ACTIONS

The advent of crisis theory is attributed to Erich Lindemann and Gerald Caplan, colleagues at Massachusetts General Hospital, who formalized the theory in the 1940s and laid the groundwork for how we practice it today.[13] German psychiatrist Lindemann started the ball rolling with his work on bereavement in the aftermath of the Cocoanut Grove nightclub fire in 1942 in Boston, noting that crises tend to share a similar progression of features; and then British-born, Harvard-affiliated Caplan extended those findings to four stages of crisis:

1. Disturbed equilibrium
2. Brief therapy or grief work
3. Working through the problem or grief
4. Restoration of equilibrium[14]

Furthermore, within this framework, there are three types of crises: developmental, situational, and existential. Since restoration of equilibrium is obviously what the helping professions are aiming for after a crisis like COVID-19, which falls squarely into the situational category of crisis typified by "events that one cannot control, prevent, or otherwise anticipate,"[15] this area of study can and should steer our efforts when managing modern-day crises, not solely but selectively.

The contemporary definition of "crisis theory"—a "group of ideas that encompasses the root of disasters, the way people behave when handling them, what causes them, how to prevent them, and how to impede one currently occurring in addition to how to resolve one"[16]—forms the foundation of crisis intervention and is thus particularly relevant to devising and implementing crisis management strategies. In a crisis, itself defined as "a period of psychological disequilibrium, experienced as a result of a hazardous event or situation that constitutes a significant problem that cannot be remedied by using familiar coping strategies," people encounter obstacles to their life goals that feel insurmountable at the time.

As a result, they experience "emotional distress," an "impaired sense of personal self-worth," an "inability to enjoy interpersonal contacts," and "impaired task performance." In turn, they may feel "a sense of disorganization, confusion, anxiety, shock, disbelief, or helplessness, which may increase as attempts to resolve the situation prove to be ineffective."[17]

Our work as helpers is to transform individuals' ineffective attempts at resolution into collective effective resolutions, using the tools and techniques social workers and psychologists are exposed to and equipped with during their education and training. Crisis theory has been applied at the individual and group level for well over half a century to deal with grief, loss, and disequilibrium. During our next society-wide crisis, we should adopt and apply its most cogent tenets, as early as possible following the crisis, in our concentrated efforts to reestablish order, organization, balance, and hopefulness in our culture at large.

ADVICE FROM BUSINESS LEADERS

The business side of crisis management is just as important as the emotional side. Even as we take care of individuals in mental crisis, we need to keep our world turning, our economy running, our operations operating. Otherwise, detrimental socioeconomic forces will just compound the crisis and people will fall further into distress of all types. How do we do that—go about "business as usual" as much as possible until we feel more comfortably in the clear?

Here's a list of the first six steps you can take to reassure your people and reinforce your organization, offered by a business owner of three full-time privatized schools and one satellite location:

1. Make your staff and your clients feel safe. Remember Maslow's hierarchy—any other criterion is superfluous if an environment of safety is not first assured.
2. Fake it 'til you make it. So many professional development texts repeat this popular-culture aphorism because it's broadly applicable. If you're feeling scared and fragile yourself, try not to show that too much to your staff, summoning your inner reserves of strength for them and allowing them to talk freely about what's happening. A problem shared is a problem halved.
3. Secure funding to ensure that your staff gets paid and your clients get served. Maslow again—if people don't know how they're going to put food on the table or access necessary services: They. Will. Panic.
4. Be open to innovation and creativity to solve unforeseen problems. When irregularities plague us, we must be willing to look beyond the regular courses of action.
5. Position yourself right in the mix, rolling up your sleeves and doing anything and everything you're asking your staff to do. Be seen. Do not hide in your office.
6. Publicly and actively join the efforts of your larger community to show that your business is interested in being part of the solution, not running from the crisis or keeping silent until you see how the chips fall.

Another helpful voice is that of Tim Ziglar, author of *10 Leadership Virtues for Disruptive Times,* who's known for what's termed his "humanizing leadership" in the foreword to his book. Coming out of the pandemic and preparing "for whatever the winds of change and challenge may bring," Ziglar states, we can be sure of three things: that we will learn and grow from the challenges, that business "will never be done the same way again," and that we will always have the choice between folding up and going home or rising up to create a better world.[18]

He goes on to advocate for "coach leadership" over management leadership as the best way to lead through times of immense change. His coach leader emphasizes 10 virtues that "never change" and thus fortify that leader and allow that leader to prosper amid disruption:

- Kindness
- Selflessness
- Respect
- Humility
- Self-control
- Positivity
- Looking for the best
- Being the light
- Never giving up
- Standing firm

"Once we understand the purpose of leadership and realize disruption is inevitable, we can prepare for it" instead of being shocked by it.[19]

Another thing we know about crisis management is that there will always be leaders at the fore like these, willing to lend their expertise and guidance. When we're facing a "next time" like "last time," we should generously borrow from them on behalf of the betterment of society.

LET'S BUILD OUR PREPARATION MUSCLES

No one knows for sure what's around the corner, but there are lots of predictions about what's most probable. Cyberattacks. Natural disasters—a parade of hurricanes, tornadoes, tsunamis, and superstorms that will just keep marching. The reverberations of climate change, like floods and rising sea levels that will engulf low-lying regions, droughts that will threaten water supplies and invite large-scale forest fires, uninhabitable areas that will lead to massive migration and emigration, dying coral reefs that will extinguish biodiversity and precipitate food scarcity and hunger for scores of populations.

Right now, California is planning for "the big one," with Los Angeles retrofitting buildings; seismologists don't know when it will occur, but they know it will. We also don't know when the next pandemic will strike, but it's certain it will. We're about to see two kinds of people in the world: those who have gone through a pandemic and those who will go through one. COVID-19 wasn't "a freak of nature," says Jennifer Nuzzo, director of the Pandemic Center at Brown University; instead, it's the new normal. "It's like the levees are built for the one-in-a-100-years crisis, but then the floods keep happening every three years."[20]

Regardless of what looms, we cannot live in a constant state of fear. But we do have to be smart about arming ourselves against the likeliest threats. There are some tangible precautions we can take in society as a whole, such as these:

- Unlimited manufacturing of and access to personal protective equipment (PPE)
- Continual development of vaccines and ongoing research and development in contagious diseases
- Building a vast and shored-up network of remote doctors and therapists
- Purchasing cybersecurity and/or ransom insurance for our businesses
- Having "disaster kits" on hand in our homes and places of business containing essential supplies, like masks, gloves, cleaning solvents, nonperishable foodstuffs, water, medicines, first-aid supplies, pet food, batteries, transistor radios, and, yes, toilet paper and paper towels
- Having evacuation routes, shelters, and emergency medical care centers in place in our local communities

Other larger-scale steps are less concrete but more all-encompassing to start training our muscles now for the marathons we may be called upon to run:

Learn from other countries. After the SARS epidemic in 2003, for instance, Taiwan set to work actively designing a master plan and creating numerous special-purpose agencies to be at the ready when another disaster struck. When COVID-19 did, the republic jumped into action, achieving far better outcomes than other nations. "They have professionals running the show. These are people who have trained for years for this,"[21] said Princeton health policy analyst Tsung-Mei Cheng in 2020.

Brace our supply chain. We haven't yet cracked the code of how to keep supply chains open and products plentiful for people just when they need them the most, but now we have the strongest impetus to do so before our chain is stressed again. We learned an awful lot during COVID about where the weak links are and how to fortify them. When we allocate enough effort to this area, as global distribution of the vaccine illustrated, we *can* untangle the knots.

Budget for disaster preparedness. Even in a severely fractured economy with exorbitant inflation, a limping stock market, and rising expenditures across the board, we found the money to help Ukraine in its time of need. We'll find the money to fund our own times of need. We always have, and we always will. But let's not wait for devastation to land—let's responsibly appropriate monies in our governments and our organizations to finance the necessary crisis measures we will surely need to enact.

Foster global cooperation. Even more than we already are, we need to foster global cooperation. By and large, despite what certain global powers may try to lead us to believe, we are not a combative people. We're competitive and we're protective, but only despots and sociopaths wield war, pestilence, and genocide as power plays. With very few exceptions, everyone in the world wants to fall in love, see their children laugh and flourish, support their family, be happy and be productive. Those with a helping mentality will feel particularly compelled to facilitate, liaise, and negotiate. Human beings long to make peace, build bridges, and forge alliances. This will all be needed, writ large, in future generations of mass crises, and if we have partnerships and preparation plans already in place, we will be far better equipped to minimize inevitable, but hopefully diminished, collateral damage.

All this talk of wide-scale infrastructure measures and international coalitions might seem quite far removed from our purpose at hand here, but it's really not; rather, it's an outline of a model you can replicate at the local organizational level—all the same principles hold. Organizational leaders in the helping professions can incorporate into your business plans *now* a crisis management budget, means of securing and supplying necessary provisions, protections against cybercrime, emergency preparedness plans for your staff and facilities, and a network of partners and allies who will support you and whom you will support in kind. You can study other organizations in your field and analyze the protocols and procedures they employed to successfully navigate COVID-19 and imitate them.

Preparation saves lives. It can also save properties, businesses, and economies. These common sensical ideas didn't feel so necessary yesterday. Today, they're both unavoidable and indisputable.

WHY HELPERS MAKE SPECTACULAR CRISIS MANAGERS

Having helpers in command of weathering a public welfare storm isn't *necessary* to weathering it, but it sure can come in handy. That's because, in essence, virtually every helping professional is a "front-line worker," hard-wired to jump in to extend assistance where it's needed and make improvements that will matter. Helpers excel at crisis management for a slew of reasons.

We're skilled at detecting warning signs and making diagnoses. Helping professionals are particularly attuned to spotting emerging problems and accurately assessing which are calling for immediate attention, which are not critical, and which are likely to resolve on their own if allowed to play out naturally. Much like a dermatologist will see a little lump on the skin and know whether it's malignant or not, your helper's X-ray vision knows where to look and how to properly name what you see.

Early intervention is a pillar of our practice. In many forms of therapy, in health care, and in education especially, we know that the earlier you can intervene in a developing issue—say, a learning disability or a speech impediment—the better. The same applies to early onset crisis situations that will benefit greatly from slowing the progression before a minor impairment can become a major hindrance. Once points of origin have been ascertained, remedies and redirection can be applied to them.

We understand the dynamics of people in trouble. Our regular application of crisis intervention methodologies in our daily work gives us a head start on other types of crisis workers. We consistently see people at their worst in wrenching situations and have learned to productively communicate with them and effectively reach them where they currently are mentally and emotionally, not where we're hoping we'll get them. Tears, frustration, rage, fear—these are the expressions we frequently see; they do not scare us, and they do not divert us one inch from our purpose.

We don't shy away from hard truths. Often during unsettling times, community leaders will try to protect the public from hard-to-swallow facts or sugarcoat them to make them go down easier. But candor is a sign of respect—it means you believe in your listener's ability to handle the truth. Helpers grasp that being honest and forthright with people about what they're really facing gives them a more direct path to facing it. Who knows how to impart bad news better than an ICU nurse? Who can lead people through loss better than grief counselors? Who will substance abusers listen to more than addiction counselors? When time is of the essence, especially, people need to be given as much information as possible to make informed decisions to protect their loved ones.

We're agile in times of adversity. Unexpected crises can come in fast and furious. When we're taken unawares by an imposing societal threat, we need leaders in place with the proven mental dexterity to immediately rank needs, juggle simultaneous tasks, and handle multiple personalities at once. Ask a schoolteacher or a juvenile justice center coordinator what it's like to deal with multiple personalities at once! We have to make quick judgment calls that consider the greater good *and* the individual good, make consequential decisions that will keep our charges secure but on point with the plan. Helpers are so deft in these areas because we are 360-degree thinkers who are adaptable and responsive. We're on the alert, primed to notice the nuances in the panoramic view, then we log what we see, keep a cool head, and get to work.

We leverage connections in crises. Helpers don't try to do things on their own because they know that the many are more powerful than the few and that one voice may not adequately represent the viewpoints of the many. Instead, their humility leads them to network with others with different areas of expertise to get things done and get the necessary players on the same page. There's another side to connection as well: helpers understand more than most how much people yearn for a sense of belonging during times of crisis, how much they need human ties to help them through dilemmas. Helpers will thus see opportunities to alleviate isolation and loneliness and open doors to those opportunities. We feel less vulnerable when we feel more connected.

We welcome external advice. Similarly, we're open to input from others on how to do our jobs to maximum effect because we don't think we're the GOAT of anything. You don't find much arrogance among helpers, and although a certain amount of take-charge blustering in leaders may come in useful at times of crisis, we would rather take the wider path that will accommodate the largest number of people in the shortest amount of time. We have been trained to closely listen to what others are telling us, to fairly judge their input, and to put the best, most humane ideas into practice. Good ideas come from all kinds of people and places, and helping professionals are open to all of them.

We know where the lifeboats are on a sinking ship. We've been there when the house is on fire, the family is falling apart, the kid is having a complete meltdown. When the bank account is empty, the insurance has dried up, and all the faith in a happy ending along with it. A lot of us have seen a lot of hard stuff. With only our instincts to guide us, with minimal resources, and with the clock ticking, we know how to get people to safety when they are submerged in pain.

We are the sentinels of human decency. Last and perhaps most important, helpers believe in being good and noble all the time, not just when tragedy strikes the deepest chords of our humanity. We strive mightily to put our best selves forward for these we serve, and we seem to have a sixth sense for drawing out others' best selves as well. Because of the evidenced dedication of helpers as civic servants, we should look to the helping professions *now* to get a jump start on the challenges that await us *later*.

When you behold some of the most difficult things we've recently gone through, on both a broad scale and a more intimate scale—9/11, the George Floyd case, Hurricane Katrina, even NFL player Damar Hamlin's January 2023 televised cardiac arrest on the football field—what outshines the tragedy is the shared humanity that rises to the top and bonds us all when faced with great hardship. There's a reason people love a doomsday-with-a-hopeful-ending plot in movies like *Armageddon*, *The Day After Tomorrow*, and *Outbreak*. We all want to believe that we will come together as a country and as a planet when faced with a cataclysmic threat, and history bears out that we will; we do. Our shared humanity when tragedy rears its awful head reveals the very best of humankind.

But what we need, and what helpers evince most, is putting that humanity on display every day, not just our worst days. If we exhibit the astounding goodness of humankind more often and more generously, letting helping professionals show us the way, that will help us get through the next crisis more than anything else. In the disruption-prone world of the twenty-first century, helpers are needed more than ever. When they are the gatekeepers of crisis management, they can do as much or more as any world leader can to keep the gates open to everything and the hope alive for everyone.

Chapter 8

Managing Personnel Issues

The role of leadership is more about managing people than managing anything else. That's because people form the backbone of your organization's structure, in the helping professions even more so than in other types of businesses, and while crises like COVID-19 and grid outages will (hopefully) be infrequent occurrences, personnel issues will arise frequently. Like, almost every day.

You're good with people—you know that. Your greatest successes have been rooted in personal connections and interrelatedness, and you wouldn't be ascending in your career if your people skills weren't first-rate. But when you become the *boss* of people, these skills are going to be called upon to be put to new use, in sometimes unfamiliar ways. It doesn't matter if you're heading a 110-person division of an agency or an 11-person crew collecting and distributing clothing to the needy for your charitable organization. You can expect to encounter personnel issues of all types and stripes, and you'll want to be as prepared as possible for those encounters.

Fortunately, the more staff situations you handle, the better you'll get at handling them until this might just become your favorite function of your job!

WHEN YOUR COLLEAGUES BECOME YOUR EMPLOYEES

When you're first promoted to a position of leadership within your current organization, it's almost inevitable that some of the people you'll be leading on Thursday are the same people you just had lunch with on Tuesday. Being the warm and personable helper you are, it's likely that you have warm and personable relationships with your coworkers. Last Sunday, you were sipping punch with Marcus at Fiona's baby shower. Last quarter, you roomed with Janelle at the company's team-building retreat. So when Marcus and Janelle are suddenly *reporting* to you, things can get, um, sticky.

Has this ever happened to you, the other way around? Has a colleague of yours gotten promoted to your supervisor? If so, the first thing to consider in this situation is how that made you feel: Did it change your relationship with this person? For better or for worse? Did you view them differently or vice versa? If you still have a relationship with this person today, are you pleased with it?

As always, firsthand experience is a great teacher, so recall your own experience to guide you in how you want to treat and talk to what's now the team you lead. And the answer is this: how you yourself would have liked to be treated and talked to by the colleague who became your boss. Even if this hasn't yet happened to you personally, call on your helper's characteristic empathy to put yourself in your former colleagues' shoes and let that empathy, more than anything in the beginning, steer your words and actions.

The second thing to consider is how to map out new rules of the road with old contacts. You absolutely want to preserve an amiable, reciprocal atmosphere of camaraderie and collegiality, but what moves up the ranks into first position now is *respect*. The new rule of the road is basically just that one word—making sure your team understands that you're now their leader and they are expected to respect your judgment, your decisions, and your new authority.

How do you "make sure" of that? You *act* like a leader first—you do and say the things a qualified and fair leader does—then you let the rest fall naturally into place. When Carolyn saunters into your office to gossip about Brett the way she used to, you politely but firmly redirect the conversation toward what Carolyn's currently working on or how she's feeling about her upcoming presentation. If you're at your regular roundtable meeting and Phil tries to take control of it the way he usually does, you thank him for his comments and then return the meeting to the next thing on the agenda. Fake it 'til you make it applies here too—you play the part of the leader until the role eventually becomes your own.

Adding this new layer of respect between your past dealings and your current dealings with your team members also entails consequences for *dis*-respect. If your directives are not followed, if tasks are not being completed properly and on time, or if someone doesn't seem to be accepting your new role, you talk to them in private clearly and candidly, making plain what you expect of them, how it's for the good of the team, and why your focus now will consistently be on what's good for the team. You usually won't have to do much more than that; in general, people respond well to guidance, especially when they feel it's being given to improve their own performance and prospects.

BEING FRIENDLY WITHOUT BEING FRIENDS

Let's take this a step further. Some of your colleagues may have been more than colleagues—they've been your friends. You and Aki have a standing tennis date every other week; he's been to your home and has broken bread at your table; you helped him through his last breakup. When you become Aki's boss, one of two things will happen:

1. You will lose your friend. The power dynamic just becomes too imbalanced, Aki just won't be able to handle that he now has to make an appointment to talk to his buddy at work, and the friendship slowly fades away into a lake of "office politics."
2. You will keep your friend, but *only* outside of work. At work, Aki must be treated just like everyone else, because if there's one thing that can poison the positive dynamics of a team, it's the appearance of favoritism. If you try to maintain a real friendship at work, visible to all around you, it's just going to backfire and blow up in your face. You will lose the respect of the people who feel like your subordinates and not your friends, as some of their peers presumably are.

The one word that applies here the most is "boundaries." To keep things fair and honest, you must draw clear, not fuzzy lines between what is and is not *appropriate*. It's okay to join your team after work for one drink; it is not appropriate to go partying with them all night. It's fine to have individual relationships with individuals on your team; it is not appropriate to make others feel left out of inside jokes or important conversations. It's good to socialize with everyone at the company picnic you planned; it is not appropriate to spend three hours at the picnic hanging with Sheila and three minutes with everyone else. You can even invite Nelson to your Super Bowl party; but it is inappropriate to laugh and chat with him on Monday about how great the game and spinach dip were in front of team members who were not invited.

With new hires or with people you never worked with before, setting boundaries in your leadership role is pretty easy. They'll just come into the situation knowing what's what, and they'll follow along with the office vibe. But with people you were or still are quite close to on a personal level, you need to be very, very careful that your inner feelings for your friends stay on the inside at work and don't seep out onto the group as a whole, because that will fracture the group.

Boundaries do *not* mean that you cannot be friendly at work with your people. Not at all. One summer morning, Josie knocked on Patrice's half-open door and asked if she could talk to her. She'd gotten a call from her son's summer camp asking her to come get him. He wasn't adapting well, and the camp coordinator had mentioned something about him possibly needing a one-to-one aide. Josie was near-frantic at the thought that her child could have serious issues and knew Patrice's background was in special education. "What do I do?" Josie asked her, near tears.

Patrice didn't hesitate a moment. She comforted Josie, got her a cup of tea, sat with her for over half an hour explaining what she could and answering Josie's questions. Josie felt comfortable coming to Patrice with this personal issue, wasn't worried about being judged as a parent, and knew Patrice would want to help. Patrice, in turn, was only too happy to be there for Josie, glad to know she was thought of in this way. At the end of their conversation, the two women hugged, and Patrice made Josie promise that she'd call her later to fill her in on how things had gone. The two weren't "friends" outside of work, but the whole encounter was very friendly.

Granted, this all sounds easier to do than it actually is, and anyone who tells you that they've got the whole formula down pat is just fooling themselves. People become friends at work. They're naturally drawn to some people they have more in common with than others, and, yes, personal relationships develop. Not only that, but creating a "family" atmosphere at work is commonplace lingo today, across all industries. How can you create a real sense of family at work without having real friends at work?

It's another balancing act you'll have to learn to master. There is a happy medium, a line you can learn to walk between who you are outside of work and who you need to be as a leader at work. You can find that middle ground. You will. If you want to be known as a respected, respectful, and unbiased leader, you must.

WHEN THOSE AROUND YOU WANT YOU TO FAIL

Life is like a game. Sometimes you're taking steps forward, sometimes taking steps back, sometimes standing still. Sometimes you're on offense, sometimes defense. Sometimes you're on a team, sometimes you're flying solo. At various times, you have opponents and you have allies. There are times when you have to compete to win the game, times when you have to cooperate to win.

In the business world, "winning" equates to becoming the new protégé, being plucked out of the crowd to advance, getting the promotion. That success can breed jealousy and insecurity in others who feel left behind, rejected, or treated unfairly because they think they deserved "the win."

Here's a tale of two men. Cole and Leo were both site directors for a large chain of occupational therapy facilities providing services throughout the

Midwest. Cole looked every bit the part of a rising executive—he was impeccably dressed and groomed, his leather briefcase gleamed, his side part was always perfectly in place—and he made it clear to all his coworkers that his objective was to eventually run the company. Leo was far more casual and informal in his dealings with people, and although he wanted to like Cole when they interacted at company functions, he was somewhat intimidated by the guy's faultless-seeming appearance and slick-seeming business sense.

Less than two years after Leo had been hired, he got the promotion to regional manager that Cole had thought was in the bag for him. According to their boss, the choice was made because Leo's people management skills had stood out, whereas Cole's sales skills were his strongest suit. So Cole was moved into a business development role, and for the next few years, he watched Leo move up and up, focusing on recruiting and retaining talent and improving service quality, while he stayed in the field selling. He was pretty good at it, but it just wasn't where he wanted to be.

Cole and Leo obviously had to work together quite often, but Cole's envy led him to want Leo to fail. It didn't matter that they were on the same team, working for the same organizational goals, Cole just didn't want Leo to succeed. Something had to change, because Leo could only tolerate Cole's resistance to his guidance, his coldness, and rumors of him bad-mouthing him and questioning his abilities behind his back for so long. It bothered Leo on a personal level—he was a sensitive guy—and he started to wonder, *Is it me? What am I doing wrong with this guy?*

At an industry conference one fall, the two men were alone on a couch during a break, and Leo flat out asked Cole what he thought about their working relationship. "You think I'm hard on you? That I judge you too harshly or have expectations of you that are too high? Maybe so," Cole admitted. "But I'm ten times harder on myself. I have far higher expectations of myself."

Leo hadn't realized—it was eye-opening to learn that Cole constantly beat himself up. *This guy needs praise like everyone else, his arrogance is just a cover for that—in fact, this guy probably needs praise* more *than anyone else.* This one conversation was the start of the two men getting to know each other a little better, on a deeper level, which led to a much-improved relationship from then on.

Leo eventually won Cole over, earning his respect as a leader, but it was a bit of a struggle. He put effort into cultivating a more authentic relationship with Cole. He didn't use his therapy skills to try to counsel or advise Cole. Instead, he dropped his own defensiveness and self-doubts in Cole's company and realized that that's what Cole wanted and needed too: to fully believe in and invest in the things he was good at, not the things he wished he were good at. Leo made a point of letting Cole know how much he valued his contributions: "You're really key to our growth right now—I couldn't do this without you. I know I'm your boss and that sometimes sticks in your craw, but you have skills that I don't, and I rely on them more than you know."

The two started doing pitches together. Leo did just fine during them, with his own knack for business development, but Cole was fantastic. People positively reacted to his polished exterior and felt reassured by his seriousness. Leo got them laughing and joking, but Cole got them to sign on the dotted line.

Ultimately, Leo came to understand Cole's motivations and showed him where his own power lay. In turn, Cole came to accept Leo's feedback as helpful rather than critical and Leo's genuine commitment to his professional development. In the process, Cole stopped viewing Leo as his "opponent," and the barrier between them fell away. The end result was an effective partnership born not of competition, but cooperation. Not breaking down, but building up.

WHEN YOU JUST DON'T CLICK WITH A TEAM MEMBER

Annette and Trent had come up in the company together, and although Trent was there longer and was something of a "company darling" because of his steady financial results, Annette was the one who was pegged to run their division when an opening arose. Annette suspected Trent thought he should have gotten the promotion on seniority alone, if nothing else, but her suspicions were never confirmed, Trent never expressed any dissatisfaction, and he seemed happy enough where he was.

The two just didn't jibe, never had. There wasn't any bad blood between them or anything like that, no outward animosity. They got along just fine—they just didn't click. This had never been an issue when they were peers. Hey, you can't hit it off with everyone, right? But now that Annette was Trent's superior, it could be an issue. It could grow into an issue. Annette was worried that her preconceived notions of Trent could cloud her leadership decisions concerning him and that their mutual standoffishness could get in the way of their aimed-for shared effectiveness.

Over lunch one day, Annette confided her worries to her mentor from another company, and her mentor gave her some very sound advice: "As long as you feel you're learning something by leading Trent, then it's a beneficial arrangement—stay in it. But as soon as the learning dries up, you're going to get frustrated with him, and it'll be time to make a change, one way or the other."

So Annette stayed the course with Trent and indeed added to her leadership suitcase by supervising someone she felt she never really grew to understand.

Their relationship remained pleasant but also on the surface—always on the surface—and Annette was never 100 percent honest with Trent because she never felt she could be. She knew she'd never won him over, like Leo did with Cole.

Eventually, Annette placed Trent under someone else's leadership. She didn't want to let him go—there was no reason to lose a perfectly capable (if not remarkable) team member just because he didn't seem to like being on *her* team—but she did come to see that she was not at her best leading him, that she was far more impactful with others on her team. She'd spent quite a while asking herself over and over, *What can I do better here? How can I break through to him?* Ultimately, she realized that her own growth was being stymied by Trent's lackluster support and static though sufficient skills, and perhaps Trent's growth, too, was also being stymied by a managerial relationship that didn't flow optimally. So in the end, she assigned him to a different manager.

If there's really very little likelihood of the working dynamic between you and one of your staffers eventually bearing fruit, it makes sense to stop trying to force the "click" and let the two of you walk in better step down parallel but different roads for the overall good of the organization.

WORKING WITH OPPOSITES

Lack of connection is one thing; working with someone who sees the world from a dramatically different viewpoint than yours and thus behaves in it dramatically differently is quite another. As a curious, open helping professional with high emotional intelligence, this doesn't have to pose a problem for you. You can like this person, enjoy this person, admire this person, but you just don't *think* like this person. That can be a good thing. That can add a fresh perspective and unexpected considerations to any scenarios you face with this person's involvement.

Vicki was the chief operations officer for a health care credentialing center, and Grace was the head of human resources. On the organizational chart, Vicki's position was one tier up from Grace's, but the two worked closely together, guided by each other's input nearly every day. Grace was all business all the time, which was maybe why she was so competent and trusted in her role—able to make objective, economic-based decisions when it came to hiring and firing. Vicki, on the other hand, was prized for her warm heart and let her "inner knowing" about people guide the majority of her management decisions.

Interestingly, even though Grace was in HR, she wasn't a "people person," and even though Vicki ran operations, she ran them more so from the base of her helper's instincts and intelligence than her financial underpinnings, of which she had no shortage.

Here's how Vicki and Grace helped rather than hindered each other with their contrasting outlooks. Grace liked when things added up, made logical sense, and rules were followed; she got upset with the staff when they didn't want to follow the plan and were always requesting extra people and higher salaries than had been allotted for the year. She took it personally, like she was the one not being respected, until Vicki helped her separate her own motives from those of the staff: they weren't trying to undo her well-laid plans, they were just trying to advocate for their own departmental needs. Over time, once Grace was able to take her personal discomfort out of the equation, she began relating better to the staff, explaining things to them from where they were coming from instead of just pointing to a report to justify her arguments.

Vicki also helped Grace see that the staff were more than countable, capital assets she was responsible for lining up and getting through the gate. Each might have a finite figure attached to their position by the company, but Vicki could anticipate their worth farther into the future, where investing more in some of them now could pay off in substantial dividends later. They started making certain personnel decisions together, with Vicki lending more qualitative considerations to Grace's more quantitative approach to assessing human capital.

For her part, Grace planted new ideas in Vicki's head about why some folks weren't returning Vicki's friendly overtures in equal measure, why they chose not to attend any nonmandatory social functions or requested private offices. It's not that they didn't like their jobs, didn't like Vicki, or didn't work well with others. They were just more reserved than Vicki was, preferring to express and comport themselves at work in ways that felt acceptable and appropriate to them. It was just their personal style, Grace explained, and had nothing to do with Vicki's leadership abilities.

Grace also helped Vicki evolve as a leader by just saying no to her sometimes. Not everyone in the company was in a position to say no to her, but Grace was, and she would whenever Vicki's well-meaning but unrealistic asks just weren't feasible. At those times, Vicki had to devise means to accomplish her goals without the concessions HR just couldn't grant her, which developed her ingenuity and honed her resourcefulness.

Vicki was long on empathy; Grace was long on practicality. Grace liked to keep to herself; Vicki wanted to be out among her team as much as possible. Vicki relished hugging and clasping hands and showing off family photos among the group; Grace was uneasy with any such outward display of affection at work. But the two women worked well together, trusted each other's judgment, and came to respect each other's differences.

The most celebrated example of a leader who invited opposing views is Abraham Lincoln. In talking about her book *Team of Rivals*, esteemed historian Doris Kearns Goodwin says of him, "By putting his rivals in his cabinet, he had access to a wide range of opinions, which he realized would sharpen his own thinking."[1]

You don't want to surround yourself with or hire only people who think like you. That will limit you; keep you in the box you already know; point you in the direction of a managerial rut. Be like Abe. Welcome divergent thinking patterns, behavioral tendencies, and coping strategies. As one person's strengths fill in another person's lacks and vice versa, you'll create a fruitful, expansive, and inclusive workplace to the benefit of all.

WHEN PEOPLE ARE RESISTANT TO CHANGE

It is very common to encounter people who are resistant to change—not just at work, but in life in general. People get used to doing things a certain way, they get comfortable with their routines, they know what "works for them." On the outside, this just looks like a structured, consistent, predictable person you can rely on to toe the line; but on the inside, this usually reflects fear of the unknown and insecurities about one's own abilities to meet new challenges. A risk-averse, fear-driven mindset will manifest in certain remarks and behaviors, as in the example of Nate. When a new task or function had to be undertaken, Nate would get someone else to handle it; when new procedures or innovations were proposed, he'd typically reply, "That's dumb." Nate was afraid of what he didn't know, and he didn't seem to know that.

Now, Nate was quite stubborn and he liked things his way, but he was also a very high performer the company valued greatly. His boss didn't want him to stagnate in the same place his whole career, not adding new skills to keep pace with the company's growth., so when a new program was being added to the organization's offerings, his boss put him in charge of training everyone who'd be implementing the program. Nate's boss thought this role would appeal to both Nate's affinity for attention and being in control—and he was right.

At first, Nate indeed offered up a lot of resistance: his plate was full, he was already working on goals with his own team. But his boss appealed to Nate's ego somewhat, explaining why his deep knowledge of the company culture, his proven commitment to their mission, and how positively staff responded to his leadership (which they did) made him a perfect fit to be a trainer (plus, it came with a healthy stipend!). Eventually, Nate found he enjoyed this role very much, and the new program was a success, due in large part to Nate's talented stewardship.

People who are resistant to change are like Tootsie Roll Pops. When you know there's a worthy prize at the center, you just have to keep wearing down the resistance layer by layer until you expose the part you believe in so that the person can believe in it as well. Each time they try and succeed at something new, it will chip away at their fear to innovate and reinforce their ability to adapt. It's worth the effort to get through the sometimes-tough exterior.

WHEN SKILL DOESN'T MATCH ENTHUSIASM

Eve had energy and vibrancy to spare. Through her work for the welfare agency, she was amazing with the kids, the parents easily opened up to her, and the sending people who referred clients to her organization always welcomed calls from her because she was upbeat, spirited, and committed.

But Eve wanted it all, and she wanted it too soon and too young. She just hadn't developed the maturity yet to handle all the things she'd eventually be faced with at the agency, and no matter how many times her supervisor reminded her that she was definitely on the right track but that she still had a way to go, Eve didn't want to hear it. She wanted a shortcut to the top, fueled by her enthusiasm.

Once in a big meeting, the county director cited an example of a worker's phenomenal performance in the field—she said it just may have been the most perceptive and skilled exchange she'd ever witnessed—and Eve actually seemed offended that the worker wasn't her. Another time, when she was giving a presentation on outreach approaches, she spent far more time telling her audience how hard she'd worked on the presentation and how late she'd stayed up to do it than on the outreach itself.

She was known to gossip about others in the breakroom, to reveal confidential details about her cases, and to overshare about her own personal life at work. More than once, coworkers heard her bragging, "I could do Christine's job right now," "I'm already better than Luther ever was."

Eve had the talent to take her where she wanted to go, but she just wasn't emotionally ready for what she'd meet when she got there. Her manager recognized all this in her—her ample potential and her unbridled passion—as well as her need for constant recognition. So she decided to play a very active role in guiding Eve's career, providing the guidance Eve didn't realize she needed.

And that's what you need to do when you have a rising star on your team who thinks they shine just a little too brightly than they actually do—yet. You get them to that "yet" with one-on-one mentoring and role-specific coaching. They're not ready for certain responsibilities now, so you prepare them with the perspectives and capacities to take on those responsibilities when the time comes.

To tutor an outstanding but overconfident employee, you'll want to be far more direct than subtle, you'll probably need a thick skin to deflect the criticisms their self-defensiveness might throw at you in response to your frankness, and you'll have to tame that "top dog" attitude somewhat as they learn to appropriately and professionally handle themselves with both the people your organization serves and the people who will one day report to them. And you'll have to do all this *without* making them feel like they have to hide their light under a bushel or extinguish the flame that everyone appreciates about them so much.

We're back on that seesaw trying to find balance again—you want to keep the team member's light intact, for sure, but you don't want them to blind others with an overzealousness that they'll certainly outgrow with some time and the proper tutelage. In mentoring others to steadily walk toward the future they envision for themselves while simultaneously corralling their zest and talents so they can be put to most productive use, your leadership talents will mature as well.

WHEN SOMEONE'S BETTER ON PAPER THAN IN PRACTICE

Wilson had all the credentials—he'd earned his degree from a good school, had the right educational background for the job, and had acquired the certifications applicable to the open position. The company hired him on the spot, signing him to a two-year contract. He set to work in the classroom instructing the trainees, and every morning, he reported with a pleasant smile, a kind word to all his coworkers, and a can-do demeanor. Whatever his director asked him to do was met with a "Yes, sure, of course," and whenever he was asked if he knew how to do something, his answer was "Yes, sure, of course."

The only problem was, he really didn't seem to know what he was doing, and the tasks his director assigned him weren't being completed properly. He didn't ask for help, he didn't admit when he was in over his head—he just carried on day after day coming to work, but not working proficiently.

It took close to half a year for it to become evident—the whole facility was overly busy, Wilson was new and surely needed some ramp-up time to assimilate—but Wilson's students just weren't learning. The other classes were ahead of his, and his teacher's surveys weren't at all promising. He'd looked so good on paper! His résumé had been so impressive! He was so easy to work with and easygoing amid the tumult that enveloped the training center some days. What should the company *do* with him?

They were reluctant to just let him go: first, they had a contract in place and the three-month trial period had already passed; second, the organization had just been sued by an employee who'd been fired, and they really weren't up for another potential lawsuit. It's a real concern these days—in today's litigious society, companies are fearful of letting people go, even people who clearly aren't making the grade.

HR came up with a possible solution. Wilson could no longer be charged with direct instruction—the entire reputation of the company rested on how well equipped the trainees were upon graduation—but that didn't mean he didn't have other strengths that could be applied in a different post. He was very amiable. He had a good sense of humor and laughed a lot. He liked to interact and knew when to talk and when to listen. He picked up on others' cues and went with the flow. Most of all, he was excited at the prospect of traveling.

"Would he consider a transfer?" His director asked him. The company had been wanting to hire a recruiter for some time now, they just hadn't gotten around to doing it yet. Would Wilson be interested in going on the road for them, at the same salary, but with travel expenses covered and with a bonus structure in place based on his output?

Wilson *was* interested. In fact, he jumped at the chance. Making this shift didn't just benefit the company; Wilson seemed much happier in his new role, without the pressure of finite instructional performance measures weighing on him. He must have known in his heart that he wasn't really skilled at doing what he'd been educated to do, and sometimes this happens—sometimes the people on your team just won't measure up to the hopes you had for them based on their qualifications on paper. Ultimately, the organization found a more comfortable place for Wilson, and he felt more comfortable being there.

GETTING LOST IN THE DETAILS

Gil was great. He really was. He worked overtime with a smile; he was eminently coachable—always eager to incorporate helpful feedback; and you could actually feel how much he wanted to do well when you were in his presence. His loyalty to the company was unmatched, and his competence never had cause to be questioned. You couldn't find a harder worker, a more dedicated employee, a staffer more willing to really get in the mud of the details and roll around in it. The things was, Gil could get so immersed in the details of his job that he could lose sight of his organization's larger mission.

An example: A family was coming in for a tour of one of the company's residential centers and an initial interview. If all went well, the family would settle on this center and the orientation would turn into an intake. But Gil didn't feel mentally ready for the Littletons' visit. The forms he'd printed out for the meeting came out a bit fuzzy because the ink cartridge was almost empty, he'd found a typo on one of the questionnaires his assistant had prepared that was really gnawing at him, and there was no more decaf left in the meeting room. What if the Littletons only drank decaf?! As a result of all this, Gil was distracted during his time with the family and not as self-possessed and persuasive as he usually was.

Often when people can't "see the forest for the trees," it's a control issue. They're frequently people pleasers who feed off approval, who have perfectionist tendencies that lead them to always prefer to do things themselves rather than delegate, and who are comforted by controlling all the minutiae around them because that's what they *can* control. There's usually some insecurity at play here as well (as a leader, you'll see how often insecurity lies at the root of many behavioral patterns). The concentration on the details keeps the individual's focus away from the heavier thoughts that might agitate or threaten them. In Gil's case, he was raised in a very unstable home with a lot of scarcity, and the effects of that on his adult need for stability, order, and precision weren't going away anytime soon.

Nor did Gil's company want him to undo the things he did so well. They adored him. He was a dream to lead, and he was always respectful to his leaders. But if he advanced to management, as they were planning, would *he* be a dream leader, would *he* garner the respect of his people?

They wanted to facilitate that outcome, elevate Gil's game, so they enrolled him in an intensive junior executive training program that would expose him to a variety of supervisory functions and give him a more comprehensive view of what company management looked like from the top. In an appropriate setting, they wanted to impart the equation: little picture = little job, big picture = big job. The minutiae would never end; you could get lost in it. If you wanted to lead, the mission had to be the central focus.

With exceedingly detailed-oriented people like Gil, if their meticulousness is curtailing their productivity and occupying too much of their attention, the aim is to expand their horizons, literally. To lead them to become wider, broader thinkers. You put something vast in front of them to force their gaze beyond their desk, their inbox, and the to-do list that must be accomplished today.

Because they're such self-directed workers who will not rest until the job is done right, they learn to rank the more consequential tasks above the less-pressing technicalities, which aren't going to derail the project anyway, in the interests of getting the job done. You can appreciate and retain their exactitude and conscientiousness even as you guide them toward channeling those attributes toward the bigger picture.

In Gil, his leadership team saw a wellspring of potential. Sending him for training was the first step in tapping that potential, followed up by taking him into top-tier meetings so he could observe the goings-on there and see the interplay of the different organizational domains in working toward company-wide goals. Step by step, once he'd been shown how to do so, he began directing his efforts toward the best uses of his time and practicing letting go of the negligible details. He delegated more to his assistant. When something wasn't perfect, he'd quickly apologize and then move on instead of trying to overcorrect the finer points himself.

When a fitting opportunity in upper management arose, Gil was named the director of business enterprises, where he's been doing a bang-up job ever since.

WHEN SOMEONE RESPECTS UP BUT DISSES DOWN

This is another common and truly unfortunate occurrence: having someone on your team who's great to the people above them and lousy to the people below them. Jennifer was like that. At the blood bank, the disposition she displayed when her superiors made their regular visits was one of nothing less than honor—she held them in the highest regard, almost fawning over them and treating them with the utmost deference.

However, when they weren't around to see how she managed her team, she was no less than awful, bossing them around like underlings at her beck and call—some of them volunteers and interns, to make matters worse!—expecting the same kind of obsequiousness she exhibited with her managers. She'd publicly scold them for missteps and yell at them for mistakes.

Eventually you'll get wind of employee dissatisfaction with a member on your team. But to compress that time gap between being unaware and then aware of something you need to know, it's good practice to talk with organizational employees at all levels, not just the one immediately under your supervision, and to distribute feedback forms to all employees about all their bosses (on an annual basis, at the least), even if the responders want to remain anonymous.

There are very few personnel dilemmas that can't be resolved reasonably, that are just downright intolerable, but this is one of them. When a servant leader makes a mockery of that title and instead treats their employees like servants or degrades or belittles them in any other way, it must be put to an immediate, unqualified stop.

The best tactic here is to face the problem head-on. No delays. No "let's wait and see." No hall passes because the worker gets things done. As soon as you become aware of the problem, you confront the individual in person, on their own turf, explaining what you've heard and then giving them a chance to explain or respond. Maintain your professionalism at all times, but don't let the person's known charm with their superiors misdirect your purpose. The target is absolutely clear and direct communication about a zero-tolerance company policy, and you make plain that if you get a whiff of such unacceptable behavior again, the individual will be terminated.

Afterward, keep an eye on things and discreetly follow up with a few of the individual's employees. If the situation doesn't improve, you must make good on your threat so that the larger team knows you have their backs and will not allow them to be disrespected by the very person entrusted with their leadership.

MANAGING STRONG-WILLED PEOPLE

To take only one more sampling of personnel issues you'll likely face as an organizational leader, let's consider the headstrong team member who's difficult to manage. You might think this is another dead end, another straightforward no-go, but it's not. In fact, it can be quite the opposite.

Bullheaded people can be challenging. They can think they can do everything better than you. They can think they're so much smarter than everyone else in the room. They can come across as obnoxious, judgmental, dismissive, and as highly critical know-it-alls. But they can *also* get things done like nobody's business; they can handle blunt honesty; they're comfortable having authority; and when they really want something, they'll hold on tight like a dog with a bone and won't let go when others would just give up and walk away. And if you get them on your side, there's no better ally.

Ryan took a liking to Tess right when he interviewed her—she was entertaining, intriguing, quirky, and sharp, and she knew her own mind. Just because he liked her personally, he realized, didn't mean she'd make a good school principal, but his gut told him to give her a try. True, the minute she'd walked into the school, she'd called it "kind of dumpy"; but when Ryan told her, "Look, I need someone who wants to be part of the solution, not sniping from the sidelines—if you're going to pitch in to help me make this place better, then I could use someone with your gusto and smarts," her eyes lit up at the invitation.

For the next several years, Ryan led Tess through a series of challenges— and watched her ace almost every one. "You think you know everything? How to fix this?" he dared her. "Good. Then prove it." And she'd set off, putting her ideas and plans into motion.

But she remained strong-minded and iron-willed every step of the way, and so Ryan still had to coach her, aiming to tone down the audacity and smugness that could put people off while still allowing her to be true to her own nature and instincts. He concentrated on two areas: (1) teaching her to direct her fierce determination and confidence toward the goals of the organization over her own interests; and (2) creating a followership, for without the backing and belief of her faculty, she wouldn't get anywhere.

Tess was tougher to lead than most, but Ryan discovered he loved leading her all the same. She never lost her rough edges or fully curbed her abrasiveness at work, but he didn't need her to change who she was; as long as she wasn't being offensive to anyone (which she wasn't), he just needed her to recognize her position in the crew at large—when to captain her own ship, her own school, and when to heed the directives of her commanding officers. And she came through. She's still with the same educational organization to this day at a very high level, considered one of its ablest leaders.

So don't take a pass on the strong-willed candidates who come across your desk. What might seem like an obstacle can be an advantage in disguise. These are the folks who will stay in the ring and never stop fighting. These are the folks who hold fast to their principles and find a way to realize their vision. They set high standards for their staff and hold themselves to higher still. They'll defend themselves to the end, yes—but they'll stand up for their people just as much. That's what makes a leader, and you can play a part in shaping that kind of leader.

EXORCISING DEMONS AND ACCENTUATING ASSETS

There are a lot of unknown personnel scenarios that can arise in any workplace, but one thing that is known is that when you work with the same team for any length of time, personal demons are going to be exposed, in one way or another, at one time or another. This includes your own as well as those of your people. Personal demons—those little imps who sit on our shoulders and whisper things in our ears that make us doubt ourselves, test our resolve, and make us feel ashamed or inadequate.

It's usually pretty easy to identify your demons, and it's usually just one big one running the show, with a B team of pesky players circling around the ringleader. You can use an exercise like Dev did with his team, asking them all to complete the sentence, "I'm not X; I'm Y." Whatever's filled in for X is the primary demon—typically a thought implanted in the brain in youth, sometimes by just one comment from one authority figure, like a parent, grandparent, teacher, or coach; and the Y variable is the aspiration—the thought repeated to oneself to disprove the demon.

Almost everyone on Dev's team was able to instantly answer. Rebecca wrote, "I'm not dumb; I'm smart." Matt wrote, "I'm not a loser; I'm a winner." Abby wrote, "I'm not unlovable; I'm lovable." Demons are not unconscious parts of our psyche that we don't have access to—they're pretty much right there on the surface when we ask them to reveal themselves, and that's good news for group leaders.

It's good news because once you know what your demons are, you can cope with them by diluting their power over you. Part of being human is that we'll probably never totally expunge or eradicate those inner thoughts that tell us we're just not good enough. But we *can* learn to nullify and neutralize them, especially in our behaviors and actions at work.

When you adequately deal with your own demons at work, you model how to do so for your team. Just like you'll learn their demons, they'll recognize yours, so when they see you restraining your defensiveness with openness to feedback, subduing your stubbornness with flexibility, or replacing grudges with forgiveness, you'll inspire them to exorcise the self-defeating tendencies that get in the way of their efficacy at work as well. This influence will likely carry over outside of work too.

Talk to your people about their demons. Share with them the ways in which you see their negative inner voice hampering their progress toward their goals. Then do the homework you need to do to learn to coach them on how to work with their demons, not futilely rail against them. Share with them your own experiences with your own self-doubts; it's not a weakness to do this—it's most definitely a strength to relate to your people on this same, mutual level.

A few months after Dev conducted his demon exercise with his team, Tim came up to him and said, "I couldn't believe it when you told us all, out loud, that you struggle with your confidence. I didn't want to hear that about my boss, and I think I maybe even lost a little respect for you in that moment. But now? Now I respect you all the more. I told my wife about the exercise, and it's really improved our marriage lately. She feels she knows me better—I feel like I know myself better."

The next step is to counter these conversations about the things that are holding your team members back with the things that make them exceptional, one-of-a-kind human beings. Just as surely as we all have a personal demon sitting on our shoulder, we all—*all* of us—have something that is exclusively and entirely our own: an essence, an aura, an internal kernel of originality, our own je ne sais quoi. It's not just one nameable characteristic that you can try to put your finger on; it's the way all *your* traits combine in *your* distinct way to make *you* an individual unlike any other. It's the part of you that is inexpressibly you.

Help your people get in touch with their most valuable assets by casually but consistently commenting on what you observe in them. No formal, across-the-desk coaching sessions here, just one person sharing with another person what you see in their conduct and their character that makes them such a vital member of your team.

Like this: "Stuart, wow. The way you just talked that guy on the phone into transferring that client here? It was such a masterful mix of firmness and gentle persuasion—really impressive finesse!"

Or this: "I couldn't have handled that any better myself, Trina. You told Roger what he needed to hear, but you did it with such sensitivity to who you know him to be. I'm going to borrow your approach next time."

Guide your people toward accentuating their strongest strengths to the max so they can apply them to the max, everywhere and with everyone in their lives. Years later, they'll be thanking you in their heads for pointing out the best in them, even if you've lost touch.

Yep, over the years of your career, you'll meet all kinds of people as an organizational leader—some won't walk their talk; some will leave at the first offer of more money; some will stay forever, safe in their predictable cocoon; and some will advance beyond you, perhaps doing incredible things at incredible service organizations.

But from the get-go, you will all have something in common: you will all have at least one personal demon that you need to lasso so you can train it to work to your advantage—motivating you to prove it wrong instead of letting it convince you that it's right; and you will all have a je ne sais quoi that makes you uniquely you. There is no other human being on this planet quite like you. So there is no other leader who will lead just like you.

Chapter 9

"Money" Isn't a Bad Word

This intentionally short chapter is basically just a permission slip to tell you that *you're allowed to make money*. Contrary to popular myth (and it is purely a myth), helping professionals who do good for the betterment of society at large are indeed allowed to do well in the process, financially and in all other ways, and anyone who tries to tell you otherwise is either looking down on your work or trying to keep you down, right where you are, without further ambition.

But there's nothing wrong with being ambitious. Absolutely nothing. Heck, it's the American way! It's okay to make a good living in return for the good work you do. It's okay to *want* to make a good living. Nevertheless, some helpers wonder if it's *not* okay—if it's "bad" to earn a good deal of money when so many of the people they've devoted their careers to have such a scarcity of it.

Chris Beckett, in another book written by a social worker who moved into management titled *Supervision: A Guide for the Helping Professions*, brings up an interesting point in this regard: he notes that in his field, there exists an "uneasy relationship with power." "Most social workers see themselves as being on the side of the powerless against the powerful."[1] As such, how can you want to ascend to a position of power when you identify as a champion of those who hold little to none of it? Is it perhaps also "bad" to desire a top-tier job and the status that comes with it, especially in light of the good you aim to do?

These are valid and not at all surprising concerns for someone with a helper's mentality. You have seen strife and want to alleviate it. You are committed to social welfare and revere the work you do on behalf of it. But you needn't have a smidge of discomfort or shame about your desire to do well in your career, because social good and financial reward are not mutually exclusive goals. They're just not. You can generate both. You can have both.

Yet some people are still uncomfortable with any or all of this: money, power, prestige, authority, status. Okay, say you're one of those people. Say your value system strongly believes in distributing wealth. Fine. Great. That works too! Because when you become successful enough to make a considerable amount of money, that almost always means your enterprise is bringing in substantial capital as well. And when your enterprise is doing well, you can use that capital to make people's lives better, make your services better, make your systems better.

So let's briefly talk about three kinds of financial prosperity that may come to you as an organization leader and why it's fine—more than fine—for you to aspire to all three.

DOING WELL FOR YOURSELF

Being rewarded copious fruits for one's labors doesn't just fall to the purview of the lawyers, doctors, tech giants, rocket scientists, Hollywood stars, and pro athletes among us. No offense to all the well-paid, often highly educated professionals out there—you keep doing what you do to defend us, entertain us, keep us healthy, and keep our devices motoring along, and we'll keep doing what we do! But what we do is important. If you're a helping professional reading this book, what you do is *important*.

And sometimes—not always, but sometimes—there's money to be made in the helping professions. There are many for-profit organizations that take care of people and can also take care of *their* people. So if you happen to be fortunate enough to advance to a place in your career where your circumstances afford you the ability to live in a nice house, drive a nice car, wear nice clothes, and send your kids to great schools, enjoy it. Rather than feel guilty about doing well, take pride in your accomplishments and grant yourself license to the financial compensation that comes in this country from doing an important job with skill and dedication.

We're not talking about greed here, of course. We're not talking about making off with millions at the organization's expense or falling prey to embezzlement or tax evasion. It *does* happen in the business world that people start out with good intentions and end up taking a wrong turn somewhere; there *are* instances of pharmaceutical companies that have saved countless lives but that have also gotten filthy rich off addiction. But when helpers are in charge of the money, there's very little risk of this type of unethical corruption, so let's just take it as a given that there's no chance of anything remotely like this happening to you.

There *is* a chance, however, that you'll make enough money to join the fancy new gym around the corner, take your partner on a long cruise, hire a landscaper, or indulge in the virtual-reality goggles you've always coveted. People who work hard should get to play hard; people who give so much are also permitted to receive. More often than not, though, helping professionals who earn a sizable living end up spending it on others—making their parents comfortable, making sure their children want for nothing, taking care of people in their lives who are less fortunate, leaving large tips.

This is fine. This is good. Again, no reason for guilt. Former Green Bay Packers quarterback Aaron Rodgers made $42 million in 2022 for playing football.[2] Do you think he felt guilty?

You didn't earn the money just by walking through the door. You earned it by becoming a successful leader who delivers effective aid to people in need of that aid. As a result of making people's lives better, you're being compensated at a level that makes your life better too.

Having said all this, you might not make a lot of money and you don't *need* to make a lot of money to keep doing a lot of good for the world. But if financial success happens to be a byproduct of your advancing career, don't begrudge yourself some of the nicer things in life that make life nicer. And if you don't want or need any of those things? You can always become an independent philanthropist and give it all away to your favored causes.

DOING WELL FOR YOUR PEOPLE

One of the most rewarding experiences you can have as a business leader is the opportunity to reward the people to whom you owe your success. Smack in between the animate person who runs the organization and the inanimate organization itself lie all the team members—the staff—who make your job possible and the organization's mission a reality.

When and if you have the chance to express your gratitude to them in the form of financial compensation, do so as often and as regularly as you responsibly can. Praise is wonderful—people love being told what a good job they're doing, how appreciated they are—but praise doesn't pay the bills. Paying them for their good work conveys how valued they are to the company, because that's simply how value is signified in the American economic system.

If the business you lead is accruing wealth, share the wealth by all means feasible. Profit sharing is a tremendous way—maybe the best way—to both engender loyalty and elicit buy-in, so if it's applicable and at all possible, institute it. If not, you can create bonus structures that recognize top performers, you can hold contests with cash prizes, you can grant great raises in great years, good raises in good years.

Employees who feel valued stay longer, work harder, and contribute more. It makes sense to take care of your people first when money is flowing, even before you take care of systems and structures, because they're the ones making the systems and structures go, it doesn't just make sense. It's the right thing to do.

Apart from all this, it just feels good to see your people doing well. To see photos of the remodeled kitchen Zara and her husband finally undertook after 12 years of homeownership, of Beverly's vacation to her ancestral homeland in Ireland. To watch Duane pull into the parking lot in his snazzy new car, having finally replaced his old jalopy with a reliable vehicle for his commute. To hear that Whitney made her first IVF appointment; and that James is sending his kid to the pricey summer program he'd been begging to attend.

You will enjoy the fruits of your labor so much more when your people are eating of the same fruit. Helpers of all types are committed to raising the standards of living and improving the quality of life of those you serve. When it's in your power to do the same for the people who serve your organization, it's an honor and a privilege to do so.

DOING WELL FOR YOUR ORGANIZATION

In the for-profit social organization sector, profit is termed "surplus." Surplus is not only highly desired—yes, even in the helping professions—it is essential to sustaining high-quality services, improving and expanding services, fairly paying the people who deliver those services, and reinvesting in the organization. Most helpers think, "I just want to make a difference. I just want to help people," so that half of the battle is already won; but the other half is having the *means* to help them. If your organization doesn't have long-term viability, then the capacity to help becomes moot—just an empty-tank wish.

If you work for or own a revenue-generating, social services–based company, then assertively seeking a surplus should be a prime objective, even as you pursue your social aims. *How* to increase your revenue stream and allocate it most strategically is a discussion for another place and time; here, the point is simply to underscore that you can make more social gains when you make more financial gains, as illustrated by a few recent examples.

Example #1: After years of working in the assistive devices industry, Shiva invented a therapeutic swing that soothes individuals suffering from disability-related anxieties. It was a lot of hard work to get the engineering just right and then get the product to market, but years after he'd built the first prototype in his garage in Sacramento, his business finally started taking off, and he found himself with net revenue to spare after covering his monthly operating expenses.

With the extra income, he was able to purchase a CRM program, hire an office manager and two sales reps, contract with a payroll company that provided direct deposit, and launch a digital ad campaign. By the end of year two in full-time business, Shiva had 36 contracts in place, supplying swings that were available for use to more than 270 people in various homes and residences.

Example #2: When circumstances beyond her control forced Olivia to shift her counseling practice online from her long-standing in-person model, she felt sure her company would suffer. She employed a dozen therapists and social workers whom she supervised under her psychologist's shingle, and she worried that she'd have to let some of them go. But her worries were unfounded. Not only did all of her standing patients stay on, but new referrals were flocking in every week.

With the new revenue stream combined with her savings on rent once she let her office space lease expire, she was able to hire two more part-time marriage and family therapists, a suicide prevention expert, and a dedicated child psychologist. Not only that, but she outfitted her team with state-of-the-art technology to accommodate the videoconferencing platform they used. Even in a time of crisis and economic downturn, Olivia and her staff were able to treat 56 more patients than they'd seen the year prior.

Example #3: An autism day school hit a record high for enrollment last year. Not everyone believes that privatized schools subsidized by the public school system budget should make a surplus, but without "good" years to counterbalance less fluid years, the facility wouldn't be able to remain in operation. The costs of highly specialized education are just too high and the needs too great. There's also a good deal of turnover, when special educators burn out or just quit, mostly because of the intense emotional demands their jobs entail.

So the day school was thrilled to have money to spend and immediately set to work making overdue improvements. The walls were painted and new carpets installed. The meeting room was redecorated to offer a comfortable, visually appealing space for visiting families. A muralist was hired to beautify the hallways and common spaces, and an unused classroom was turned into a serenity room outfitted with soft toys, yoga mats, relaxing games, and therapeutic tools.

Staff-wise, a part-time nurse's assistant was hired to lend the full-time nurse a hand, and the school brought in an art therapist three days a week. They also made arrangements for a local musician to come in two days a week to offer music lessons to the students. They started with an electric guitar, a drum set, and a flute. If next year's enrollment stays high, they plan to add more instruments over the summer, hire another assistant behavior analyst, maybe even purchase a second minivan to take the kids on field trips.

Example #4: A home health agency operated three satellite locations in Horry County, South Carolina, and two in Georgetown County. With the massive influx of retirees moving to the area in recent years, the agency could barely keep up with the demand. But company ownership had anticipated the market growth based on population forecast reports over the last decade and had been planning for just this opportunity to blossom.

Registered nurses had already been interviewed and were on on-call status. The current full-time aides had been shown a five-year raise structure, and the part-time aides had been promised promotion to full-time positions. The operations director had been networking with specialists all over town to meet anticipated needs in such areas as wound care, postsurgical rehab, at-home cardiac care, nutritional counseling, and palliative care, and the accounting department had been working for months to formalize procedures with Medicare and various insurance companies.

When increased income started flowing in as expected, the company was able to upgrade in ways both small (artisan lotions and soaps for clients) and large (starting a 401k for employees and offering a better health insurance plan, both of which attracted more experienced, higher-quality service providers).

It comes down to simple math. A service organization needs more capital to feed and grow its service line, so it needs to bring in more revenue. No stigma attached. If we don't generate enough income to keep our businesses solvent and sound, it doesn't matter how big our hearts are. A dollar in the helping professions, though, is different than a dollar in most corporations: a dollar for us equates to more books in the library or more home visits we can make or more trips to the equine therapy farm. Each dollar has goodness on its face. And because every dollar we make uplifts lives, we can be proud to make—no, to *earn*—each and every one.

This book isn't about getting rich, no. It's about getting the life you want by what you're willing to give to it . . . and if you end up getting a nice lifestyle in the mix and being in a position to grant the same to others, then you've hit the jackpot.

But in the helping professions, "richness" applies mostly to the stature of the organizations that fall within those professions—the (hopefully far-ranging) extent of their reach to people who will benefit most from what they offer, the (hopefully expansive) circle of diversity and inclusiveness that characterizes their practices, the (hopefully unshakable) equality with which they treat, guide, and assist the populations they were created to serve. In this way, you, your people, and your organization should be as rich as possible!

We live in a capitalist society—that's just the way it is. And within this framework in which we all operate and to which we all contribute, money is the principal tool that funds our hopes and dreams. It's a tool like any other—like a software program, online banking, drive-thru windows—that makes things easier for people. Capitalism isn't supposed to work for just the few. In embracing its power, you can further its ability to work for the many by using financial gains to spread the wealth, reallocate funds, reinvest in vital services, and effect societal change.

Helping professionals can and should be able to do good *and* do well. Because the better we do, the more good we can do.

Chapter 10

Succession Planning and Growth

Rounding out your leadership journey are two imperative components of management that should never leave your line of vision for as long as you're a leader with vision: (1) succession plans for the company and (2) the continued growth of the company. These are both equally important and, as always and at core, they both ultimately rely on the people who form the heart of the organization.

SUCCESSION PLANNING: BUILDING UP YOUR WORKFORCE TODAY FOR TOMORROW

Succession (*not* the way the Roys do it on the HBO series!) should be your initial area of attention when projecting the growth of your company in any way, shape, or form, because succession planning—that is, intentionally and strategically creating a lineup of promising and talented team members to advance to roles of leadership—is all about having people in place (hopefully, the right and best people) to both take over positions when others leave and to promote to positions when the need arises.

The need will arise more often than you anticipate, and if you're short on "reserve players" to take the field when opportunities present themselves, you'll fall short of your growth goals. Simply put, without bench strength, you'll drop the ball.

There are three ways to fortify your bench: (1) prepare current middle-management leaders to take over upper-management positions when they are vacated (or created); (2) equip current team members with the skill set they'll need to advance to middle management within your organizational structure; and (3) hire from the outside, with your eye specifically trained on new hires who seem to possess the characteristics and capabilities most aligned with your organization's values and purpose.

The first two options obviously fall under the umbrella of "promoting from within," the preferred path. However, the third option also carries advantages by breathing new life into and bringing freshness to what may be a longstanding and reliable, but nevertheless slightly stagnant or musty organizational model.

What can cause an organization to become stagnant or stalled in its growth? Let's start by talking about an unfortunate but somewhat common issue you may face when you yourself assume a position that's placed higher on the organizational chart than someone who used to run the show.

Heroes of the Past Who Can't Be Heroes of the Future

We all want to honor the organizational pioneers who came before us, grant them the loyalty and gratitude they're due, bring them along on the planned rise upward. But sometimes we can't keep them in positions of leadership when the mom-and-pop shop (the way a lot of helping organizations start out) transitions into a mid- or large-sized company because they are too resistant to that transition.

Something happens that calls for significant growth in the organization's constitution—maybe you got bought out or you won a huge contract with a sudden influx of clients or a radical shift in the industry transforms the way this sector will now do business (like the move to virtual instead of physical delivery of services)—and it becomes clear to you pretty quickly as a member of the "new guard" who will be managing this transition that it's going to be an uncomfortable growth spurt for some of the organization's "old guard," the heroes of yesterday's model that's being reconceptualized, revamped, or rebuilt in front of their eyes.

You can spot these individuals by their opposition to innovation and progress. They'll say things like, "We're getting too big too fast. We're trying to do too much." To the tune of Bruce Springsteen's "Glory Days" in the background, they'll reminisce about better times of fewer departments, fewer people, and fewer responsibilities. They're happier with the past than they are with the present, and they seek more of your time and energy than you can spare.

It's not that there's anything wrong with people wanting to stay where they are—in fact, all organizations need and can benefit from the stability provided by a corps of proficient workers on the ground levels. It's just that sometimes the very people who used to lead or inspire us don't have what it takes to move into the future.

Sometimes it's a matter of ambition. They know what they know, and they show no interest in knowing more. Sometimes it's a matter of skill. They've reached their highest level of achievement and just aren't equipped to advance within a more sophisticated and complex organization. And sometimes it's a matter of fear. They're afraid of the challenges of that sophistication and complexity.

What it isn't, however, is a matter of age. Toni likes to tell the story of her grandmother, who worked retail for a high-end designer for years, writing up all her sales on hard-copy receipt pads. When automatic cash registers came in, her boss worried that she'd flounder, but she took to the new system just fine and remained a top seller on the floor into her 80s. On the other hand, Toni also knows of a 30-year-old guy who simply refused to transition from his black book of contacts to Salesforce when his company adopted the software. Award-winning, record-setting group leader that he'd been, he walked away rather than accept something new in his professional orbit.

And that's what it comes down to when someone you admire for their past performance just isn't going to remain a leader amid present circumstances: acceptance. You just have to accept that they're not able or willing to change and make personnel decisions on that basis. So long as they're not openly antagonistic to the shifts underway or interfering with organizational goals, you can keep them on in the most suitable position for them, recognizing and respecting the contributions they have made, acknowledging and appreciating them for who they are, and always treating them with dignity and fairness.

But these are not the people you're going to promote, no matter how long they've been with the company or how many laurels they can rest on. They can remain benchwarmers—comfortably sitting still where they are—but they're not going to become part of your bench strength.

Promote from Within . . . Whenever Possible

Okay, so maybe you can't promote everyone from within. Some people won't have leadership potential and some with that potential will take it elsewhere before you have a chance to mobilize it. However, whenever you can, it's a *very* good idea to line your bench with team members who are already in the fold.

From the employee's side of things, they have a shortcut to already knowing the organization—not just the big stuff, like culture and chain of command, but the little stuff, like how to submit expense reports and what to do when the printer is on the fritz. By showing interest in the available promotion, they're simultaneously showing awareness of what they'd be getting into—who they'd be reporting to, what the new job entails—so surprises are minimized, and expectations are well managed.

They joined your team by committing to its mission, with the hopes of moving up within it, so when the first appropriate opportunity to advance becomes available, granting them that opportunity right off the bat (instead of first launching a search outside and then making them feel second best when they eventually get it) energizes their career momentum and solidifies their allegiance.

From management's side of things, the advantages of promoting from within include already knowing the candidate's work ethic, strengths, weaknesses, and performance output. This is a huge benefit, because no matter how qualified or impressive an outside hire can look on paper, you really have no way of knowing how they will perform and interact with your team until after you've made that investment in them.

By eliminating ramp-up time, you keep productivity apace (not so with external hires, who take up to two years to get up to speed).[1] And by showing your team that internal promotion is the preferred approach at your organization, everyone works harder, recognizing that they can advance too, and plans for a longer-term tenure with the company.[2]

Studies show that external hires cost more (not just salaries,[3] but recruitment[4] and training[5] expenses), induce animosity and hostility in people who feel passed over (causing up to 35 percent of those people to either quit or consider quitting),[6] receive significantly lower marks in performance reviews,[7] and are 61 percent more likely to be fired.[8]

Internal hires, in contrast, produce lower turnover, higher morale, and greater job satisfaction. A full 70 percent of employees report that they prefer to be managed by "a seasoned company vet."[9] In a nutshell, internal succession rewards good performance, and that's exactly what should be rewarded in the business marketplace. So if any of your current staffers want to climb the ranks, let 'em climb!

Having said all this, succession is *not* an automatic process. The assistant director doesn't just automatically become the next director, and the COO isn't just a shoo-in for the next CEO if the individual is not ready, if their skill set will not readily transfer, or if they're just not a viable prospect for the next linear link in the chain. In other words, internal promotions should proceed on the basis of merit, always picking the strongest candidate you have on hand, not necessarily the "next in line" candidate.

And it should be noted that some jobs, like company accountant or data analyst, simply require certain training or expertise that might not be available among your current staff. With these qualifiers in mind, though, you can pretty much bet on the fact that following a promote-from-within guideline will create the most loyal following among your workforce.

Hire for Attributes over Background

The more you promote from within, the more openings you'll have available, and that's when it's time to give serious consideration to *how* you want to hire at your organization as much as *who* you want to hire. The corporate world hires for revenue—it seeks profit maximizers, generators of the bottom line. But it's a better practice to hire for growth. That means looking for people who possess certain qualities and exhibit personality tendencies that suggest they will be very active, enthusiastic, and dynamic participants in the singular culture you advocate for daily.

An impressive alma matter, a string of initials after a name, and a bulleted list of past accomplishments are all very fine, but you need a bench filled with self-motivated, enterprising team members who are eager to learn, grow, expand, and evolve with the company and for the company. There are steps you can take to narrow down the field and increase your chances of finding the right player for the right position from the start.

Interview Tactics

Hiring is a little like speed dating: You meet as many people as you can in a limited amount of time, learning as much as you can about them in that time, as you search for a suitable fit. Then, after what's usually just one encounter, you're supposed to make a long-term commitment to a special someone that carries significant repercussions. Sounds crazy, right? Who'd get married after just one date? But hiring is also an art, and as with any art, the more you practice it, the more finesse you will develop to reduce the risk of, well, divorce.

To draw a more composite portrait of the candidate beyond the sketchy evidence often gleaned from one sit-down, you'll want to be strategic with your time and discerning with your judgment. The interviewee should talk more than you do (so you can assess what they reveal), the person who will be the candidate's direct supervisor should certainly be included in the interview, if not also a would-be peer (so you can gather multiple opinions), and taking the candidate on a tour of your facility while you're chatting is highly advisable (so you can observe mannerisms and comfort level, interaction or lack thereof with others, amount of curiosity displayed and type of questions posed).

You can also employ specific techniques, like one interesting approach recommended specifically for helping professionals called "motivational interviewing," which purports to identify people "most open to change and growth" through conducting "a particular type of conversation aimed at strengthening a person's own motivation and commitment to change."[10]

You're not just interviewing to fill a position, though. When engaged in succession planning, you're interviewing to find the next great leader to add to your cadre. To zero in on a person's growth potential, then, spend less time talking about the job they're applying for today and more time talking about the job they want in your organization *next*.

Ask them what position most appeals to them and why, the timeline they have in mind, and what they plan to do to earn the role. Ask them what drew them to your organization in particular and why they think they have what it takes to eventually ascend to its top level. Their responses will tell you if they've got fire and drive, if they're looking beyond the job of today and onto tomorrow's shared horizon with you.

One of the very best uses of your time with a potential new hire is to guide them on a search for the next job they want on the very day you hire them for this job. That way, both of you already have your eyes on their future, you've already signaled your long-term interest in them, and you've already given them direction toward and authority over their own advancement. They'll not only accept your offer, they'll stay.

Hiring for Balance

If you've managed any kind of group before—a wait staff, a Pop Warner team, an after-school club—you've no doubt noticed that skill levels run high, low, and all over the place in every single group member. And that's a good thing, a blessing really, for how would anything get done anywhere if everyone were just fast or just exacting or just a math whiz or a virtuoso muralist?

Diversity on a work team isn't just preferable, it's essential if you want tasks completed properly, functions fulfilled optimally, and client needs met individually and personally. No one personality type or skill set can accomplish all that; for that, you need a collection of variously talented people, each of whom brings their own assets to the collective table. They bring their deficits, too, and that's precisely why it's expedient to populate your team with members who can balance one another out, supply the yin to the yang, and achieve overall equilibrium.

Say you lead a team of half a dozen department directors. They're all at the same middle-management level, all working in the same role, they just each have their own region to run. But they operate as one coordinated unit, regularly collaborating and depending on one another to meet departmental goals.

You don't want all six of them to have the same strong suits. In that case, you're going to experience gaps where they're not as strong, whether it's on the customer service side, the financial side, or the business development side. So when hiring or promoting to those positions, if you purposely assemble a group of people who each shine in distinct areas, their combined but contrasting strengths will be far more powerful in application than the same strength multiplied by six.

It's pretty basic, really. If you have someone who's got a really soft exterior that works well for their staff, balance that out with someone a little tougher, someone who's good with breaking bad news and holding the staff accountable. And if you have someone who's really strong with money management, counter that with someone who excels in service delivery initiatives. Have them work together often so they can learn from one another and borrow each other's fortes when needed. You want all your bases covered with the right person in the right position that will most strategically apply their top talents.

Hiring for Redundancy

And now for something totally contradictory (that's really just complementary)! Having just advised you to search out differences among your team members so you can leverage them to their best advantage, it must be said that intentional sameness serves a purpose too. What this means is, you don't want to have just one individual on your team who knows how to do their job at maximum effectiveness (i.e., one quarterback who consistently avoids getting sacked, one linebacker who excels at interceptions, one kicker who thrives under pressure). No, you want at least one backup player for each key position, someone already waiting on the bench, trained and ready to come in as replacements or reinforcements are needed.

When you're manning the second and third strings for succession planning, look for people who make you think, *She reminds me of Silvio—that's what he said when I was interviewing him too.* Or, *Hank's analytical thinking is like Vivian's; they both approached a similar problem in the same way.* Or even, *That's exactly how I was when I first got here.* Look for similarities among team members that indicate who would do well in Terrence's role when he retires and who should be groomed to succeed Kimber once she's transferred to Minneapolis in February.

This is the complete opposite of what "redundancy" often means in the business world (i.e., firing when there's a surplus of people with the same job functions), and it's very similar to understudies in the theater world, waiting in the wings to go on when they're called. If you've ever seen a traveling Broadway show or a performance when one of the stars is out for the day, you'll notice how uncannily alike the actors in the same parts are: how their singing voices have the exact same range and tonality, how their delivery mirrors each other, how they elicit the same reactions from the audience.

That doesn't mean your redundancy hires can't bring their own flair to their role. It just ensures that the show will still go on when any of your current supporting and lead cast members move on, move up, or take to another stage.

A Sample Scenario

Just a quick example of someone who was hired on the basis of their attributes instead of their formal training. Gary indeed had his special education certification when he was hired as the associate director of a school for the Upward Academy, but he was actually a gym teacher at the time, a natural fit for his lifelong participation in athletics, his competitive spirit, and his rugged appearance.

At first, Melanie worried that his stereotypical "jock mentality" would work against him—most people don't think of athletes as the wisest or most sensitive people in the world—but just last year, she'd hired a gruff-seeming, but totally kindhearted former police officer to run one of her schools, and he was working out beautifully. He didn't shy away from trouble, he understood the necessity of crisis intervention, he was able to keep the students in line, and that's what she needed in her alternative education schools. She needed people who could take the heat but also lead with fairness and follow regulations.

The same thing happened with Gary. His real-life experiences transferred uncommonly well to the school management setting, where his coaching tactics and his "results, results, results" mindset turned the school culture around in record time. Before him, there was desk flipping, cursing in class, and multiple suspensions. After he instituted a behavior modification system entirely of his own making, that all stopped. His compassionate helper's approaches knew how to motivate the students, and his passionate outcomes-driven temperament commanded their respect.

He'd had zero leadership training, had never taken a business course, and he was not a behavior specialist. But on the job, he became all of that and more, learning to harness his powerful blend of sense and sensitivity. He ended up taking over for Melanie when she left the company and stayed on for 10 more years as the organization's senior-most business leader and special education expert advisor.

Train, Train, Train

If there's one place to put the majority of your attention as a leader of a service-oriented staff, it's here, in training them, both existing employees and newer hires alike. It's a concentration on "growing your own talent" instead of "bringing in new talent," and it's a concentration that will pay off time and time again as you need to fill role after role.

Not everyone who works for your organization is going to want or have the capacity to be a leader, but when you spot noticeable up-and-comers, you'll want to point your spotlight on them.

You do so by supporting them in their current job, of course, which has a dual purpose: first, you want them to gain complete mastery over their position (there's no boss more respected on the planet than one who knows your job inside and out and can do it in your absence); and second, as you support them, you're modeling how a skilled leader coaches and teaches for when they assume those functions one day. But you also want to prepare them for the future job you ultimately have in mind for them, right from the start.

This entails immersing them in the company culture, instructing them on the finer points of the organization's business model, including them in management meetings and making them privy to management decisions, and investing in their continuing education now in skills they don't even have a current need for but will in the foreseeable future. It involves providing them with the tools and resources they'll need in their future with the organization and giving them a certain degree of autonomy over how they choose to migrate toward that future. It requires a time commitment on your part to set a regular mentoring schedule.

You obviously can't take each and every budding leader under your wing and train them personally, but you can make training a regular part of your own staff's efforts with their staffs. So the lead teacher in a school would start training the other teachers to become leads early in their tenure. The district manager would hold training seminars for their associate managers to prep them for running the district eventually. And the customer service director would design workshops and seminars for their customer service reps in preparation for their subsequent roles.

The standouts will become apparent rather quickly, as they're the ones who will start flexing their newly developing muscles a bit, taking the initiative in group settings, and experimenting with making some decisions on their own instead of running everything past their superior.

This *can* be unsettling for some people—training their own employees to do their own jobs, but if you make mentoring and knowledge sharing seminal to your company culture, it transforms a potentially competitive situation into one in which the higher-ranking team members are actually assisted, rather than threatened by the additional duties their employees will be able to take on to lighten their own load.

Not that it's always smooth sailing. Not only do people learn and progress at varying rates, but they learn differently as well. Some will absorb book learning; some will respond best to sensory learning; and some will learn only by doing, not by observing or being vocally coached.

So throw your trainees into the fire every once in a while. Two outcomes are possible, and both benefit the organization. Either the trainee handles it well—okay, great, lesson filed away, move on to the next—or they don't handle it well, which creates an ideal teaching moment for you at a time when the trainee's misstep doesn't have any real consequences yet, when you're still there as their safety net.

Walk them through the scenario, teach them how to do better next time, and point out the value of learning from our mistakes. We all probably learn more from our mistakes than our successes, anyway, so mistakes should be welcomed during training exercises, not a source of shame in the least.

One operations director was known for throwing his people in the deep end of the pool significantly before they were ready to swim there, and initially, his trainees weren't thrilled with him for it. Later, though, they came back to him with gratitude: "I'm glad you tested me that way because now I feel like I'm equipped to handle anything." When you prod your people into challenging terrain, their latent abilities unfurl and their self-confidence escalates.

And fear—fear is okay too; in fact, it's actually constructive because it shows that your trainees care enough not to fail. Fear almost always becomes a motivator instead of a paralyzer, at least in promising leaders. Barbra Streisand and Adele are both famous for intense stage fright; Frank Sinatra and Elvis were rumored to be riddled with nerves before concerts. But all these legends managed to get out there and do what they do better than anyone else, no doubt more to prove their abilities to themselves than to anyone else. You won't have to ask this of high achievers; high achievers will demand this of themselves.

That's what you want in the people you hand select for your line of succession. They can make mistakes, they can be afraid to fail, but as long as they push themselves through the training ground—even with all its stumbling blocks, potholes, and land mines—they'll come out the other side leaders in the making. Leaders of your making.

Plan for Setbacks in the Plan

No matter how cleverly you interview, how well you line your bench, and how effectively you train the rising stars to rise, "the best-laid plans of mice and men often go awry," as the poet Robert Burns was well aware of over 200 years ago. So just consider this a given—that plans don't always go according to plan—and since it's not something you can fight, it has to be something you can accommodate.

Succession plans can be interrupted by a variety of factors: family needs, spouse transfers, health issues, earlier-than-anticipated retirements, and, of course, unexpected new opportunities that arise and lure people away, sometimes to the surprise of you both. When a link in your planned chain suddenly falls away, you obviously need to bridge the gap and reinforce the chain as seamlessly as you can. This is all the more reason to have several individuals, not just a single individual, already lined up for promotion.

There should definitely be a scheduled handoff meeting (multiple meetings, if possible) during which the departing team member sits with their replacement in the actual office space in which they'll be working and literally hands off everything that person will need to hit the ground running, explaining it all in elaborate detail—the entire filing system, the logs and assessment tools, all the forms, procedure manuals, and paperwork. The replacement should be personally introduced to all the external people they'll be working with. The replacement should come prepared with a list of questions and a means to record answers.

And you can bet the questions will continue after the person has assumed the role, so it's optimal to make arrangements with the departing member to remain available for a transitional period of time, either in a part-time contracted advisory role for a bit or just accessible via phone or email.

Transition periods can be bumpy even in the best of circumstances, but the wrinkles can usually be ironed out when you give people time to adjust (and a good deal of your personal attention while they're doing so). So what of the other kind of snag that can impede your succession plan? What do you do when someone you've chosen for succession is struggling to the point where it just doesn't look like things are going to work out?

Here again, you want to allow enough time to adapt to a new job description, but you don't want it to be *too* much time either. Two years is too long—an ineffectively run position for that long will surely hurt the organization—so a good rule of thumb is one year. If you see positive signs of real and measurable growth in the span of that year, it's probably worth sticking with your investment in this person. However, if they're not zinging along at a smooth clip in the role by the second year, it's time to let them go or demote them.

Do a Postgame Analysis

And then it's time to take a good long look at what went wrong so you can up your succession planning game in future. When anyone on your team doesn't stick with the team for whatever reason, ask yourself the hard questions and answer them honestly, with input from your own trusted team of advisors. Did Sabine really leave because she needs to care for her ailing mother at home, or was she dissatisfied here? What did we see in Tyler that really wasn't there? Or was it there and we just failed to bring it out in him? If we kept Venus on too long, why didn't we cut our losses earlier, and what kind of procedure can we put in place to avoid doing this again?

When filling integral positions, many candidates will balk if you tell them it's on a six-month-trial basis. They won't want to upend their lives, possibly relocate, or make any purchases if the job feels unsteady to them, like they're on "probation" for something they haven't even done yet. But in the event that a new hire proves to be an unsuitable fit, offering a sufficiently attractive severance payout within a certain amount of time can usually resolve the issue.

To avoid possible lawsuits for terminations, you want to have ample documentation proving that issues were discussed on multiple occasions and solutions were attempted. You might not be able to avoid "bad hires" completely as an organizational leader, but these are some of the things you can do to protect the organization from prolonging unfortunate situations.

Lots of time is often poured into preplanning and not enough into postplanning. As you would with any project or program you oversee, conduct a review of results after the fact to reveal useful information and insights you can use going forward to inform your ongoing succession strategies. Analyze the quality of your preparation. Make a list of things you could have done better. Determine if you should have been relying on broader evidence or on finer-grained aspects to assess how a person's performance was coming along.

When you have the courage to explore what role you played in some stage of your succession planning going awry, you won't be left wondering why when someone you pinned your hopes on detaches from the organization.

Transaction vs. Connection

There's something extremely special about the helping professions that doesn't characterize all professions—it's the preeminence of *connection* in our work and in our lives. It's what drives us the most, unites us the most, and inspires us the most. It's what we spend all our effort building and what builds us up in kind. It's why we opt to join one team and not another, why we're attracted to one mission over another. At its core, connection is what defines helping professionals. It is what we're all about.

Most professional hiring processes, in contrast, are about transaction. They're transactions in which one party offers another party something of monetary value, and if the price is right, the purchasee signs on the dotted line. In so doing, they contract to produce something of monetary value for the purchaser.

All people crave connection, it's true. No matter one's job, we all seek out partners and friends, and we all want to feel we matter to those around us. But in professions that are more objective than subjective—for example, stockbrokers, bankers, manufacturers, carmakers, analysts, researchers, programmers, actuaries, pilots—it's safe to assume that deciding where and for whom to work will primarily be determined by the proposed terms of the transaction.

Even in the world of sports, where passions run extremely high and where fans and players form extremely loyal bonds, transaction dominates. There are some exceptions to the rule, when megastars like Derek Jeter or LeBron James are significantly influenced in contract negotiations by personal attachments; but as a rule, when an athlete is signed, that player hire is transactional.

Sure, maybe they'd like to stay on this team for the duration of their career and enjoy the personal rewards of feeling enfolded into a franchise, but they have been bought for the results they're expected to immediately produce and for the revenue their name or star power can bring in. If they don't live up to club-owner expectations, they know they can be traded away in a heartbeat, so they have to protect themselves by fielding other offers for money and glory.

Your hiring practices are completely different. To a helping professional, connection trumps all other considerations, and you will attract and retain the very people you want when they can sense that they're being invited into a warm and close-knit family and will be treated like a beloved family member, with all the goodwill, support, rapport, encouragement, and belief in them that that implies. It's not signing a job contract—it really isn't; that's just a formality to helpers. It's establishing and then nurturing a connection that grows stronger every day and is enriched every day by their presence.

Where there's connection, people commit themselves for the long haul. They stay when they feel vital to the whole. They are fulfilled when they feel valued and appreciated. They will fight for their ideas when they know someone wants to hear them, and they will fight for you when you've shown genuine care for their best interests.

Connection. If all your succession planning is designed atop this foundation, you will build a house so solid and impenetrable that it's incapable of crumbling, even without you. In fact, the best indicator of successful succession planning is when the place continues to hum along just fine when you're on vacation or when you eventually leave. That means you've empowered other highly competent people to make highly competent decisions. It means you've raised a productive, passionate, purposeful family. It means you've built something truly worthwhile that will be self-sustaining even once you yourself are succeeded.

GROWTH: KEEPING YOUR ORGANIZATION RELEVANT AND VITAL

Succession planning and growth go hand in hand—you can't have one without the other because your people create the growth, and the growth nourishes the people. And growth is mandatory these days, no longer optional in any kind of business marketplace, even in the helping professions. The world is in a constant state of flux, and you simply must be able to go with the flow or else you're going to get stuck in a dam, drown in the rapidly moving waters, or get tossed up on the shore as an extraneous, inconsequential dinosaur.

Growth does not mean abandoning tried-and-true methods that have served your organization well, forcing your people to be uncomfortable or inauthentic, or changing your brand with each passing fad. But it does mean staying abreast of significant developments in your field that look like they're going to stick around, keeping pace with evolving industry benchmarks, and updating processes and procedures to align with contemporary definitions of best practices. Here are a few ways to keep both your organization and yourself growing.

Stay Open-Minded and Adaptable

In our discussion of your helper's natural emotional intelligence in chapter 4, we touched upon the mental agility that profoundly benefits an organizational leader: being open to new approaches, exhibiting flexibility in unfamiliar situations, regaining your footing when you're thrown off-balance by modernizations that invade predictable patterns to which you've grown accustomed. There's nowhere you will use this mental faculty more than in formulating growth plans for your organization.

Look what's happened to the taxi industry now that ride-sharing companies like Uber and Lyft have taken center stage. Consider how DoorDash and GrubHub have completely shaken up Pizza Hut's and China Palace's former lock on Friday-night dinner deliveries. When businesses don't adapt along with current market forces, they lose their force.

To keep the door to your mind open, the first thing you need to do is stave off the close-mindedness that can ensue from "believing your own press" and not seeing your own blind spots. Leaders who have been in their positions for a while—even really decent people, truly committed helpers—can develop a case of "poweritis," the symptoms of which include a touch of arrogance and a spoonful of overestimation of oneself.

But the best leaders, like Abraham Lincoln with his cabinet of rivals, guard against the trappings of their own power by making it safe for dissident voices to speak up against any misjudgments they may be making and bringing to light considerations and concerns they may not be seeing. Remember to invite contrasting opinions, let people shoot down your ideas, create a space for debate and discourse, and do your best to not be defensive during these discussions. The person who points out the flaw in your plan at the outset is far more helpful to you than someone who does so after you've sunk a quarter million dollars into a new flawed project.

Being adaptable to changing circumstances, accommodating a wide range of viewpoints, and showing interest in the motivations of people around you pave the way for new opportunities. Likewise, not having an open mind to new things, people, and products blocks the way to new opportunities.

Eastman Kodak may as well have had a monopoly on the U.S. photography market in the late twentieth century, but it didn't pivot well at all to the advent of digital photography. Ironically, Kodak invented the first digital camera in 1975, but company leadership was resistant to plowing forward with what would soon become a worldwide revolution, so it missed the wave when it hit in the early 2000s and eventually filed for bankruptcy in 2012. The company is still around, but it's a shell of its former self, with recent ventures totally unrelated to the market it used to own.[11]

Open-mindedness not only keeps us on the map of an ever-changing world, it helps us address the intricacies of a wide array of situations more effectively because our ears are open to outside ideas and our eyes are open to creative innovations and novel solutions. When we stay broad of mind, we're on the lookout for openings we can guide our organizations through and toward new vistas. That keeps things vibrant, lively, and interesting for everyone. That keeps our companies on the cutting edge and competitive.

Basically, there are no disadvantages and only advantages to an open-minded approach to leadership. You don't have to go it alone. You can ask for help and advice and guidance when foraying into foreign territory. But when newness knocks on your door, it would be foolish to ignore it. It's not going away, but if you don't accept it and adapt to it, *you* just might.

Keep Educating Yourself

We discussed in chapter 5 the value of lifelong learning, and one of the best ways to stay on a growth track is to continue to educate yourself. Eleanor Drago-Severson, an esteemed voice in the educational leadership sphere, defines "growth" as "the cognitive, emotional, intrapersonal, and interpersonal capacities that enable us to better manage the complexities of leading, learning, teaching, and living." She goes on to say, "Leaders who sustain this kind of growth themselves are then better able to support it in others."[12]

Devote effort to keeping yourself informed and up-to-date about happenings in your field, yes, but also about evolving managerial practices and tactics that will make you a better leader and a better helper. Attend conferences. Join a professional group of peers. Take classes. Listen to podcasts and watch TED Talks. Given the current climate, read things like "When Teams Hit Rough Waters," *Leadership in Turbulent Times*, and *The Eight Paradoxes of Great Leadership: Embracing the Conflicting Demands of Today's Workplace*.[13]

Don't neglect the power of curiosity, the fraternal twin of open-mindedness, as it leads to a yearning to discover answers and active investigation of concepts new to you. Einstein once said, "I have no special talent. I am only passionately curious." That curiosity led him to keep probing deeper until he unlocked some of the secrets of the universe. Previously mentioned Microsoft CEO Satya Nadella is also a proponent of curiosity, which led him to shift the powerhouse from a "know-it-all" to a "learn-it-all" enterprise.[14] When the L in your leadership style stands for "learning," it's a surefire formula for success.

Failure *Is* an Option

And yet success is never guaranteed. Indeed, when you're trying new things—engaging in new growth techniques—they're not always going to work. It's statistically impossible and, to be honest, not necessarily desirable. If you pull off every new idea with a 100 percent pass rate, you're likely aiming too low, proceeding too conservatively, or innovating too little.

It's okay to try and fail. You don't want to duplicate errors two or three times, no, but when anticipated outcomes fall short, you can both handle it and then take from it what to never do again. Think of failure as a gift you unwrap to expose a narrower range of solutions that might work better or a clearer path forward to more fertile ground. It's better to take a chance, to swerve out of your lane a bit and avoid a near-miss than to never deviate from your lane and languish at the wheel. It's what you would tell your children so that they can learn and grow. It's what you would tell your staff, so it's what you should tell yourself.

Failure can actually be success in disguise. Have you heard the story of Spencer Silver, the 3M chemist who was trying to invent a new type of superglue but instead came up an adhesive that had stickiness but easy removability? It turned into the Post-it Note, and Post-it Notes became one of the biggest game-changers to ever hit the marketplace.[15] Failures can thus be instructive stepping stones to solutions that never would have materialized without the failures.

Remember Thomas Edison's 10,000 defeated attempts at refining the light bulb cited as an example of resilience earlier in the book? He didn't see things that way: "I have not failed. I have just found 9,999 ways that do not work."[16] You won't need to fail thousands of times; just one misstep will lead you to make giant leaps forward to where you want to go.

Nourish the Culture and Promote the Mission

Everyone's talking about culture and mission these days—as redundant as these discussions are, we'd be remiss to not at least cover them here, because they really are important. Like, supremely important. To season a dish, you need salt and pepper. To form a marriage, you need two partners. To compose, you need both a writing implement and a blank surface. And to breathe life into an organization that is otherwise just a sign on the door or a Google listing, you need a customized culture and a pointed mission.

Think of a company's culture as its personality, its ambience, its essence, and its mission as the key that starts its engine. Actually, the mission is both the motivating force that propels the enterprise *and* the destination to which the enterprise is always traveling. Though both are intangibles, the first is a legacy that lives on regardless of who's manning the ship—it has an identity of its own—and the second can be captured in both word and deed.

A company's team needs the culture as the floor to stand on. It's what orients them in this particular environment, it's the foothold that anchors them and keeps them steady at work. The mission provides them with direction—where they should aim their attention, time, and energy, the North Star that should consistently guide their steps.

If you're the one responsible for conceptualizing and establishing the culture and crafting and implementing the mission, it's an amazingly creative and invigorating undertaking. This is your chance to visualize your dream company and then color in all the parts the way only you would. Or if the culture and mission are already in place when you advance to top management, you can refine them as you see fit, making it a really fun and inclusive process by asking for company-wide input or holding a contest for new additions or inspired language. Either way, you want to be able to stand behind every single component of your culture and every single word of your mission, so proud of and committed to them that you want to shout it from the rooftops.

In today's world, you do that through social media, blogs, published interviews, and press exposure. You let the public know about the culture you have built and what your mission is doing for the public. This is not the place to be humble; this is the place to boast of your organization's accomplishments so that it's known as a good place to work and one that's doing good in the world.

Information sharing is key to becoming a thought leader or respected innovator in your field. Toyota has perhaps the most famous culture on the planet, named the "Toyota Way." As successful and profitable as the automaker has remained for decades, it freely shares knowledge and technology with the industry, known for allowing both partners and competitors to tour its plants, observe its mechanical lines, and analyze its practices.

When questioned about this surprising transparency, the attitude of Toyota's executive team has basically always been this: You can replicate our processes, but you'll never replicate our culture. And it's true. Though an inordinate number of studies have been done about this particular culture, no one else has yet cracked the code that Toyota seems both to have invented and to have down pat. The company is an admirable example of remaining at the very top of its field by staying unwaveringly true to the one-of-a-kind culture that defines it and stands firm for its people.

A healthy, vibrant culture that your team believes in is a prerequisite to fulfilling your mission. What are the signs of an ailing company culture? Steady turnover; interoffice gossip, complaining, or cliques; people afraid to share honest, constructive feedback; people doing the minimum instead of going the extra mile; heads down at desks in isolated concentration instead of a lively workforce infused with interaction, collaboration, and smiling faces. And most damaging of all, people working just for themselves, prioritizing their own needs over organizational goals.

This is unsustainable. Not only will the floor fall out, you will have no floor. Nobody knows what they're standing on or what they're standing for. In this extreme case, you have to rebuild your culture piece by piece, getting buy-in from your team members with every nail and board by making them part of the work crew assembling a new structure they want to inhabit.

If you have an enfeebled culture, nursing it back to health by all means within your power is a task that moves to the top of your list, so that your people are utterly clear on what they're doing, why they're doing it, and for whom they're doing it. If your people have lost their way, *you* are the compass that must redirect them to your shared home and the motto framed above its doorway.

And then you continue to nourish that culture and reinforce that mission until they regain their strength. Sometimes only a little boost is needed, sometimes a lot. Just keep your eye on the health and vigor of both culture and mission, the way you would for a house plant or a fish tank, on the lookout for *any* signs of malnutrition or malady that could impede growth. Feed them both equally and ceaselessly. When both thrive, so do the people living and breathing them.

Replication Plus Innovation

Many organizations grow by sprouting new limbs on their tree—that is, by adding new locations, new channels, or new outlets for the same service delivery. And this is a pretty smooth process when you have a well-oiled, fine-tuned, effective model in place that you can simply replicate in another place. Indeed, replication is a mainstay of business growth and a direct route to multiplying your footprint in your market, much the way enterprises like Starbucks, CVS, and Subway regularly open new franchises in places where they're most likely to succeed.

Sometimes the head office owns the franchises, and sometimes the franchises can be purchased independently, but what's being erected here is a replicated blueprint of a model that's already been proven to work.

If replication applies to your organization, it should be incorporated into your growth plans. Costs are minimized and start-up processes are streamlined when you already have a business plan that runs well, a staffing structure that fits, any relevant suppliers and vendors on hand, even a floorplan that works for your operation.

Say your company hosts three outreach clinics in the same town. To reach more people in need, you're planning to open two more locations in two different neighboring towns next year. Well, you already know how to do this, don't you? You're already doing it and doing it well, so now it's just a matter of doing *more* of it.

That's the simple way of looking at replication. As long as you don't try to get too big too fast—as long as you calculate for manageable growth and don't overestimate your market viability (like Krispy Kreme did, just to take one example)—replication is a relatively safe and cost-effective way to further your mission.

Replication doesn't have to mean duplication, by the way. The great thing about the helping professions over an enterprise like KFC or Marriott—where the Colonel's original recipe has to be followed identically in each store or every hotel room is decorated exactly the same from Providence to Provo—is that the helping professional put in charge of the new site will put their own stamp on the "new addition" to your company house to individualize and customize it.

No principal is going to run a school exactly the same way as any other principal. No physical therapist treats their patients just like every other PT. And no counselor talks and relates to their patients like any other counselor out there. So the company provides the structure and the stability, but the people you entrust the replicated site to are given a good deal of latitude to adorn and embellish it as they see fit to maximize its reach and impact in its particular location with its particular population.

You don't want to stop at replication, though. Replication alone will grow your organization's width, but to deepen its imprint, you also need to introduce new offerings now and then to stay at the forefront of your field and buoy company momentum. If a chain like Chipotle never added new items to its menu, patrons would eventually come less and less often if, for example, the latest superfoods weren't incorporated, vegan options weren't available to accommodate this growing market, or keto-friendly wraps weren't offered as an alternative to the higher-carb standards.

Similarly, you'll want to add new curriculum materials, launch new programs, create new trainings, or introduce new specialization areas—whatever it is that is related to what you're already known for but also divergent enough to qualify as fresh, innovative, leading-edge, and timely to and for the market you serve.

It can be as targeted as adding the latest piece of therapy equipment to your rehab centers or as grand as adding an entirely new type of accreditation you grant. Sometimes your clients will point you to a lack in the market that you can fill; and sometimes you'll create a new option that will point your clients to a lack they didn't even know they had. It's not novelty for the sake of novelty: it's newness in the name of progressing your mission, maturing your brand, and enhancing your value.

Who hasn't been warned at one time or another not to put all your eggs in one basket? This applies across the board in businesses of all types. You don't want to have just one service offering. Just one vendor. Just one source of referrals or just one big client. It may work for a while, but it won't work for long.

Better to replicate and innovate, to diversify and disperse, to combat obsolescence with opportunity. However you want to word it, the idea is to hold fast with one hand to the bedrock that sustains and supports your organization while reaching out with the other to new prospects and potentialities that will keep you in the black and at the summit of your area of expertise.

The Best Idea in the Room Wins

All the growth doesn't fall to you all of the time. That's an awful lot of pressure. When you've cultivated a true sense of teamwork in your organization, you'll find that you galvanize others to spark new ideas and stimulate growth along with you. The best ideas can come from anyone, anywhere, at any time. And whatever the best idea is? That's the one you should go with. Doesn't matter if it came from the cafeteria lady, the building supervisor, your admin, or your aunt.

Actor Bryan Cranston tells this great story about rehearsing for an episode of *Seinfeld* in which the dentist character he portrayed, Tim Whatley, gives Jerry nitrous oxide to knock him out for a procedure.[17] When the rest of the cast and crew were elsewhere on set working on another scene, Cranston was prepping for his scene when he heard a voice above him. A guy on a ladder adjusting a light said, "Hey, you know what would be funny? If you first took a hit of the laughing gas before you gave it to him."

Cranston agreed and waited until the cameras were rolling to try out the prank. Not only did it crack Jerry up (something Cranston takes great pride in accomplishing), but show lead Larry David immediately recognized the comic brilliance of the ad-lib and left it in the scene. Even with all that mega-talent in the same room, the lighting guy came up with the best laugh. So the lighting guy's idea made it into the final version of the episode.

Look to your team to help you elevate and augment the important work you're charged with doing. They'll support you in attaining your goals in the most unexpected and incredibly serendipitous ways.

Allow Others to Shine Brighter than You

An organization will blossom across its entire field when everyone within it is recognized for the distinct talents they contribute to the whole and is given the opportunity to apply them. Lots of bosses are intimidated by their staff members who know more than them or outperform them in some areas. As a helper, it's likely you don't think that way, but if ever a drop of hubris trickles into your mind about a team member's skill level greater than you own, replace that threat by embracing their aptitudes. Not only does this improve the organization's overall potency to be staffed with all kinds of people who have all kinds of strengths, but you look better when your people look good. Your team's results are a direct reflection of your leadership, and so the more they shine, the more you do as well.

Never hold back your praise because of a bruised ego. Never give your people a reason to think that they have to hide their light. Never neglect an opportunity to laud a standout accomplishment that just increases the goodwill across your team and makes someone feel really good. This isn't the same as exaggerated flattery or butt-kissing, but when acknowledgment has been earned, grant it vocally and heartily. Others will notice that you openly recognize achievement on your team and work to gain your notice all the more.

Stand for Your People's Greatness

All of this has been building up to the same message you've hopefully been hearing again and again in this book: it's all about your people. Whether or not your growth plans flourish, the caliber and constancy of the players lining your bench, the reputation and standing your organization holds in your field, how long your organization remains in business and the sheer quality of the business it conducts, the kind of difference it's making in the lives of the people you serve. It all depends on your people—it all comes down to them.

Yes, you get some of the credit for the health and vitality of your organization because you're the one leading it and them, but your team members are the ones executing your plans, upholding your policies, engaging with your client base, and generating the results you've mapped out for them. Thus, standing for them—for the greatness inside each and every one of them—is how your organization will remain standing strong.

This looks like fighting for them when they need protection, giving them a voice when they don't feel heard, encouraging them when they doubt their own power, and rewarding them when they excel. Publicly applaud their accomplishments, regularly let them know how much and why they are prized so highly, invest in their future, and promote them as soon as they're ready to take on more responsibility. Believe in them—sometimes even more than they believe in themselves.

You'd be hard-pressed to find a bad head of a good operation or a good head of a bad operation. That's because a skilled leader is always lifting people up, giving them opportunities to heighten their skills, inspiring them to want to do more, to become the very best versions of themselves they can be. A skilled leader knows whose shoulders they stand on, and it's not just the former bosses and leaders who mentored and trained them. It's also those who they're mentoring and training now.

Remember, you can't be a leader without a band of trusty followers. They're your single most valuable asset, and they don't just staff the helping profession organization. They *are* the organization.

If you take only one thing from this chapter, let it be this: there's no better way to both keep your bench strong and keep your company growing than to champion your people. They're the ones who will take over when you're gone. They're the ones who will carry on the legacy. They're the ones holding the future. And if you're very, very lucky, you're the one who put a lot of them there.

Conclusion

What Kind of Leader Do You Want to Be?

There are many labels for types of leadership that apply to the helping professions.

The American Association of Critical Care Nurses supports "authentic leadership" as a necessity for establishing "a healthy work environment."[1]

Chris Beckett's book *Supervision: A Guide for the Helping Professions* talks about the distinctions between "clinical supervision" and "accountability supervision."[2]

Tim Ziglar's "coach leadership" was introduced in chapter 7, with Ziglar believing that "the ability to help your staff grow, perform at their best, and achieve success is one of your most important roles as a leader, if not your most crucial role."[3]

Nicki Weld espouses what she calls "transformative supervision" in her book *A Practical Guide to Transformative Supervision for the Helping Professions: Amplifying Insight*, which examines such key factors as the role of observation and questioning, the importance of working with emotions, and exploring intuition. Here's an appetizing taste of what she means by the transformative function:

> We live in a world that requires the best of us. Supervision has been increasingly providing important opportunities for us to learn and develop that support this. It is time now to bring supervision to a new place by building in more of a transformative function so we can continue to ensure we are being all we can be in the complexity of the world that we live in. Change begins with us, and the task of challenging ourselves to transform what needs to improve both around and within us is our responsibility.[4]

And Jean East is one of the many thought leaders who employ the term "transformational leadership" in their approaches, with the beautiful subtitle of her book—*Transformational Leadership for the Helping Professions: Engaging Head, Heart, and Soul*—even making room for the pure humanity of the tools that helpers rely on most. She understands that "leadership work in the service or helping professions requires a strong knowledge base, a set of skills and processes, and way of being in the world. The intersection of these three elements is clearly a complex process."[5]

It doesn't matter which leadership style you choose to adopt—all that matters is that you believe you can be a spectacular leader in your profession, that you already *are* a leader, on the basis of your "way of being in the world" that is yours and yours alone.

Do you know how many times people say, "But I'm only a social worker," "I'm only a classroom aide," "I'm only an assistant therapist," "I'm only a youth coordinator"? *Far* too many times, in far too many situations. Helping professionals put limits on themselves all the time, their natural humility and selflessness leading them to believe they're "only" this or "only" that. The limits are nothing but self-imposed restrictions you've allowed to pen in your potential and tamp your sparkle.

Gender is becoming less and less of any issue every day, as we learned in chapter 2. Being just a single individual with a single mission is no longer inadequate to make a tremendous mark on society, as we learned in chapter 3. You already have everything you need and everything it takes to dazzle, induce, and triumph, as we learned in chapters 1 and 4. You are a servant leader, one of the most noble and honorable roles a human being can assume. You make ethical decisions where others take the easy way out. You persist where others quit, accept challenges that others refuse, assist where others turn away.

If you want to lead a helping organization someday, make your ambitions known. Start putting out there in the world the intention you want to actualize. Find a mentor who will groom and champion you. Study up on areas in need of improvement, and broadcast the multitude of skills and talents you've already aced. Take a chance on yourself and believe in yourself the way you do for others. Bring the best of yourself to work every day because your best is the best there is.

Leadership is not a faraway star to pray on, a holy grail you'll never unearth, or an object of wish fulfillment. It is an attainable, accessible, doable opportunity that lies on the other side of this page. It's not about having an MBA or a PhD. It's not about pedigree or prestige or power. It's about you and what's in your heart, your head, and your soul.

In the eloquent words of John Quincy Adams, "If your actions inspire others to dream more, learn more, do more, and become more, you are a leader."

You see yourself in these words, don't you? Of course you do. You inspire others. You do it every day in a hundred different ways. It's time to put that inspiration to work on a broader scale. To look beyond the office you're currently sitting in to explore what awaits—no, what you can *create*—beyond that door. It's time to spread your glorious wings and soar to your highest altitude.

It's time to be the leader you were born to be.

Notes

INTRODUCTION

1. Carolyn Dewar, Martin Hirt, and Scott Keller, "The Mindsets and Practices of Excellent CEOs," McKinsey & Co., October 25, 2019, https://www.mckinsey.com/capabilities/strategy-and-corporate-finance/our-insights/the-mindsets-and-practices-of-excellent-ceos.

CHAPTER 1

1. "The Academic Backgrounds of the World's Most Powerful CEOs," Study.eu, December 13, 2017, https://www.study.eu/article/the-academic-backgrounds-of-the-worlds-most-powerful-ceos.

2. Dan Rasmussen and Haonan Li, "The MBA Myth and the Cult of the CEO," Institutional Investor, February 27, 2019, https://www.institutionalinvestor.com/article/b1db3jy3201d38/The-MBA-Myth-and-the-Cult-of-the-CEO.

3. In Irina Ivanova, "MBAs in Management Lead to Lower Employee Pay, Study Finds," *CBS News Moneywatch*, April 4, 2022, https://www.cbsnews.com/news/mba-degree-management-lower-worker-pay-study/.

4. Jason Villarreal, "The Importance of Seeing the Whole Picture," *TechNative*, November 7, 2019, https://technative.io/the-importance-of-seeing-the-whole-picture/.

5. Staff, "The Teachers Who Aren't Coming Back to School This Year," Chalkbeat.org, September 6, 2022, https://www.chalkbeat.org/2022/9/6/23220508/teachers-leaving-the-profession-quitting-teaching-reasons.

6. Cork Gaines, "Then and Now: What NBA Coaches Looked Like When They Were Players," *Business Insider*, April 1, 2019, https://www.businessinsider.com/nba-coaches-who-played-2019-3.

7. Content Team, "Standing Up for Your People," MindTools.com, accessed November 20, 2022, https://www.mindtools.com/aoae1dw/standing-up-for-your-people.

8. Katty Kay and Claire Shipman, "The Confidence Gap," *The Atlantic*, May 2014, https://www.theatlantic.com/magazine/archive/2014/05/the-confidence-gap/359815/.

9. Naomi Cahn, "Do Women and Men Have a Confidence Gap?" *Forbes*, February 26, 2020, https://www.forbes.com/sites/naomicahn/2020/02/26/do-women-and-men-have-a-confidence-gap/?sh=58b12d8e7bd2; and Christina Pazzanese, "Women Less Inclined to Self-Promote Than Men, Even for a Job," *Harvard Gazette*, February 7, 2020, https://news.harvard.edu/gazette/story/2020/02/men-better-than-women-at-self-promotion-on-job-leading-to-inequities/.

10. Nadzeya Shutava, "Leadership Self-Efficacy and Self-Doubt: A Look at Women in the Workplace," OurPublicService.org, November 3, 2022, https://ourpublicservice.org/publications/leadership-self-efficacy-and-self-doubt/.

CHAPTER 2

1. Barra quotes from Mary Barra, "Mary Barra: Five Lessons from the Kitchen Table," *Duke Today*, May 8, 2022, https://today.duke.edu/2022/05/mary-barra-five-lessons-kitchen-table.

2. Neal E. Boudette, "G. M. Expects Production to Return to Normal This Year as a Chip Shortage Eases," *New York Times*, February 1, 2022, https://www.nytimes.com/2022/02/01/business/gm-earnings.html.

3. Dale Buss, "Barra Already Ranks as GM's Most Important CEO Since Alfred Sloan," *Forbes*, January 31, 2021, https://www.forbes.com/sites/dalebuss/2021/01/31/barra-already-ranks-as-gms-most-important-ceo-in-a-half-century/?sh=658438c43481.

4. Julianne Pepitone, "How This Woman Beat the Odds and Rose to the Top at the Office of the Surgeon General," MSNBC, October 12, 2021, https://www.msnbc.com/know-your-value/how-woman-beat-odds-rose-top-office-surgeon-general-n1281322.

5. Katelyn Fossett, "A Record Number of Women in State Legislatures," *Politico*, December 2, 2022, https://www.politico.com/newsletters/women-rule/2022/12/02/a-record-number-of-women-in-state-legislatures-00071897.

6. Carrie Blazina and Drew DeSilver, "A Record Number of Women Are Serving in the 117th Congress," Pew Research Center, January 15, 2021, https://www.pewresearch.org/fact-tank/2021/01/15/a-record-number-of-women-are-serving-in-the-117th-congress/.

7. Robin Bleiweis and Shilpa Phadke, "The State of Women's Leadership—and How to Continue Changing the Face of U.S. Politics," AmericanProgress.org, January 15, 2021, https://www.americanprogress.org/article/state-womens-leadership-continue-changing-face-u-s-politics/.

8. "Countries with Female Leaders," World Population Review, accessed November 15, 2022, https://worldpopulationreview.com/country-rankings/countries-with-female-leaders.

9. "NASA Organizational Structure," NASA.gov, accessed February 19, 2023, https://www.nasa.gov/about/org_index.html.

10. Penn Medicine, Historical Timeline, UPenn.edu, accessed November 15, 2022, https://www.uphs.upenn.edu/paharc/timeline/.

11. Reynolds-Finley Historical Library, "The Life of Florence Nightingale," UAB.edu, accessed November 15, 2022, https://library.uab.edu/locations/reynolds/collections/florence-nightingale/life.

12. American Red Cross, "American Red Cross Guide to Services," 2011, https://www.redcross.org/content/dam/redcross/atg/PDF_s/GuideToServices.pdf.

13. Janine Solberg, "Taking Shorthand for Literacy: Historicizing the Literate Activity of US Women in the Early-Twentieth-Century Office," *LiCS*, vol. 2, no. 1 (March 2014): 1–28, https://licsjournal.org/index.php/LiCS/article/view/787/597.

14. Jessica Lyn Gladden, ed., "The Creation and Development of the Social Work Profession," chap. 1 of *Social Work Leaders Through History* (New York: Springer Publishing, 2018), p. 5, https://connect.springerpub.com/content/book/978-0-8261-4645-8/chapter/ch01.

15. Nili Tannenbaum and Michael Reisch, "From Charitable Volunteers to Architects of Social Welfare: A Brief History of Social Work," School of Social Work, University of Michigan, Fall 2001, https://ssw.umich.edu/about/history/brief-history-of-social-work.

16. "50 Notable Social Workers in US History," BestMSWPrograms.com, accessed November 23, 2022, https://www.bestmswprograms.com/great-american-social-workers/.

17. "Jane Addams–Biographical," The Nobel Prize, NobelPrize.org, December 8, 2022, https://www.nobelprize.org/prizes/peace/1931/addams/biographical.

18. All information on Mary Richmond from: Gladden, ed., "The Creation and Development of the Social Work Profession," chap. 1 of *Social Work Leaders Through History*; "50 Notable Social Workers in US History," BestMSWPrograms.com; and "Mary Ellen Richmond (1861–1928)—Social Work Pioneer, Administrator, Researcher and Author," Social Welfare History Project, Virginia Commonwealth University, 2011, https://socialwelfare.library.vcu.edu/social-work/richmond-mary/.

19. Arlisha R. Norwood, "Biography: Dorothea Dix," National Women's History Museum, https://www.womenshistory.org/education-resources/biographies/dorothea-dix; and Gladden, ed., "The Creation and Development of the Social Work Profession," chap. 1 of *Social Work Leaders Through History*.

20. "50 Notable Social Workers in US History," BestMSWPrograms.com.

21. Ibid.

22. Elizabeth Boyle, "The Feminization of Teaching in America," MIT Program in Women's and Gender Studies, accessed December 1, 2022, https://stuff.mit.edu/afs/athena.mit.edu/org/w/wgs/prize/eb04.html.

23. Ibid.

24. Genevieve Carlton, "A History of Women in Higher Education," Best Colleges, March 15, 2021, https://www.bestcolleges.com/news/analysis/2021/03/21/history-women-higher-education/#:~:text=In%201836%2C%20Wesleyan%20became%20the,U.S.%20between%201836%20and%201875.

25. Jessica Bryant, "Women Continue to Outnumber Men in College Completion," Best Colleges, July 8, 2022, https://www.bestcolleges.com/news/analysis/2021/11/19/women-complete-college-more-than-men/.

26. "Top Ten Most Influential Women in American Education," Minds Matter Colorado, January 28, 2019, https://www.mindsmatterco.org/top-ten-most-influential-women-in-american-education/.

27. Audrey Dentith, "Women's History in Education in the United States," Adult Education Research Conference, 2016, https://newprairiepress.org/aerc/2016/roundtables/4.

28. "Alice Elvira Freeman Palmer," *Encyclopedia Britannica*, https://www.britannica.com/biography/Alice-Elvira-Freeman-Palmer.

29. "Top Ten Most Influential Women in American Education," Minds Matter Colorado.

30. Maya Riser-Kositsky, "Education Statistics: Facts About American Schools," *Education Week*, updated January 7, 2022, https://www.edweek.org/leadership/education-statistics-facts-about-american-schools/2019/01#:~:text=the%20Broad%20Center%20.-,STUDENTS,for%20the%20fall%20of%202022.

31. Mitra Toossi, "A Century of Change: The U.S. Labor Force, 1950–2050," *Monthly Labor Review*, May 2002, table 4, https://www.bls.gov/opub/mlr/2002/05/art2full.pdf.

32. Ibid., table 1.

33. "Women in the Workforce Statistics," Team Stage, accessed December 1, 2022, https://teamstage.io/women-in-the-workforce-statistics/.

34. Cited in "27 Shocking Women in the Workplace Statistics," What to Become, September 13, 2022, https://whattobecome.com/blog/women-in-the-workplace-statistics/.

35. Ibid.

36. Kasee Wiesen, "How Many Nurses Are There in the U.S.—2022 State Wise Data," Nursing Process, 2022, https://www.nursingprocess.org/how-many-nurses-are-there-in-the-us.html.

37. "Social Workers," *Occupational Outlook Handbook*, U.S. Bureau of Labor Statistics, 2022, https://www.bls.gov/ooh/community-and-social-service/social-workers.htm.

38. Alyssa Middleton, "Women in Social Work, Leadership, and Management: A Complete Guide," MSW Online, August 5, 2021, https://mastersinsocialworkonline.org/resources/women-in-leadership/.

39. Maya Riser-Kositsky, "Education Statistics: Facts About American Schools," *Education Week*, updated January 7, 2022, https://www.edweek.org/leadership/education-statistics-facts-about-american-schools/2019/01#:~:text=the%20Broad%20Center%20.-,STUDENTS,for%20the%20fall%20of%202022.

40. Middleton, "Women in Social Work, Leadership, and Management."

41. Nicole Lipkin, "Why Women Are Natural Born Leaders," *Forbes*, November 19, 2019, https://www.forbes.com/sites/nicolelipkin/2019/11/19/why-women-are-natural-born-leaders/?sh=50d5c7506641.

42. Ibid.

43. Jack Zenger and Joseph Folkman, "Research: Women Score Higher Than Men in Most Leadership Skills," *Harvard Business Review*, June 25, 2019, https://hbr.org/2019/06/research-women-score-higher-than-men-in-most-leadership-skills.

44. Jemma Roedel, *She Thinks Like a Boss: Leadership: 9 Essential Skills for New Female Leaders in Business and the Workplace* (independently published, 2021).

45. Alexis Krivkovich et al., "Women in the Workplace 2018," McKinsey & Co., October 2018, https://www.mckinsey.com/featured-insights/gender-equality/women-in-the-workplace-2018.

46. Corinne Post, Boris Lokshin, and Christophe Boone, "Research: Adding Women to the C-Suite Changes How Companies Think," *Harvard Business Review*, April 6, 2021, https://hbr.org/2021/04/research-adding-women-to-the-c-suite-changes-how-companies-think.

47. Georges Desvaux, Sandrine Devillard-Hoellinger, and Pascal Baumgarten, "Women Matter," McKinsey & Co., October 4, 2017, https://www.mckinsey.com/~/media/McKinsey/Business%20Functions/Organization/Our%20Insights/Gender%20diversity%20a%20corporate%20performance%20driver/Gender%20diversity%20a%20corporate%20performance%20driver.pdf.

48. Joanne Cleaver, "How Can the Talent Pipeline Bottleneck Be Cleared?" SAGE Business Researcher, October 24, 2016, https://wilson-taylorassoc.com/wp-content/uploads/2012/04/Women-in-Management-%E2%80%93-SAGE-Business-Researcher.compressed.pdf.

49. Leslie Shaffer, "Female CEOs, Board Members Super-Charge Company Returns: Credit Suisse Report," CNBC, September 25, 2016, https://www.cnbc.com/2016/09/25/female-ceos-board-members-super-charge-company-returns-credit-suisse-report.html.

50. Janelle Jones, "5 Facts About the State of the Gender Pay Gap," U.S. Department of Labor Blog, March 19, 2021, https://blog.dol.gov/2021/03/19/5-facts-about-the-state-of-the-gender-pay-gap.

51. Sarah O'Brien, "Here's How the Wage Gap Affects Black Women," CNBC, August 22, 2019, https://www.cnbc.com/2019/08/22/heres-how-the-gender-wage-gap-affects-this-minority-group.html.

52. "Women in the Workforce Statistics," Team Stage, https://teamstage.io/women-in-the-workforce-statistics/.

53. Soledad Pérez-Sánchez, Sara Eichau Madueño, and Joan Montaner, "Gender Gap in the Leadership of Health Institutions: The Influence of Hospital-Level Factors," *Health Equity*, vol. 5, no. 1 (2021): 521–25, https://www.ncbi.nlm.nih.gov/pmc/articles/PMC8409238/#:~:text=Women%20accounted%20for%2052.2%25%20of,%25%20CI%203.02%E2%80%934.92).

54. Georgina Gonzalez, "Women Hold Only 15% of CEO Roles in Healthcare Organizations," *Becker's Hospital Review*, November 29, 2021, https://www.beckershospitalreview.com/hospital-management-administration/women-hold-only-15-of-ceo-roles-in-healthcare-organizations.html.

55. Middleton, "Women in Social Work, Leadership, and Management."

56. Riser-Kositsky, "Education Statistics."

57. Andre Perry, "Education Needs More Ambitious Women," *Hechinger Report*, August 18, 2020, https://hechingerreport.org/column-education-needs-more-ambitious-women/.

58. Josh Moody, "An All-Women Executive Leadership Team," Inside Higher Ed, April 8, 2022, https://www.insidehighered.com/news/2022/04/08/celebrating-all-female-executive-leadership-team.

59. Karolina Edman, "Why We Need to Talk About the Confidence Gap," Universum, September 11, 2021, https://universumglobal.com/blog/why-we-need-to-talk-about-the-confidence-gap/.

60. Katty Kay and Claire Shipman, "The Confidence Gap," *The Atlantic*, May 2014, https://www.theatlantic.com/magazine/archive/2014/05/the-confidence-gap/359815/.

61. See, for example, Stéphanie Thomson, "A Lack of Confidence Isn't What's Holding Back Working Women," *The Atlantic*, September 10, 2018, https://www.theatlantic.com/family/archive/2018/09/women-workplace-confidence-gap/570772/; and Christine L. Exley and Judd B. Kessler, "The Gender Gap in Self-Promotion," National Bureau of Economic Research, October 2019, https://www.nber.org/papers/w26345.

62. Naomi Cahn, "Do Women and Men Have a Confidence Gap?" *Forbes*, February 26, 2020, https://www.forbes.com/sites/naomicahn/2020/02/26/do-women-and-men-have-a-confidence-gap/?sh=7ec76c5b7bd2.

63. Jo Miller, "The Soul-Crushing Truth About Women and Self-Promotion," *Forbes*, April 29, 2021, https://www.forbes.com/sites/jomiller/2021/04/29/the-soul-crushing-truth-about-women-and-self-promotion/?sh=aa6460e6906b.

64. In Susie Gharib, "Hershey's CEO on Professional Growth and Women in Business," *Fortune*, January 3, 2018, https://fortune.com/2018/01/03/hersheys-ceo-michele-buck/.

65. Anu Madgavkar et al., "Human Capital at Work: The Value of Experience," McKinsey & Co., June 2, 2022, https://www.mckinsey.com/business-functions/people-and-organizational-performance/our-insights/human-capital-at-work-the-value-of-experience.

66. Laura Guillen, "Is the Confidence Gap Between Men and Women a Myth?" *Harvard Business Review*, March 26, 2018, https://hbr.org/2018/03/is-the-confidence-gap-between-men-and-women-a-myth.

67. James Doeser, "Racial/Ethnic and Gender Diversity in the Orchestra Field," League of American Orchestras, September 2016, p. 4, http://www.ppv.issuelab.org/resources/25840/25840.pdf.

68. For commentary on the advantages of anonymizing job applications, see, for example: Stefanie K. Johnson and Jessica F. Kirk, "Research: To Reduce Gender Bias, Anonymize Job Applications," *Harvard Business Review*, March 5, 2020, https://hbr.org/2020/03/research-to-reduce-gender-bias-anonymize-job-applications; and Ulf Rinne, "Anonymous Job Applications and Hiring Discrimination," IZA World of Labor, https://wol.iza.org/articles/anonymous-job-applications-and-hiring-discrimination/long.

CHAPTER 3

1. Naomi Blumberg, "Malala Yousafzai," *Encyclopedia Britannica*, accessed December 2, 2022, https://www.britannica.com/biography/Malala-Yousafzai.
2. "Malala Yousafzai," United Nations Messengers of Peace, accessed December 2, 2022, https://www.un.org/en/messengers-peace/malala-yousafzai.
3. "Greta Thunberg," *Encyclopedia Britannica*, accessed December 10, 2022, https://www.britannica.com/biography/Greta-Thunberg.
4. Olivia Lai, "18 Powerful Greta Thunberg Quotes to Inspire Climate Action," Earth.org, January 13, 2022, https://earth.org/greta-thunberg-quotes-speeches-to-inspire-climate-action/.
5. Ibid.
6. In Brian MacQuarrie, "Malala Yousafzai Addresses Harvard Audience," *Boston Globe*, September 27, 2013, https://www.bostonglobe.com/metro/2013/09/27/malala-yousafzai-pakistani-teen-shot-taliban-tells-harvard-audience-that-education-right-for-all/6cZBan0M4J3cAnmRZLfUmI/story.html.
7. James Clayton and Jasmin Dyer, "Ukraine War: The TikToker Spreading Viral Videos," BBC, March 5, 2022, https://www.bbc.com/news/technology-60613331.
8. "*The Los Angeles Times*' History," *Los Angeles Times*, September 21, 2012, https://www.latimes.com/la-mediagroup-times-history-htmlstory.html.
9. Travis M. Andrews, "Charli D'Amelio Is TikTok's Biggest Star: She Has No Idea Why," *Washington Post*, May 26, 2020, https://www.washingtonpost.com/technology/2020/05/26/charli-damelio-tiktok-star/.
10. Emily Graham, "10 Teachers You Should Follow on Social Media," Teacher Lists, January 4, 2021, https://www.teacherlists.com/blog/teachers-you-should-follow-on-social-media/.
11. Hanna Kerr, Richard Booth, and Kimberley Jackson, "Exploring the Characteristics and Behaviors of Nurses Who Have Attained Microcelebrity Status on Instagram: Content Analysis," *Journal of Medical Internet Research*, vol. 22, no. 5 (May 2020), https://www.ncbi.nlm.nih.gov/pmc/articles/PMC7284411/.
12. Estelle, "10 Incredible Stories of Heroism in the Midst of Tragedy," Listverse.com, September 22, 2021, https://listverse.com/2021/09/22/10-incredible-stories-of-heroism-in-the-midst-of-tragedy/.
13. Melissa Chan, "'I Just Did What Anybody Would Do': 5 Heroes Who Gave Us Hope in 2017," *Time*, December 7, 2017, https://time.com/5052840/2017-hero-shooting-hurricane-fire/.
14. In R. Eric Thomas, "Maxine Waters Does Not Feel Vindicated Yet," *Elle*, February 1, 2018, https://www.elle.com/culture/career-politics/a15947361/maxine-waters-does-not-feel-vindicated-yet/.
15. Dan Moskowitz, "The 10 Richest People in the World," Investopedia, updated December 13, 2022, https://www.investopedia.com/articles/investing/012715/5-richest-people-world.asp.
16. Rachel Makinson, "How Spanx Founder Sara Blakely Created a Billion-Dollar Brand," *CEO Today*, October 28, 2021, https://www.ceotodaymagazine.com/2021/10/how-spanx-founder-sara-blakely-created-a-billion-dollar-brand/.

CHAPTER 4

1. "What Is Servant Leadership?" Greenleaf Center for Servant Leadership, accessed December 15, 2022, https://www.greenleaf.org/what-is-servant-leadership/.

2. Nathan Eva et al., "Servant Leadership: A Systematic Review and Call for Future Research," *Leadership Quarterly*, vol. 30, no. 1 (February 2019): 111–32, https://www.sciencedirect.com/science/article/pii/S1048984317307774.

3. "What Is Servant Leadership?" Greenleaf Center for Servant Leadership.

4. Zita Lagos Sánchez, "Soft Skills and Warmth in Nursing," *Horizonte de Enfermería*, vol. 24, no. 1 (2013): 32–41, https://revistas.uc.cl/wp-rev/en_us/horizonte-de-enfermeria/soft-skills-and-warmth-in-nursing-definition-design-and-features/.

5. Naomi Blumberg, "Bob Ross," *Britannica*, updated October 25, 2022, https://www.britannica.com/biography/Bob-Ross.

6. Jacqui Palumbo, "New Bob Ross Documentary Complicates the Legacy of an Artist Who Painted 'Happy Little Trees,'" CNN, August 24, 2021, https://www.cnn.com/style/article/bob-ross-netflix-documentary-culture-queue/index.html.

7. Kendra Cherry, "What Is Emotional Intelligence," Verywell Mind, updated November 7, 2022, https://www.verywellmind.com/what-is-emotional-intelligence-2795423.

8. All of the information that follows on Goleman's four EI components comes from, unless otherwise noted: Leslie Riopel, "Emotional Intelligence Frameworks, Charts, Diagrams & Graphs," *Positive Psychology*, March 12, 2019, https://positivepsychology.com/emotional-intelligence-frameworks/; and Crystal Ott, "What Is Emotional Intelligence?" Ohio State University Extension, Ohio4h.org, https://ohio4h.org/sites/ohio4h/files/imce/Emotional%20Intelligence%20Background.pdf.

9. Quoted in Andrea Ovans, "How Emotional Intelligence Became a Key Leadership Skill," *Harvard Business Review*, April 28, 2015, https://hbr.org/2015/04/how-emotional-intelligence-became-a-key-leadership-skill.

10. Daniel Goleman, "What Makes a Leader?" *Harvard Business Review*, January 2004, https://hbr.org/2004/01/what-makes-a-leader.

11. Raelene Morey, "How 5 Emotionally Intelligent CEOs Handle Their Power," Pagely, July 4, 2018, https://pagely.com/blog/emotionally-intelligent-ceos/.

12. Vahid Kohpeima Jahromi et al., "Active Listening: The Key of Successful Communication in Hospital Managers," *Electron Physician*, vol. 8, no. 3 (March 2016): 2123–28, https://www.ncbi.nlm.nih.gov/pmc/articles/PMC4844478/.

13. Arlin Cuncic, "What Is Active Listening?" Verywell Mind, November 9, 2022, https://www.verywellmind.com/what-is-active-listening-3024343.

14. Jean F. East, *Transformational Leadership for the Helping Professions: Engaging Head, Heart, and Soul* (United Kingdom: Oxford University Press, 2018), p. 187.

15. Both examples in this section from: "Top 50 Listening Leaders," Sideways6, accessed December 12, 2022, https://ideas.sideways6.com/article/the-top-50-listening-leaders.

16. In Ashley Elizabeth, "What Is Grit and How to Develop It for a Successful Life," Lifehack, accessed December 12, 2022, https://www.lifehack.org/884651/what-is-grit.

17. Jeff Stibel, "10 People Who Didn't Give Up," *Business Journals*, August 16, 2016, https://www.bizjournals.com/bizjournals/how-to/growth-strategies/2016/08/10-people-who-didnt-give-up.html.

18. Deborah Perkins-Gough and Angela Duckworth, "The Significance of Grit," *Educational Leadership: Journal of the Department of Supervision and Curriculum Development*, N.E.A 71 (January 2013): 14–20, https://www.researchgate.net/publication/272078893_The_significance_of_grit.

19. Claire Robertson-Kraft and Angela Lee Duckworth, "True Grit: Trait-Level Perseverance and Passion for Long-Term Goals Predicts Effectiveness and Retention Among Novice Teachers," *Teachers College Record*, vol. 116, no. 3 (2014), https://www.ncbi.nlm.nih.gov/pmc/articles/PMC4211426/.

20. Perkins-Gough and Duckworth, "The Significance of Grit."

21. In John Antonakis, Marika Fenley, and Sue Liechti, "Learning Charisma," *Harvard Business Review*, June 2012, https://hbr.org/2012/06/learning-charisma-2.

22. Elizabeth, "What Is Grit and How to Develop It for a Successful Life."

23. In Andrew Pistone, "Three Retired NBA Superstars Who Were Cut from Their High School Teams," GMTM, June 21, 2022, https://gmtm.com/articles/nba-players-who-were-cut-from-their-high-school-teams.

24. "8 Famous People Who Overcame Obstacles," Familius, accessed December 15, 2022, https://www.familius.com/8-famous-people-who-overcame-obstacles/.

25. Rafly Gilang, "Everything Martha Stewart Has Done Sincer Her Prison Release," *The Things*, August 19, 2021, https://www.thethings.com/everything-martha-stewart-has-done-since-her-prison-release/.

26. Raffi Berg, "Benjamin Netanyahu, Israel's Comeback Leader," BBC News, November 4, 2022, https://www.bbc.com/news/world-middle-east-18008697.

27. Patrick Kingsley, "Lapid Concedes in Israel, Paving the Way for Netanyahu's Return to Power," *New York Times*, November 3, 2022, https://www.nytimes.com/2022/11/03/world/middleeast/israel-netanyahu-election.html.

28. "Why Teaching Without Passion Is a No-Win Situation," Misfit Teachers, accessed December 15, 2022, https://misfitteachers.com/teaching-without-passion-nowin/.

29. Bill Smoot, "Passion and Awareness: What Great Teachers Have in Common," HigherEdJobs, February 27, 2013, https://www.higheredjobs.com/blog/postDisplay.cfm?post=412.

30. David Robson, "How a 'Growth Mindset' Can Lead to Success," BBC, March 13, 2020, https://www.bbc.com/worklife/article/20200306-the-surprising-truth-about-finding-your-passion-at-work.

31. Jodie Cook, "7 Signs You Have Found Your Calling," *Forbes*, October 21, 2020, https://www.forbes.com/sites/jodiecook/2020/10/21/7-signs-you-have-found-your-calling/?sh=3f8928107b98C.

32. Michele W. Gazica and Paul E. Spector, "A Comparison of Individuals with Unanswered Callings to Those with No Calling at All," *Journal of Vocational Behavior* 91 (2015): 1–10, https://www.sciencedirect.com/science/article/abs/pii/S0001879115000901?via%3Dihub.

33. Kate Torgovnick May, quoting Dave Isay in "7 Lessons About Finding the Work You Were Meant to Do," Ideas.TED.com, April 29, 2016, https://ideas.ted.com/7-lessons-about-finding-the-work-you-were-meant-to-do/.

34. Elizabeth, "What Is Grit and How to Develop It for a Successful Life."

35. Lauren C. Howe, Jon M. Jachimowicz, and Jochen I. Menges, "To Retain Employees, Support Their Passions Outside Work," *Harvard Business Review*, March 30, 2022, https://hbr.org/2022/03/to-retain-employees-support-their-passions-outside-work.

36. Joseph Guinto, "Hot Pants, Love Potions, and the Go-Go Genesis of Southwest Airlines," *Texas Monthly*, July 2021, https://www.texasmonthly.com/news-politics/southwest-airlines-50-anniversary/.

37. Kris Swank, "Herb Kelleher," Reference for Business, accessed December 16, 2022, https://www.referenceforbusiness.com/biography/F-L/Kelleher-Herb-1931.html

38. In Todd Wickstrom, "Love at Work: Herb Kelleher and Southwest Airlines," Medium.com, February 24, 2020, https://medium.com/groove-enhancers-leadership-academy/herb-kelleher-and-southwest-airlines-1b6d9042beaa.

39. Janice Tazbir and Patricia Kelly, eds., *Kelly Vana's Nursing Leadership and Management* (United Kingdom: Wiley, 2021), p. 3.

CHAPTER 5

1. "15 Famous Mentoring Relationships," PushFar, accessed December 23, 2022, https://www.pushfar.com/article/15-famous-mentoring-relationships/.

2. Susan Jekielek et al., "Mentoring: A Promising Strategy for Youth Development," *Child Trends Research Brief*, Research Gate, February 2002, https://www.researchgate.net/publication/234682682_Mentoring_A_Promising_Strategy_for_Youth_Development_Child_Trends_Research_Brief.

3. "Lead Better by Knowing When to Follow," Wharton@Work, September 2012, https://executiveeducation.wharton.upenn.edu/thought-leadership/wharton-at-work/2012/09/know-when-to-follow/.

4. Terina Allen, "Want to Be a Good Leader? Learn to Follow," *Fast Company*, November 28, 2018, https://www.fastcompany.com/90273002/want-to-be-a-good-leader-learn-to-follow.

5. Brian J. Brim, "Strengths-Based Leadership: Building Compassion in Followers," Gallup, updated September 30, 2021, https://www.gallup.com/cliftonstrengths/en/250931/strengths-based-leadership-building-compassion-followers.aspx.

6. Rasmus Hougaard, Jacqueline Carter, and Nick Hobson, "Compassionate Leadership Is Necessary—but Not Sufficient," *Harvard Business Review*, December 4, 2020, https://hbr.org/2020/12/compassionate-leadership-is-necessary-but-not-sufficient.

7. "Adapt or Die: Eight Businesses That Transformed Their Business Models to Survive," Hiscox, accessed December 29, 2022, https://www.hiscox.co.uk/broker/

about-hiscox/news/adapt-or-die-eight-businesses-transformed-their-business-models-survive.

8. "10 Benefits of Continuous Education for Career Advancement," EHL Insights, accessed January 1, 2023, https://hospitalityinsights.ehl.edu/15-benefits-continuing-education.

9. Adam Bryant, "How to Be a C.E.O., from a Decade's Worth of Them," *New York Times*, October 27, 2017, https://www.nytimes.com/2017/10/27/business/how-to-be-a-ceo.html.

10. Mohd Abdul Moid Siddiqui1 and Ayesha Farooq, "Mergers and Acquisitions: Failures and Causes, an Evidence-Based Approach," *International Journal of Interdisciplinary Research and Innovations*, vol. 7, no. 2 (April–June 2019): 147–52, https://www.researchgate.net/profile/Mohd-Abdul-Moid-Siddiqui/publication/361366467_Mergers_and_Acquisitions_Failures_and_causes_an_evidence-based_approach/links/62ac51ca40d84c1401b1f219/Mergers-and-Acquisitions-Failures-and-causes-an-evidence-based-approach.pdf.

11. Hadas Gold, "Appeals Court Backs AT&T Acquisition of Time Warner," CNN Business, February 27, 2019, https://www.cnn.com/2019/02/26/media/att-time-warner-merger-ruling/index.html.

12. David W. Garrison, "Most Mergers Fail Because People Aren't Boxes," *Forbes*, June 24, 2019, https://www.forbes.com/sites/forbescoachescouncil/2019/06/24/most-mergers-fail-because-people-arent-boxes/?sh=2e911e4c5277.

13. All statistics in this paragraph from: Bailey Maybray, "How Many Startups Fail," *The Hustle*, December 19, 2022, https://blog.hubspot.com/the-hustle/how-many-startups-fail; and Josh Howarth, "What Percentage of Startups Fail?" Exploding Topics, November 30, 2022, https://explodingtopics.com/blog/startup-failure-stats.

14. Johnny Dodd and Wendy Grossman Kantor, "She Gives Retreats to Moms Fighting Cancer," *People*, November 21, 2022, p. 121.

CHAPTER 6

1. "Budget Basics: National Defense," Peter G. Peterson Foundation, June 1, 2022, https://www.pgpf.org/budget-basics/budget-explainer-national-defense.

2. "How Much Has the U.S. Government Spent This Year?" Fiscal Data, accessed December 29, 2022, https://fiscaldata.treasury.gov/americas-finance-guide/federal-spending/.

3. Riser-Kositsky, "Education Statistics."

4. Ibid.

5. "Expenditure on Education as a % of GDP in the United States (2010–2020)," GlobalData.com, July 2022, https://www.globaldata.com/data-insights/macroeconomic/expenditure-on-education-as-a-of-gdp-in-the-united-states/.

6. "Compulsory Education Laws: Background," FindLaw, June 20, 2016, https://www.findlaw.com/education/education-options/compulsory-education-laws-background.html.

7. Heather Stewart, "Children Denied Education in the United States of America," NAFSA, January 25, 2017, https://www.nafsa.org/blog/children-denied-education-united-states-america.

8. Edward Glaeser, *The Triumph of the City* (New York: Penguin, 2011), p. 254.

9. TED Talks Education, PBS, May 7, 2013, https://www.pbs.org/wnet/ted-talks-education/speaker/ken-robinson/.

10. Pedro Noguera, "Equity Isn't Just a Slogan," Holdsworth Center, July 8, 2019, https://holdsworthcenter.org/blog/equity-isnt-just-a-slogan/.

11. "16 Facts About Gun Violence and School Shootings," Sandy Hook Promise, accessed January 3, 2023, https://www.sandyhookpromise.org/blog/gun-violence/16-facts-about-gun-violence-and-school-shootings/.

12. Robin Levinson-King, "Sandy Hook 10 Years On: How Many Have Died in School Shootings?" BBC News, December 14, 2022, https://www.bbc.com/news/world-us-canada-63911172.

13. Lauren Camera, "School Shootings Hit Highest Level on Record, Federal Data Shows," *U.S. News*, June 28, 2022, https://www.usnews.com/news/national-news/articles/2022-06-28/school-shootings-hit-highest-level-on-record-federal-data-shows.

14. Naaz Modan and Kara Arundel, "School Shootings Reach Unprecedented High in 2022," K–12 Dive, December 21, 2022, https://www.k12dive.com/news/2022-worst-year-for-school-shootings/639313/.

15. "Calculate Probability of Dying in School Shooting Usual Spatial Statistics," Stack Exchange, accessed January 3, 2023, https://stats.stackexchange.com/questions/577071/calculate-probability-of-dying-in-school-shooting-using-spatial-statistics.

16. Jillian Peterson and James Densley, "What School Shooters Have in Common," *Education Week*, October 8, 2019, https://www.edweek.org/leadership/opinion-what-school-shooters-have-in-common/2019/10.

17. For example, Amy Rock, "44% of K–12 Parents Fear for Their Children's Safety at School, Poll Finds," *Campus Safety*, September 6, 2022, https://www.campussafetymagazine.com/safety/k-12-parents-fear-children-safety-at-school/.

18. "16 Facts About Gun Violence and School Shootings," Sandy Hook Promise.

19. Quoted by Ross Clennett, "Jack Welch: How He Justified His Famous 'Fire the Bottom 10%,'" RossClennett.com, October 3, 2020, https://rossclennett.com/2020/03/jack-welch-how-he-justified-his-famous-fire-the-bottom-10/.

20. "The Standout Schools That Can Inspire Us All," *The Age*, August 24, 2022, https://www.theage.com.au/national/victoria/the-standout-schools-that-can-inspire-us-all-20220824-p5bcbh.html.

21. Cited in "Teachers: The Lifeblood of Your School's Success," ISM, September 18, 2013, https://isminc.com/advisory/publications/the-source/teachers-lifeblood-your-schools-success.

22. "These 5 Education Leaders Are Changing the World," World Savvy, November 15, 2021, https://www.worldsavvy.org/these-5-education-leaders-are-changing-the-world/.

23. Alana Semuels, "Good School, Rich School; Bad School, Poor School," *The Atlantic*, August 25, 2016, https://www.theatlantic.com/business/archive/2016/08/property-taxes-and-unequal-schools/497333/.

CHAPTER 7

1. See, for example, Ralph Ellis, "Over 333,000 Healthcare Workers Left Jobs in 2021, Report Says," WebMD, October 24, 2022, https://www.webmd.com/a-to-z-guides/news/20221024/over-333000-healthcare-workers-left-jobs-in-2021-report-says; Gaby Galvin, "Nearly 1 in 5 Health Care Workers Have Quit Their Jobs During the Pandemic," Primary Care Collaborative, October 4, 2021, https://www.pcpcc.org/2022/01/07/nearly-1-5-health-care-workers-have-quit-their-jobs-during-pandemic; and Marissa Plescia, "If 1 in 5 Healthcare Workers Have Quit, Where Have They Gone?" *Becker's Hospital Review*, February 11, 2022, https://www.beckershospitalreview.com/workforce/if-1-in-5-healthcare-workers-have-quit-where-have-they-gone.html.

2. Adam Jeffery, "New Yorkers Stop and Give Daily Thanks and Gratitude for Coronavirus Frontline Workers," CNBC, April 5, 2020, https://www.cnbc.com/2020/04/05/new-yorkers-stop-and-give-daily-thanks-and-gratitude-for-coronavirus-frontline-workers.html.

3. Eliza Goren, Shefali S. Kulkarni, and Kanyakrit Vongkiatkajorn, "The *Washington Post* Asked Readers to Describe 2020 in One Word or Phrase: Here's What They Said," *Washington Post*, December 18, 2020, https://www.washingtonpost.com/graphics/2020/lifestyle/2020-in-one-word/?utm_campaign=wp_post_most&utm_medium=email&utm_source=newsletter&wpisrc=nl_most&carta-url=https%3A%2F%2Fs2.washingtonpost.com%2Fcar-ln-tr%2F2dafe7f%2F5fdcda929d2fda0efb8c6cdc%2F5e95e40bade4e25735f27dba%2F8%2F72%2F5fdcda929d2fda0efb8c6cdc.

4. Holly Ellyatt, "Last Responders: Mental Health Damage from Covid Could Last a Generation, Professionals Say," CNBC, February 10, 2022, https://www.cnbc.com/2022/02/10/covid-pandemic-mental-health-damage-could-last-a-generation.html.

5. Corrie Pikul, "Depression Rates Tripled and Symptoms Intensified During First Year of COVID-19," News from Brown University, October 5, 2021, https://www.brown.edu/news/2021-10-05/pandemic-depression.

6. "Mental Health and COVID-19," Mental Health America, April 2022, https://mhanational.org/mental-health-and-covid-19-two-years-after-pandemic.

7. Citing a FAIR Health report in "Teen Mental Health: A Vulnerable Stage of Life," SOS Children's Villages Illinois, accessed January 8, 2023, https://www.sosillinois.org/teen-mental-health-a-vulnerable-stage-of-life/.

8. Christine Vestal, "COVID Harmed Kids' Mental Health—and Schools Are Feeling It," Pew, November 9, 2021, https://www.pewtrusts.org/en/research-and-analysis/blogs/stateline/2021/11/08/covid-harmed-kids-mental-health-and-schools-are-feeling-it.

9. "New CDC Data Illuminate Youth Mental Health Threats During the COVID-19 Pandemic," CDC Newsroom press release, accessed January 8, 2023, https://www.cdc.gov/media/releases/2022/p0331-youth-mental-health-covid-19.html.

10. Sarah Klein and Martha Hostetter, "Building Better Systems of Care for People with Mental Health Problems," The Commonwealth Fund, June 24, 2021, https://www.commonwealthfund.org/publications/2021/jun/building-better-systems-care-people-mental-health-problems.

11. "New CDC Data Illuminate Youth Mental Health Threats," CDC Newsroom press release.

12. Klein and Hostetter, "Building Better Systems of Care for People with Mental Health Problems."

13. Brienna Thompson, "Crisis Theory & Intervention: History, Indication, and Effectiveness," *Abstract Elephant*, June 2020, https://abstractelephant.com/2020/06/30/crisis-theory-and-intervention/.

14. Summarized by Dustin K. MacDonald, "Crisis Theory and Types of Crisis," DustinKMacDonald.com, June 13, 2016, http://dustinkmacdonald.com/crisis-theory-types-crisis/.

15. Thompson, "Crisis Theory & Intervention."

16. Sam N., M.S., "Crisis Theory," PsychologyDictionary.org, April 7, 2013, https://psychologydictionary.org/crisis-theory/.

17. Cheryl Regehr, "Crisis Theory and Social Work Treatment," in Francis J. Turner, ed., *Social Work Treatment: Interlocking Theoretical Approaches* (New York: Oxford University Press, 2011), pp. 134–43.

18. Tim Ziglar, *10 Leadership Virtues for Disruptive Times: Coaching Your Team through Immense Change and Challenge* (Nashville, TN: Nelson Books, 2021), p. 6.

19. Ibid., pp. 7–8.

20. Apoorva Mandavilli, "New Infectious Threats Are Coming. The U.S. Probably Won't Contain Them," *New York Times*, September 29, 2022, https://www.nytimes.com/2022/09/29/health/pandemic-preparedness-covid-monkeypox.html.

21. Christina Farr and Michelle Gao, "How Taiwan Beat the Coronavirus," CNBC, July 15, 2020, https://www.cnbc.com/2020/07/15/how-taiwan-beat-the-coronavirus.html.

CHAPTER 8

1. Ellen Fried, "An Extraordinary President and His Remarkable Cabinet: An Interview with Doris Kearns Goodwin About Lincoln's *Team of Rivals*," *Prologue*, Spring 2006, https://www.archives.gov/publications/prologue/2006/spring/interview.html#:~:text=Perhaps%20equally%20surprising%20was%20what,and%20Bates%20as%20attorney%20general.

CHAPTER 9

1. Chris Beckett, *Supervision: A Guide for the Helping Professions* (London: SAGE Publications, 2021), chap. 4.
2. Joe Rivera, "Aaron Rodgers Contract Breakdown," *Sporting News*, October 30, 2022, https://www.sportingnews.com/us/nfl/news/aaron-rodgers-contract-breakdown-packers-qb-making-2022/vhmld1afzqbmgrdl26nmsltb.

CHAPTER 10

1. Susan Adams, "Why Promoting from Within Usually Beats Hiring from Outside," *Forbes*, April 5, 2012, https://www.forbes.com/sites/susanadams/2012/04/05/why-promoting-from-within-usually-beats-hiring-from-outside/?sh=2b52b2b536ce.
2. Jeff Hader, "It's Official: Promoting Leaders from Within Is the Best Approach," *Inc.*, April 29, 2021, https://www.inc.com/jeff-haden/its-official-promoting-leaders-from-within-is-best-approach.html.
3. Adams, "Why Promoting from Within Usually Beats Hiring from Outside."
4. Herbert L. Lemaster, "Should You Promote Managers Internally or Hire from Outside," Clark Schaefer Hackett Business Advisors, February 4, 2020, https://www.cshco.com/articles/should-you-promote-managers-internally-or-hire-from-outside/.
5. Jason Carney, "Pros and Cons to Internal Promotion vs. External Hiring," HR Daily Advisor, July 1, 2019, https://hrdailyadvisor.blr.com/2019/07/01/pros-and-cons-to-internal-promotion-vs-external-hiring/.
6. Hader, "It's Official: Promoting Leaders from Within Is the Best Approach."
7. Adams, "Why Promoting from Within Usually Beats Hiring from Outside."
8. Carney, "Pros and Cons to Internal Promotion vs. External Hiring."
9. Hader, "It's Official: Promoting Leaders from Within Is the Best Approach."
10. Colleen Marshall and Anette Søgaard Nielsen, *Motivational Interviewing for Leaders in the Helping Professions: Facilitating Change in Organizations* (New York: Guilford Press, 2020), pp. 12–13.
11. Magdalena Petrova, "What's Behind Kodak's Pivot to Pharmaceuticals?" CNBC, August 22, 2020, https://www.cnbc.com/2020/08/22/kodak-pivots-to-pharmaceuticals-whats-behind-the-move.html.
12. Eleanor Drago-Severson, *Helping Educators Grow: Strategies and Practices for Leadership Development* (Cambridge, MA: Harvard Education Press, 2012).
13. Eleanor Drago-Severson, Christy Joswick O'Connor, and Jessica Blum-Destefano, "When Teams Hit Rough Waters," *Learning Professional*, vol. 39, no. 4 (August 2018): 54–58, https://learningforward.org/wp-content/uploads/2018/08/when-teams-hit-rough-water.pdf; Doris Kearns Goodwin, *Leadership in Turbulent Times* (New York: Simon & Schuster, 2018); and Tim Elmore, *The Eight Paradoxes of Great Leadership: Embracing the Conflicting Demands of Today's Workplace* (Nashville, TN: HarperCollins Leadership, 2021).

14. Adam Grant, "Microsoft CEO Satya Nadella: How Empathy Sparks Innovation," Knowledge at Wharton, February 22, 2018, https://knowledge.wharton.upenn.edu/article/microsofts-ceo-on-how-empathy-sparks-innovation/.

15. Nick Glass and Tim Hume, "The 'Hallelujah Moment' Behind the Invention of the Post-it Note," CNN, April 4, 2012, https://www.cnn.com/2013/04/04/tech/post-it-note-history.

16. Scott Cowley, "Thomas Edison and Michael Jordan Were Failures," *Business Insider*, September 16, 2010, https://www.businessinsider.com/thomas-edison-and-michael-jordan-were-failures-2010-9.

17. Justin Page, "Bryan Cranston Tells the Story of How He Made Jerry Seinfeld Laugh Once During a *Seinfeld* Episode," *Laughing Squid*, December 6, 2017, https://laughingsquid.com/bryan-cranston-made-jerry-seinfeld-laugh/.

CONCLUSION

1. In Tazbir and Kelly, eds., *Kelly Vana's Nursing Leadership and Management*, p. 3.

2. Beckett, *Supervision*.

3. Ziglar, *10 Leadership Virtues for Disruptive Times*, p. 5.

4. Nicki Weld, *A Practical Guide to Transformative Supervision for the Helping Professions: Amplifying Insight* (United Kingdom: Jessica Kingsley Publishers, 2012), p. 17.

5. East, *Transformational Leadership for the Helping Professions*, introduction.

Acknowledgments

My life's work wouldn't be possible without the people who make my life work. I want to extend my profound appreciation and boundless gratitude to the many people who contributed in many different ways to this long-dreamed-of, now-realized book:

To all the students, families, clients, patients, and colleagues I've had the honor of working with throughout my career—thank you all so much for giving me a purpose.

To Joe B., who has shown me that family isn't defined by blood and who has taught me about humility, patience, loyalty, and unconditional love.

To my wife, Sharyn, the kindest person I've ever met, whose undying support and love makes everything in life so much easier. Despite all my faults, you never ask me to change, and I'm so happy and lucky to have you.

To my three beautiful daughters, each amazing in their own way, who bring so much joy to my life. I couldn't imagine doing anything without you.

To my parents, who have taught me invaluable life lessons, each in their own way, and have shaped me into the man I am today: my father, with his humor, quickness, structure, and grit; my mother, with her creativity, kindness, people skills, and warmth; and my second mother, who serves as a stellar example to me of strength and integrity.

To my sisters, Amy and Cindy, my two best friends since the day I was born, the first two people who believed in me—without you, I wouldn't have been able to accomplish anything, and so I owe you everything.

To Ellyn, my mentor, my champion, and my friend. Thank you for teaching me how to lead and to love your people. This book is my attempt to pay forward everything you imbued in me.

To Tony and Greg, my friends first, my business partners second. I couldn't ask for better cotravelers on this road we have chosen, and I respect and admire both of you more than I can say as educational leaders, fathers, and brothers-in-arms.

To Adrian, my technology guru and incredible friend. You are such a calming and wise influence in my life, a confidant who is always there for me.

To Dan McNeill, for your initial support in drafting this book and your devoted efforts to helping it take shape.

To all my friends and family members who have enriched my life beyond measure.

Last, circling back to my sister Cindy, who serves a dual role in my life. You've been answering my sentences since I was a baby. You've brilliantly put all my words and ideas to paper for me throughout my career, and you always make me sound smarter and more eloquent than I actually am. There is no me without you, and this book certainly wouldn't have made it to print without you.